Hittin' the Prayer Bones

Hittin' the Prayer Bones

MATERIALITY OF SPIRIT IN THE PENTECOSTAL SOUTH

Anderson Blanton

The University of North Carolina Press
CHAPEL HILL

This book was sponsored by the postdoctoral fellows
program at the Center for the Study of the American South,
University of North Carolina at Chapel Hill.

© 2015 The University of North Carolina Press
All rights reserved

Designed and set in Miller by Rebecca Evans
Manufactured in the United States of America

The paper in this book meets the guidelines for permanence
and durability of the Committee on Production Guidelines for
Book Longevity of the Council on Library Resources.

The University of North Carolina Press has been a member of the
Green Press Initiative since 2003.

Cover illustration: photo of x-ray originally published in
Dr. John Eggert, *Einführung in die Röntgenphotograph* (1923).

Library of Congress Cataloging-in-Publication Data
Blanton, Anderson.
Hittin the prayer bones : materialities of spirit in the pentecostal
south / Anderson Blanton. — 1 [edition].
   pages cm
Includes bibliographical references and index.
ISBN 978-1-4696-2397-9 (pbk : alk. paper)
ISBN 978-1-4696-2398-6 (ebook)
1. Pentecostalism—Appalachian Region, Southern. 2. Appalachian
Region, Southern—Religious life and customs. 3. Material culture—
Religious aspects—Christianity. 4. Christianity and culture—
Appalachian Region, Southern. I. Title.
BR1644.5.U6B56 2015   277.5'7082—dc23
2015002752

This book was digitally printed.

*This book is dedicated to
Brother Aldie and Sister Dorothy,
who learned me on the breath.*

Contents

Acknowledgments xi

Introduction 1

CHAPTER 1 Radio as "Point of Contact" 11
Prayer and the Prosthesis of the Holy Ghost

Interlude SERMON 1 Sister Julie's Preachin' 36

CHAPTER 2 Prayer Cloths 52
Remnants of the Holy Ghost and the Texture of Faith

Interlude SERMON 2 Sister June's Bulldog Preachin' 105

CHAPTER 3 Preaching 115
The Anointed Poetics of Breath

Interlude SERMON 3 The Breath of Brother Pearl—
"Are You Ready?" 150

CHAPTER 4 Standin' in the Gap 156
The Materialities of Prayer

Altar Call 185
If You Ain't Blas-ah-phemed the Holy Ghost

Notes 187

Bibliography 207

Index 217

Figures

1 The circulation of ethnographic material 6
2 Radio station coverage map 7
3 Illustration of the "Point of Contact" from the healing treatise 24
4 Iconic image of famous healer Oral Roberts 25
5 Hanky-Panky, 1886 74
6 Ectoplasmic materialization 77
7 Advertisement from the Red Ash Coal Company, ca. 1900 92
8 Prayer cloths 98

Acknowledgments

BEFORE CALLING DOWN THE healing power of the Holy Ghost, some charismatic faithful invoke a passage from the book of Matthew: "For where two or three are gathered together in my name, there am I in the midst of them" (18:20). When multiple voices come together in one accord in the act of communal prayer, a sacred sound in excess of the mere sum of individual cries is unleashed into the spaces of the everyday. In much the same way, the present work is indebted to the support and participation of many individuals who have made this process of ethnographic writing possible. I am grateful to Kevin "Bossman" Grogg and family for allowing me to use their beautiful farm in southern West Virginia as a research base during ethnographic fieldwork. My time on the farm spent mending fences, fixing old hay bailers, and tending gardens taught me a great deal about the exigencies of the material world and the perpetual process of mending, patching, and creative substitution in southern Appalachia.

During the write-up phase of this project, my efforts to describe the intimate relationships among prayer, healing, and technology was strengthened by my interactions with faculty in the Department of Anthropology at Columbia University, especially Marilyn J. Ivy, Brian Larkin, and Michael Taussig. John Pemberton's work on the voice and the object has provided a constant source of inspiration, and the influence of this teaching resonates throughout this text. Likewise, my attempt to craft an interpretation that poetically conjures the phenomena in question has been enlivened by many spirit-infused conversations with Allen Shelton. Of all my academic colleagues and mentors, my collaborations with Ward Blanton on the question of technology and the production of sacred presence have been most fruitful. For their remarkable assistance with the book illustrations, I am grateful to Byron Russell and Dr. Kristin Futterlieb. The process of manuscript revision was made possible through the Social Science Research Council's "New Directions in the Study of Prayer" research initiative. This research grant was administered through the Center for the

Study of the American South located at the University of North Carolina at Chapel Hill. The copyediting process and final manuscript revision was generously facilitated by the Max Planck Institute for the Study of Religious and Ethnic Diversity in Germany under the directorship of Peter van der Veer. Finally, it was only through a longing to hear the laughter of my wife, Sally, that I was able to complete *Hittin' the Prayer Bones*.

Hittin' the Prayer Bones

Introduction

"HITTIN' THE PRAYER BONES" is a phrase invoked in charismatic Christian worship spaces throughout southern Appalachia. Evoking a long history of Christian devotional exercises, this phrase viscerally describes the importunate act of falling down upon one's knees in the performance of prayer. Hittin' the prayer bones is a percussive genuflection that literally sounds an embodied technique of divine communication. Even before the mouth begins to give voice to a prayer, the body itself, in a sudden coincidence with an external object, opens a communicative space between the sacred and the everyday. In this moment of collision between the enlivened bone and the wooden floorboard, the curative efficacy and miraculous power of the Holy Ghost is materialized within the space of charismatic worship.

In this way, the miraculous appearance of the Holy Ghost, a seemingly intangible and ethereal entity, can never be fully abstracted from this striking sound unleashed between the subject and the object in the performance of divine communication. The percussive noise produced through this technique of the body-in-prayer also resonates with the rapid, disjointed hand claps that pierce the entangled voices during performances of communal prayer, and the bony knuckles of a brother or sister as he or she raps the wooden church podium to mimic "God knockin' on that heart's door" during the altar call of the worship service. The sound of the bone is not only used as a crucial embodied metaphor of prayer within spaces saturated with "Holy Ghost'n'*par*" (power), but the rattling sound of those dry bleached bones in the valley becomes a sermonic touchstone to describe the enlivening potentiality of the Spirit in a world where the living waters of charisma have dried up. While scanning the airwaves of southern Appalachia on any given weekend, for instance, one is sure to tune in to a disembodied radio voice speaking of those dry bones and the quickening power to come:

> Ever-body that can, stand up an' help us,
> Sister Jackson wants "These Bones."

These bones are definitely gonna rise again.
You know, I thank so much about Elisha.
An' they went out thar an' buried him.
An' then how they come by ta bury a man [*Chuckles under his breath*]
Happened ta lay'em down right on Elisha's bones.
When they saw a troop of men comin' along. [*Audience response: Amen!*]
Kindly scared'em, they dropped'em on Elisha's bones,
An' 'at man sat straight up! [*Hallelujah! Clapping of hands*]
"There's somethin' alive in here!" [*Visceral, vehement voice, energetic*] [*Whoo!*]
Ya know one day after awhile,
The Lord's gonna step out on tha clouds a'glory.
They gonna be alotta dead bones gonna raise up.
Ah' praise God, I tell ya what [*Congregation member cries out, "Whoop-Glory!"*]
They's somethin' alive gonna come outta there!
I don't know what it's gonna be,
But somethin's commin' outta tha grave,
The grave is not gonna hold. [*That's right. Yes!*]

Immediately after the brother's final words, a song begins, sung with the accompaniment of guitar, tambourine, piano, and rhythmic clapping.

THESE BONES

Well my God decided to make'em a man
These bones gonna rise again
With a little bit of mud and a little bit of sand
Yea these bones gonna rise again
My God decided to make a woman too
Yea these bones gonna rise again
Well my God knows just what to do
Said these bones gonna rise again
And well I know it, indeed I know i
I know it, these bones gonna rise again!

The resonance of the bone extends to another recurrent motif within the charismatic space of worship, the performative description and evocation of suffering and corporeal breakdown in a world of sin. Here visceral accounts of gnarled arthritic joints, hip and knee replacements, broken bones, bones held together with steel frames and metallic screws, and the agonizing progression of cancer down to the very marrow of the bones fill the worship space with stories of pain and suffering in a world of fleshly bodies "got down."[1] The preeminent performance in these charismatic communities is a communal hittin' of the prayer bones that instantiates the miraculous healing power of the Holy Ghost into the participants' ailing bodies and everyday experiences.

Exploring the intertwined practices of prayer, faith, and healing, *Hittin' the Prayer Bones* attends to that particular sound of the sacred produced through "hittin' the prayer bones" and other material and technological conduits of the Holy Ghost. My ethnography is an attempt to hear the sound of the Holy Ghost in that abrupt space of coincidence between subject and object, spirit and matter. Taking cue from the charismatic phrase itself, my research moves outward from techniques of the body to investigate the materialities of prayer within the space of enthusiastic worship. In this way, the "prayer bone" also includes other crucial material underpinnings of divine communication such as prayer cloths and technologies of sound reproduction such as radio. Throughout the project, I describe the way prayer, even within a historically iconoclastic Pentecostal tradition that overtly postulates no mediated grace and the immaterial nature of divine communication, subsists upon a material underbelly that actively organizes and inflects the way divine communication is experienced and understood by the charismatic faithful. As Marcel Mauss presciently states in *On Prayer* (English translation published in 2003), "Prayer in religions whose dogmas have become detached from all fetishism, becomes itself a fetish."[2]

Exploring the materialities of divine communication, my research responds to a recent body of scholarship on the question of religious experience and its specific relationship to technological mediation.[3] These investigations into the material and technological resonances of the bone in religious experience have been much inspired by the work of Birgit Meyer. Her concept of "sensational forms," or the specific ways in which embodied experiences of religious presence are organized within particular religious communities and media environments, resounds throughout this ethnography.[4] Meyer's notion of sensational forms is useful not only because it emphasizes how somatic experiences of the transcendent are produced through authorized sensory regimes, but also because this critical concept challenges studies in the anthropology of media to describe the ways devotional objects and media technologies *themselves* play a forceful role in the organization of religious experience. Expanding upon this aspect of Meyer's term, my research emphasizes the question of the material actuality of devotional objects and media technologies in the production of sacred presence.

In addition to the more contemporary reflections on what Hent de Vries calls the "interfacing" or inextricable relationship between religion and media, my research on faith healing has been inspired and challenged by a classic body of ethnological scholarship exploring the relation between artifice and healing efficacy.[5] In these ethnological descriptions, it is precisely through a performance of sleight of hand or other form of trickery, what Mauss and Hubert call "the moment of prestidigitation," that an experience of curative force is released between the patient and the healer against the broader background of communal belief.[6] Yet, as these ethnographic accounts describe, it is often the case that both the audience and the patient demonstrate a critical awareness of the legerdemains performed by the healer. A translation between the discontinuous experiential frames of the patient-healer dyad and the concomitant release of healing efficacy, however, seems to take place *despite* this communal suspicion of potential artifice at the heart of the curative technique.[7]

Inspired by this early ethnological conundrum that outlines an intimate relationship between the artifice of the healer and the instantiation of curative efficacy, *Hittin' the Prayer Bones* describes the phenomenon of contemporary practices of healing prayer mediated through apparati such as radio, as well as other devotional objects, with these older ethnological resonances in mind. Articulating the way that contemporary practices and embodiments of faith healing subsist and make their appearance through technologies and objectile media *exterior* to the "believing" subject, my research departs from the majority of scholarly approaches on the practice of faith healing that have either sought to debunk the curative practice by revealing the technological artifice associated with the healing performance or relegated the curative force of the faith cure to some interiorized black box mechanism such as the placebo effect or so-called psychological suggestion.[8] By focusing on the exteriorities inherent in the performance of "faith," my research returns to early anthropological questions of the moment of prestidigitation, applying these insights to the contemporary phenomenon of faith healing.[9]

Related to these materialities of divine communication, my research on the prayer bone also contributes new ethnographic descriptions to a burgeoning body of scholarship interested in the objectile dimension of devotional practices. Works such as historian Colleen McDannell's *Material Christianity: Religion and Popular Culture in America* articulate the importance of material devotions in the process of religious subjectivization and the perpetuation of religious communities. By focusing upon the sensation of tactility and Christian healing techniques of manual imposition, my research articulates the way objects such as radios and prayer cloths play a crucial role in the reproduction of charismatic communities and the production of sensations of Holy Ghost presence. Tracking the circulation of material devotional objects within charismatic communities, my research also extends a body of classic ethnological theory on the religious force of compulsion that is generated through the exchange and movement of objects.[10]

This ethnography is based upon two years of fieldwork with charismatic radio preachers and their in-studio congregations, as well as dispersed members of the listening audience out in that nebulous space of what is referred to by the broadcasters as "radioland." I began my project in the summer of 2007, conducting site visits to radio stations and churches and scanning the airwaves throughout southern West Virginia, southwestern Virginia, and eastern Kentucky. It was during this summer pilot research that I located radio station 105.5, WGTH, "The Sheep," in Richlands, Virginia, and first met Brother and Sister Allen. Their hour-long live charismatic broadcast, *The Jackson Memorial Hour*, was to become the centerpiece of my research into the materialities of divine communication. A small Christian radio station, WGTH is located in the heart of southern Appalachia, and its broadcast signal is capable of reaching into portions of western North Carolina, eastern Tennessee, southern West Virginia, and eastern Kentucky (see figure 2).

In terms of participant observation within the immediate space of the live studio of the radio station, I spent over 135 hours at the station conducting research. While in the live studio, I paid close attention to techniques of prayer and performances of worship, especially as they related to technologies within the studio, such as the microphone. An overarching question within this technological environment was, In what ways, if at all, did the microphone and associated technologies of radio broadcasting actively organize the charismatic worship environment and concomitant practices of devotion?

One of the numerous facets of my research made possible through the openness and generosity of Brother and Sister Allen are the eighty-five cassette tape recordings of their worship broadcasts that they have sent

FIGURE 1
The circulation of ethnographic material

to me through the mail over the past four years. Not only have these tapes enabled me to keep abreast of the developments among the congregation members I came to know during fieldwork, but some of my richest ethnographic material in relation to ritual organization around the radio apparatus has been gleaned from these recordings. Moreover, the Allens have given me access to their collection of over thirty years of recorded charismatic worship broadcasts from the time period when Sister Dorothy's father, Brother George Jackson, preached over the radio. This charismatic radio archive has proved invaluable, allowing me to hear both the development of Brother Aldie's sermonic style over a period of twenty years and the continuities in performance styles and techniques of healing prayer. In this way, it is not so much my capacities in ethnographic observation but the remarkable generosity of the Allen family that has enabled this project.

My interest in the practices of charismatic healing prayer often led outside the spaces explicitly oriented around the radio apparatus as I followed preachers whom I had met within the context of the radio station to other spaces such as church services, tent revivals, prayer meetings, and baptisms. It was in spaces such as these that I realized early on in my fieldwork that my research frame on the materialities of prayer needed to be expanded to encompass the pervasive use of prayer cloths as a physical conduit for the power of the Holy Ghost. Another unanticipated opportunity for ethnographic analysis emerged from what became a constant source of curiosity and interest during the course of my fieldwork, the phenomenon of radio tactility. In this ritual of divine communication, the sick patient out in "radioland" touches the radio as a conduit for efficacious healing power. The more I attempted to think about the specificities of this technologically mediated practice of prayer and healing in many charismatic communities in southern Appalachia, the more I realized that

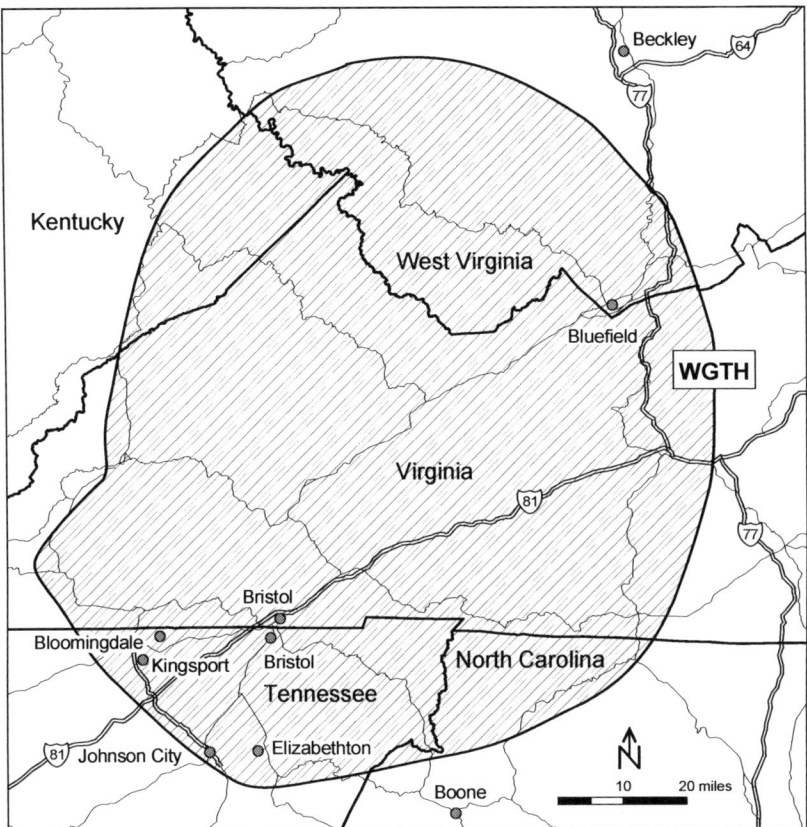

FIGURE 2 Radio station coverage map (Map design by Dr. Norbert Winnige)

the key moment of these radio broadcasts was intimately linked to broader practices of healing prayer that were disseminated on a national scale in the heyday of what has been called the Charismatic Renewal.[11] In this way, some of the crucial healing performances within the so-called folk religious practices of southern Appalachia suggested an intimate link of oral-folk transmission with larger mass-mediated religious movements of the twentieth century. In order to explore all the implications of healing radio tactility within the radio stations in southern Appalachia, it was necessary to broaden my research to include an analysis of specific practices of prayer broadcast on a national scale during the healing revivals of popular charismatic figures such as Oral Roberts. My interest in radio tactility within the worship contexts of southern Appalachia necessitated that I expand the scope of my project to include instances of this practice on a wider national scale and also challenged me to begin thinking about the broader histories of faith healing and efficacious techniques of prayer in an age of mechanical reproduction. Far from taking my research into the isolated and preserved recesses of uncorrupted practices of so-called old-time religion in Appalachia, the preeminent ritual practice among these small gospel radio stations called for a sustained engagement with a history of prayer in the modern world that is intimately extended and organized by forces of technological mediation. Thus, just as my ethnography moves between spaces of transmission (radio station) and reception (private home) in an attempt to hear the sacred resonances of the Holy Ghost, my narration of the materialities of prayer constantly oscillates between the specificities of curative practices in southern Appalachia, on the one hand, and broader international Pentecostal practices on the other.

Exploring the forces of attraction between performances of healing prayer and the radio apparatus, chapter 1, "Radio as 'Point of Contact': Prayer and the Prosthesis of the Holy Ghost," tracks the miraculous power of the Holy Ghost and its particular mediations through the radio loudspeaker. Through this exploration of prayer translated by the radio apparatus, this chapter also introduces key performances of charismatic worship and techniques of prayer that recur throughout this work. Articulating the phenomenon of "radio tactility" as an efficacious point of contact for the communication of healing virtue, this section moves comparatively between theurgical practices in southern Appalachia and broader Pentecostal practices of the twentieth century. While grounded in the contemporary practice of curative radio prayer among charismatic communities in southern Appalachia, this chapter also recalls formative practices of faith during the Charismatic Revival of the early 1950s, when millions of listeners tuned in to Oral Roberts's *Healing Waters* radio broadcast and were instructed to put their hands on the radio during the healing prayer.

Chapter 2, "Prayer Cloths: Remnants of the Holy Ghost and the Texture of Faith," describes the remarkable metamorphosis of a mere rag into a sacred cloth receptacle for the healing and apotropaic power of the Holy Ghost. Tracking the circulation of anointed fragments of cloth for the purposes of healing and divine protection, this section articulates the relation between the movement of materialized prayers and the compelling narrative force of testimony. Through ethnographic descriptions of the process of manufacture and use of these sacred cloth remnants, this chapter describes the "texture of faith" as a particular desire to instantiate the fleeting voice of prayer. Tracing the movement of these sacred rags, I demonstrate the unanticipated emergence and force of faith in and through the exterior object. Suggesting a profanation at the heart of Holy Ghost power, this chapter describes the "patching-in" of materialized prayers into the threadbare fabric of everyday life.

In chapter 3, "Preaching: The Anointed Poetics of Breath," the ethnographic ear is prosthetically extended by radio loudspeakers and systems of voice amplification into a sacred soundscape that is punctuated by a particular technique of respiration practiced in southern Appalachia and within the African American church throughout the American South. In this sermonic performance, the faculties of articulation are *inspired* by the breath of the Holy Ghost. This possession, in turn, unleashes a divine poetic fluency that is characterized by a guttural and percussive gasp for breath at the end of the chanted sermonic line. Through the explosive force of this nonrepresentational noise that erupts from the anointed bodily techniques of the preacher, the power-filled presence of the Holy Ghost announces itself within the charismatic milieu. With gestures to other similar forms of rhythmic breath among African American communities opening a space of comparative leverage, I propose that the mouth of the radio loudspeaker—a crucial technological force in the oral transmission of this performative style—announces the anointed poetics of breath in particularly compelling ways.

Performances of healing prayer in southern Appalachia often require a physical body to literally "stand in the gap" between the sacred and the everyday. Revisiting classic ethnological theories on the contagious transmission of force, chapter 4, "Standin' in the Gap: The Materialities of Prayer," explores the place of material objects in the performance of divine communication and the practice of faith. Tracking between the devotional specificities of the practice of "standin'-in" within the context of southern Appalachia and the broader mass-mediated performances of healing prayer during the Charismatic Renewal, this section also articulates Oral Roberts's famous notion of "the point of contact" as a physical conduit for the transmission of healing power.

Recalling those rattling resonances of the very dry bones, the prophet Ezekiel reminds us that the bone itself has a capacity to register the sound of the sacred word and the divine breath in specific ways: "And he said unto me, Son of man, can these bones live? And I answered, O Lord God, thou knowest. Again he said unto me, prophesy upon these bones, and say unto them, O ye dry bones, *hear* the word of the Lord" (Ezekiel 37:3–4, King James Bible, my italics). Yet the bone has not only the sensitive capacity to register the presence of the sacred in particular ways, but also the power to announce or signal this divine presence through the production of *sound*: "So I prophesied as I was commanded: and as I prophesied, there was a noise, and behold a shaking, and the bones came together, bone to his bone" (v. 7).

Interpreting this passage, which resounds in charismatic sermons and songs throughout southern Appalachia quite literally, my project attends to the production of *numinous* noise in and through the technological and objectile media of charismatic worship. Like the sound of the bone that announces the presence of the spirit, a basic premise of my ethnography is that manifestations of the Holy Ghost, sonic or otherwise, can never be abstracted from the material objects, bodily techniques, and media technologies that are used to both disseminate the gospel and access communicative relays between the sacred and the everyday. One of the challenges of this ethnography, therefore, is to hear the specific resonances of the object itself in the organization and enframement of religious experiences of divine presence.[12]

The attempt to hear the sound of the sacred is also beholden in particular ways to the resonance of the bone.[13] More specifically, the capacity of human audition is made possible through the translations of three tiny bones (the hammer, the anvil, and the stirrup) as they resonate at the interface between the exterior environment and the sensitive structures of the inner ear. That the process of hearing is contingent upon a bone suggests the ways that the capacities of the human sensorium are always imprinted, cauterized, extended, and organized by technological environments that are seemingly exterior to the "natural" perceptual faculties of the subject. The experience and perception of prayer, therefore, an act intimately associated with capacities of human and divine audition, is transformed in different technological environments and historical epochs. Taking another oft-invoked phrase within the charismatic worship milieu, "His ears are not too heavy to hear the cries of his people" (Isaiah 59:1), this ethnography explores the specific ways efficacious prayer and other practices of divine communication are experienced and understood when the sound of prayer is "heard" by the artificial ear of the microphone, amplified by the mechanical mouth of the loudspeaker, and communicated across vast expanses through "wireless" apparati. Through the artificial ear of the microphone, a kind of prosthetic extension of a human sensory capacity, *Hittin' the Prayer Bones* attends to the contemporary technological resonances of that ubiquitous passage from the book of Romans (10:17): "Faith cometh by hearing."

CHAPTER 1

Radio as "Point of Contact"
Prayer and the Prosthesis of the Holy Ghost

I

Emerging from the black-veiled surface of the radio, the tremblings of her voice filled the room with an intimate presence, like the warmth of words whispered directly into the ear. These tremulous sounds—winding, careening, and twisting like the snake-path roads following the mountainsides and hollers of southern Appalachia—were punctuated every few seconds with a guttural gasp of breath. So clearly audible, the sound of these gasps made it seem as if the fleshy organs of vocalization themselves were incarnated by the mechanical lungs of the loudspeaker. Combined with the undulating flow of her voice, these guttural punctuations began to form a rhythmic and songlike cadence, so that to the ear of the attentive listener, the sound of the loudspeaker oscillated between the palpable cadence of rhythm and the emergent meaning of articulated words.

> SISTER VIOLET: The dead in Christ is gonna rise up—agh
> Amen.
> These old bones—agh
> They're gonna rise again one day after-awhile—agh
> Amen.
> When this is all over, and that Gabriel blows that trumpet—agh.
> Ooohh, get ready while ya can—agh
> God is a'tellin' ya, "Come On!"
> Come.
> When he calls—agh
> Don't turn him away.
> How can ya do except the Spirit draw-ye.
> The Spirit will draw you.
> Like-at Sister said when she come to that altar.

> The fire was in her shoes—Amen. That's your fire shut up in your
> bones—agh
> Amen—thank-God for that sweet Holy Ghost!
> Amen—agh!

Scanning the airwaves of southern Appalachia on any given Sunday, the radio loudspeaker is certain to voice the communal prayers, energetic singing, and "anointed" preaching styles that characterize the ecstatic performances of so-called folk religion in Appalachia. Unlike the highly produced, syndicated Evangelical programs that also retain a daily place within the Appalachian ether, these charismatic broadcasts are recognizable by their spontaneous and improvisatory style. The guiding principle of these live broadcasts, repeated time and again during each worship service, is "Just obey the Lord." Implicit in this phrase is a profound sense of expectation and anticipation that the miraculous power of the Holy Ghost will instantiate itself within the ritual milieu, taking possession of the faculties of speech and bodily control for the purposes of healing physical ailments and blessing the listening faithful.

These charismatic radio broadcasts maintain a vague liturgical structure, yet this form is often deferred, interrupted, or completely derailed according to the precarious contingencies introduced into the worship context by the miraculous power of the Holy Ghost. When the "power falls," it often "anoints" the preacher with a particular poetic style characterized by a rhythmic delivery of sentences punctuated by guttural grunts and gasps for breath, while at other times the spirit is "quenched" and withholds the *charismata* of rhetorical inspiration.[1] When the Holy Ghost power reaches ecstatic intensity, the anointing becomes so excessive as to completely enrapture the body of the speaker, initiating a "fallin' out in the spirit" that renders speechless the mouth of the preacher. This evocative phrase describes the sudden and precipitous collapse of the body into an inanimate mass whose only sign of life is the gentle, silent, undulation of respiration. To those not present but listening on the radio, the abrupt silencing of an anointed voice usually signals that an in-studio congregate has fallen out, as if their consciousness were suspended in that nebulous space between transmission and reception. The power of the spirit can take on myriad manifestations and self-effacing intensities, and the structure of the broadcast must be flexible enough to accommodate these precarious potentials of the Holy Ghost.

Centrally located within the southern Appalachians, radio station

105.5 FM, WGTH, "The Sheep," provides a good example of the small independent radio stations located throughout this region. Transmitting from southwestern Virginia, the signal of this station is capable of reaching the listening faithful throughout portions of southern West Virginia, eastern Kentucky, western North Carolina, western Virginia, and eastern Tennessee. As if to mimic the improvised spontaneity of the charismatic worship services that take place within the live studio of this station, the building itself was originally constructed as a domestic residence, but it has been converted with minimal alteration into a radio station. The space of the "live" studio clearly suggests its earlier domestic organization, with its brick fireplace, now usurped by a wooden podium that functions as both a support for the single studio microphone and an altar for the participants of the worship service. A large window in this room reveals a dilapidated storage shed and an outmoded satellite dish resting wirily in the backyard, its rusted face still gazing expectantly toward the heavens. On the wall opposite the window, a bare incandescent bulb mounted in a porcelain housing looks strangely out of place. The sudden muted glow of this bulb signals to the live studio congregation that the sounds within this converted space are now being broadcast to the listening audience out in what is referred to as "radioland," a nebulous space where the totality of the dispersed listening audience is imagined as a single community. Two reclaimed church pews, well-worn and stained from years of use, and fifteen mismatched chairs provide seating for the members of the live studio congregation. Though sometimes young children are present in the studio, the congregation is primarily made up of white working-class individuals (truck drivers, cafeteria cooks, miners, waitresses, and mechanics, among others), generally ranging in age from forty-five to seventy. Women have a slight majority in terms of attendance and participation within the live studio. Underneath the naked bulb sits a piano that often gives instrumental accompaniment to the lively singing of hymns.

During the week, live charismatic worship services are interspersed with local news, obituaries, church announcements, and syndicated Evangelical programming such as the *Back to the Bible Broadcast*. In addition, local businesses such as funeral homes, banks, restaurants, and farming supply stores advertise on this station. On the weekend, however, the programming features a higher concentration of charismatic worship services and preaching. On Saturday and Sunday, the radio station is bustling with energy as preachers, instrument-toting musicians, and faithful congregants pass in and out of the studio in slots of airtime ranging from thirty minutes to an hour. One of the most popular weekend broadcasts is the *Jackson Memorial Hour*, airing during the prime Sunday listening time from 11:00 A.M. until noon. The main organizers of this worship service, Brother Aldie Allen and Sister Dorothy Allen, have been preaching on the radio for over forty-three years. The Allens took over the program from Dorothy's father, Brother George Jackson, who began broadcasting in the mid-1950s on a radio program called *The Little Mountain Preacher*. Brother Aldie, the main preacher during this broadcast, had his conversion experience while listening to the voice of Brother George issuing from the radio loudspeaker.

As these brief historical details suggest, many of the self-proclaimed "old-time Gospel" worship practices in Appalachia are intimately related to the technology of radio. A significant proportion of the charismatic faithful in this region grew up listening to worship services mediated over this apparatus. The prominent practice of radio listening, in combination with the aurally saturated metaphors of early Christianity ("Faith cometh by hearing," as an example), significantly influences the way many of the charismatic faithful, broadcasters and radio listeners alike, experience and understand practices such as intercessory prayer, faith healing, and glossolalia.

Like many of the charismatic broadcasts in this region, the *Jackson Memorial Hour* is oriented around the healing of physical illness. The key ritual performance and climax of emotional intensity in such radio programs is organized around the practice of faith healing. In order to create an efficacious milieu for miraculous cures, the force of the Holy Ghost must be instantiated into the worship context. Various theurgical apparati are set in motion in a *precarious* attempt to "get a prayer through" to the divine ear. As noted by Max Muller in his series of Oxford lectures, "On Ancient Prayers," the word "prayer" has an important etymological similarity with the word "precarious." This analysis is helpful within the context of this study because it suggests the emergence of faith as a kind of burden or threat to the automatic efficacy of the magical incantation. An elementary contingency and potential breakdown, therefore, resides within the performance of prayer. Moreover, this supposed burden of faith gets to the core of significant debates within the emergent disciplines of comparative religion and ethnology. These debates described how the automatic efficacy of the magical and materialized incantation undergoes a gradual process of "abstraction," "spiritualization," and "interiorization" through an ever-increasing technological control of the contingencies of the natural environment. Through this process of abstraction, the materialized and automatic efficacy of incantation becomes the precarious practice of prayer directed toward autonomous spiritual agents. Despite these earlier forecasts, however, material conduits always seem to insinuate themselves into the contemporary worship context in a tactile attempt to mitigate the precariousness of prayer. Thus, a panoply of charismatic techniques of the body, material objects, and media technologies are simultaneously engaged to make manifest the presence of the Holy Ghost. Such material and ideational entanglements summon a physicality shared by both the spirit and the radio voice, a commonality that is necessary for successful faith healing.

Several times during the course of the *Jackson Memorial Hour*, the members of the studio congregation, referred to as "prayer warriors," are called to circle around the microphone and pray for the sick listeners out in "radioland." The altar mentioned during such healing prayers refers to the microphone and microphone stand as well as the wooden table they rest on. Congregants of the radio church occasionally kneel down in front of the microphone during moments of conversion and supplication. As the prayer warriors approach and place their hands upon the wooden platform, the sensitive microphone crisply perceives brisk pops, cracks, creaks, and thuds as hands are placed near the microphone and as the microphone is adjusted. This call for participation in the healing prayer also includes the listening audience. Both the isolated sick in need of a cure and the distant worshipper who wishes to contribute to the theurgical efficacy are called on to "lay your hand on the radio as a point of contact and pray with us." As if to mimic the early radio sets that had the capacity to both transmit and receive, the radio loudspeaker becomes a two-way conduit for divine communication.[2] For listeners out in radioland, it is as if the radio loudspeaker can simultaneously amplify or extend prayers from the everyday to that sacred space somewhere else *and* receive the miraculous transmission of healing force from the sacred to the everyday.

While these preparations for healing prayer are taking place, Brother Aldie further organizes the prayer by assigning "stand-ins" and arranging the most efficacious manual positioning for the communication of Holy Ghost power. Once again, the level of spontaneity and creative improvisation that characterizes these ritual preparations is worth noting. While observing these preparations, one is reminded of the creative informality of rural farmers who use whatever materials are at hand (garden hoses, tin cans, bailing twine, rusted washing machine parts, and so on) to get a tractor up and running again before the rain falls upon the hay. "Standin' in" the gap between the everyday and the sacred, poetic techniques of prayer and material conduits of the spirit are mobilized through a consecrated performance of what Stewart calls, in describing a local cultural poetics, "foolin' with thangs."[3]

Among charismatic practices in Appalachia, one member of the congregation who is present in the studio becomes the bodily substitute for a patient who is to be prayed for but not physically present. Blood relations usually provide the most efficacious "stand-ins" or conduits for the prayer, though some members of the congregation are believed to possess particular connections to certain categories of illness and patients and may be employed as stand-ins in these cases. For example, one older sister was believed to have a special gift as an embodied conduit for sick children; therefore, when the congregation prayed for a distant child who had no kinship bond in the studio, she was often called upon to stand in and thus become a physical medium for healing power on behalf of the ailing child.

Radiating outward like spokes around the hub of the microphone-altar, the outstretched arms and downward-facing palms of the studio worshippers demarcate a sacred circle for the communication of Holy Ghost power. As if to amplify the efficacious connectivity of the spirit through tactile contact, the body in communication with divine powers and the material mediations of the radio apparatus mimic one another almost without distinction. In this way, the haptic and proprioceptive sensations of the outstretched or uplifted "holy hand" seem to amplify the technical capacities of the microphone. Speaking forcefully toward the center of this sacred wheel, Brother Aldie begins the prayer: "Father God we call . . . ." Like the sudden illumination of the exposed electric bulb protruding from a wall in the makeshift studio, his short invocation signals all the prayer warriors to commence praying their own specific prayer out loud.

What follows is a technique of prayer that is practiced in charismatic worship services throughout Appalachia. Because of the striking entanglement of articulated words created in this communal performance of divine communication, I have termed this practice "skein prayer." Borrowed from the terminology of weaving and textiles, the word "skein" denotes both a bundle of yarn and the act of tangling or coiling thread. Thus, the phrase "skein prayer" suggests that there are elements of manual technique and haptic sensation intertwined with the oral performance of prayer. As the prayer progresses, this atmosphere of language grows dense like the haze of coal dust: the bituminous unction of industrial modernity. As these atmospheres thicken, so does the explosive potential. In this entanglement, the possibility of articulation is immersed in a seething skein of noise.

As if this vociferous entanglement of dismembered words were not enough to secure the attention of the divine ear,[4] the noise of the skein prayer is augmented by vocal exercises such as wailing, crying, and the most prominent and practiced form of these vocalizations, the undulating "Whooo." As if to further thematize the disarticulation of language and immersion into the buzz of noise, the mouth cedes its function of *articulous* and simply cries out, voicing a basic capacity of the vocal organs.[5] Skein prayer, according to many charismatic practitioners in Appalachia, is one of the most efficacious theurgical techniques to "get a prayer through" to the divine ear. Suddenly, this pulsating flow of skein prayer is cut through with the only clearly discernible sound, the percussive *pop* of hands rapidly clapped together in disjointed bursts of five to fifteen beats. If only for an instant, these percussive cracks pierce through the entangled thickness of noise. There is an important structural similarity between the overall aural effect of the communal skein prayer and the practice of speaking in tongues, or glossolalia. In both cases, the most efficacious forms of prayer are those that can be registered by the human ear but whose plenitude of meaning remains unavailable. To observe this performance of skein prayer in the space of the live studio, one is moved, perhaps even threatened, by the emotionally charged, ecstatic space that is produced. However, the translation of this performance through the radio apparatus produces a significantly different experience—an experience, moreover, that seems particularly apt for the ecstatic moment of skein prayer.

The performance of skein prayer in the live studio differs subtly from the way that this efficacious prayer is "traditionally" practiced. Whereas the ritual of skein prayer within the space of the church or revival tent is usually performed by each congregation member, whether positioned within the space in the rows of chairs or pews or perhaps gathered around the body of the sick patient, the performance of this type of entangled prayer within the live studio is specifically organized and oriented around the artificial ear of the microphone. As if to use the artificial amplifications of the electro-mechanical ear/mouth to enhance the efficacy of this theurgical technique, the prayer warriors gather around the microphone/altar.

The skein prayer oriented around the microphone suggests yet another entanglement: an intertwining between the technological infrastructure of the apparatus and the precarious hearing capacities of the divine ear. Early Christian anxieties around the potential for the divine ear to become "heavy," "dull," or "deaf," and thus unable to hear "the cries of the people," suggest the historically and technologically contingent modes for understanding and experiencing divine hearing capacities, angelic messengers, divinatory speech, sacred postal economies, disruptive demons, oracular noise, and so on.[6] Charismatic practitioners self-consciously utilize the radio apparatus to amplify "the cries of the people." Yet this amplification reacts back upon the pious subject with unanticipated consequences and attunes particular modes of religious sensation. Within this charismatic context, the radio apparatus is an important component of what Birgit Meyer has recently termed the "sensational form."[7] Senses of transcendence are inflected, attuned, and augmented in particular ways by the religious mediations within the worship context. Embodied techniques and pious training combine with material mediations of the divine to produce the ecstatic sensation of what Hent de Vries, emphasizing the intimate relation between instrumental artifice and the miraculous, calls the "special effect."[8]

The theurgical orientation around the microphone simultaneously facilitates a benediction upon the ears of the listening faithful out in radioland and an amplification of the exigent intercessory cry toward heaven. The prayer warriors in the radio station anticipate the simultaneous voicing of their prayer somewhere else in the nebulous and diffuse space of radioland. The very organization of the prayer, even before the tongues have tangled and the percussive pops have cut through the skein, thus prefigures a peculiar experience of simultaneity or doubling somewhere else. This basic detail concerning the different orientation and conception of the charismatic skein prayer reveals how the radio apparatus inflects or augments experiences and performances of divine communication. Skein prayer voiced into the artificial ear of the microphone is not merely the replication of "normal" charismatic worship practices "over" the radio, but a profound alteration, reconceptualization, and reembodiment, through the transforming process of technological mediation.

As the skein prayer is translated from the space of the live studio to the mouth of the loudspeaker at home, the listener, whose capacity for hearing is extended by the artificial ear of the microphone, experiences this moment in a condition of "blindness."[9] The technical capacities of the radio do not convey any visual information about the prayer. There is no visual grounding to help orient and locate the voice issuing forth from the loudspeaker. Alternatively, when this type of prayer is experienced within the space of the studio or church, for example, the participant is able to differentiate and organize this otherwise cacophonous tangle of noise by visually identifying the positions of other congregants' bodies. Likewise, if the congregant has her eyes closed and hands raised in a posture of prayer, she is able to differentiate and locate these voices by differing proximity and intensity of sound, reverberations created by architecture or surroundings, physical contact with other church members, and so on. Rather than detracting from the somatic and emotional power of prayer in the presence of a church space, this distinction may be useful to emphasize the different sensory registers and sense ratios that are invoked, attuned, and trained in what may seem to be the same practice. In comparison to the architectural space of the church, worship through the radio invokes, attunes, and trains significantly different sensory registers and sense ratios.

Issuing from nowhere, this compelling force of sacred noise gains a new quality and intensity of disorientation through the radio. This vertiginous "special effect" of the radio apparatus foregrounds and attunes the sense of hearing at the expense of other perceptual capacities. This is not to say that the body of the listener loses all perceptual and embodied orientations in the private domestic space. Listeners are still experiencing this "canny" environment through the embodied orientation of the senses (seeing the table upon which the radio sits, feeling the fabric of the couch, or smelling the food cooking). This feeling of embodied familiarity, we might add, could nevertheless further contribute to the strange sensation of aural disjuncture between the noise issuing from that peculiar elsewhere of the apparatus and the privacy of the everyday domestic space. The sacred noise of skein prayer rends the mundane and habituated "radio texture" that is usually associated with practices of radio listening within the domestic space.[10] Uncanny in the strict sense of the term, the ecstatic noise of skein prayer demarcates a numinous space within the intimate interior of the home.[11]

One could add to the disorienting force of the "disembodied" skein prayer the technical failure of the microphone that is voiced by the loudspeaker. At moments, the noise of the prayer reaches such sonic intensities that the sensitivities of the microphone are unable to clearly register the sound. This technical inability to process the boisterous prayer generates a strange distorted noise that is sounded through the mouth of the loudspeaker . Like the stones in the book of Luke, the technical capacities of the apparatus themselves cry out, adding to the efficacy and sensorial impact of the prayer.[12] This technological failure is voiced by the loudspeaker as a violent hiss of wind and static and a bending or distortion of the skein voices.

Just as there are moments during the performance of prayer when the technological media fail to "faithfully" register the din within the studio, there are many instances following the gradual lull and decrescendo of the skein prayer when the pastor declares, "That prayer ain't gone through yet. Keep prayin'!" When a member of the congregation senses that the prayer has not "gone through," the prayer warriors resume the prayer until everyone is satisfied that the theurgical transmission has reached the divine ear. Communication breakdown between the divine and the everyday is often attributed to the obstructing influences of the devil and his "dark principalities," as well as the burden of unbelief among the radio congregation and the listening audience. Likewise, the negative force of unbelief is said to "quench" the Holy Ghost, preventing the anointing power from entering the space of worship. Though many times the skein prayer is performed with no tangible manifestations of the spirit within the studio, there are occasional moments of ecstatic irruption when the numbing buzz of prayer unleashes the miraculous power of the Holy Ghost.

II

Many faithful listeners in radioland claim to have been miraculously healed as a result of hearing the skein prayer mediated through the radio apparatus. Sister Violet, a faithful listener to charismatic broadcasts and occasional participant in the space of the live studio, gave a testimony to the miraculous cure of her severely infected index finger while listening to the radio:

> When my fanger was in bad shape,
> you know, Sister Dorothy was a-prayin'.
> She was a-prayin' one Sunday mornin' on there [the radio] for me.
> And I felta-sucha par [power] a-shakin' my radio.
> And I just lifted my hands up,
> and then I realized that I had my fanger on the radio,
> and my fanger began ta straighten out.
> And, you know, somebody's gotta pray the prayer of faith for ye.
> And I felt her, and then I realized my fanger was straight....
> You know, we need to tell, and stand up and tell what God does for us.
> And may God bless ya—I don't wanna take up no more time.[13]

As Sister Violet testifies into the microphone for an unseen audience, her performance completes a circuitry of efficacious prayer. It is as if the healed body of the patient tracks back to the mechanical origin of the prayer. Recounting the miraculous event and thus tracing the infrastructure of the radio broadcast, the healed patient returns to the material source of transmission. Her "live" in-studio appearance in the technological space of transmission is voiced into the self-same microphone that once registered a prayer on her behalf. The anointed body of Sister Violet embodies a forgotten technical potentiality of the radio apparatus; the magnetic interface of the radio's transducer is capable not only of reception but of transmission as well.[14]

Sister Violet's experience of "presence" entails sensations that are in excess of the merely instrumental capacities of the medium. Thus, the haptic and kinesthetic descriptions given by Sister Violet point to a specific effect of radio listening that transcends the informational content of the broadcast. Not only are the sounds of Sister Dorothy's praying voice translated by the apparatus; Sister Violet *feels* the physical proximity of Sister Dorothy, and this specifically in relation to the somatic awareness of bodily disfigurement and proprioceptive sensations of raised hands.

Likewise, faithful listeners out in radioland also respond to radio's production of presence by actively participating with the broadcast. During interviews, listeners often describe how they interact with the worship service by clapping their hands and singing along with the studio congregation. Several listeners claimed to actively encourage the radio preacher with exhortations such as, "Preach it Brother!" and "Come On!" This type of participation with the radio broadcast is accompanied by ecstatic manifestations, such as the listener who called in to the broadcast to testify that she received the anointing while doing house chores and suddenly began "just a-jumpin' and a-shoutin' all over the kitchen." The sound issuing from the radio loudspeaker produces an experience of calling or demand upon the listener that is in excess of the informational content of the broadcast.

As Theodor Adorno notes, a basic characteristic of the radio apparatus is that during the experience of listening, the instrumental/material aspects of the radio apparatus (studio microphones, transmitters, receivers, electrical grids) are forgotten or repressed.[15] Through habitual use and a longing for the unmediated, the machinations and material details of the instrument fade into the background.[16] This inability to actively conceptualize the infrastructure of broadcasting, therefore, creates a sensation of actuality—that an unmediated voice is present in the space of listening directly addressing the listener in his or her singularity. As I have suggested, this sensation is also described as the experience of the isolated radio listener suddenly singled out by a speaker who seems to be actually present in the space of listening.[17]

And yet it is not merely this capacity to forget that produces the most profound sensations of presence, but a kind of doubled awareness that simultaneously recognizes the instrumental machinations of the apparatus and a vague sensation of something else at work behind the apparatus. This rupture, or special effect, that is produced when sensory capacities are augmented and extended by media such as radio brings us closer to understanding the moment when Sister Violet's radio trembled with divine power.

To be sure, the charismatic faith-healing tradition is saturated with metaphors and practices of touch. Throughout many charismatic radio broadcasts, the phrases "he needs a touch from the Lord" or "touch her, Lord" are employed as metaphors of divine healing and miraculous intervention. Accounts within the New Testament of "laying on of hands" and various instances of efficacious communication of divine healing through tactile contact are interpreted literally and translate into a plethora of tactile practices within worship. The performance of healing prayer is intimately and crucially linked to a frenetic drive to tactility.

In this way, the contagious potentiality of the Holy Spirit could become communicated through tactile contact with the radio loudspeaker. The specificities of charismatic radio tactility, however, cannot be merely collapsed into a more general charismatic drive to healing touch. The act of touching the radio receiver in order to facilitate both the efficacious reception and the transmission of Holy Ghost power is generally referred to as a "point of contact." Though this crucial theologico-technical term has spread out—a propensity of all sacred force—to encompass a significant inventory within the charismatic reliquary (anointing oil, photographs, letters, television sets, prayer stamps, prayer cloths), the key concept of "point of contact" itself was, in fact, formulated within the context of healing prayer mediated over the radio apparatus. Oral Roberts, arguably the most significant proponent of both the charismatic healing revival and Pentecostal faith-healing movements during the twentieth century, coined this phrase as a theologico-technical term that helped to mitigate the distance from both the ear of the faithful radio listener and the efficacious healing virtue of the Holy Ghost. The term "theologico-technical" suggests that the point of contact is both a specific theurgical technique that augments or amplifies the efficacy of the prayer, as well as a theological claim upon the nature of divine communication and faith. According to Roberts,

God brings certain "instrumentalities" into the world to provide material conduits for divine force, allowing the patient to "turn faith loose" through an act of tactile contact.

Though most of the faithful must employ an actual piece of technology to unleash their faith and thus instantiate healing virtue, Roberts himself claimed to have been given as one of his *charismata* a specific "sense of discernment" in his right hand that allowed him to "detect" the presence of illness-causing demons. This presence was discerned through tactile sensations of pressure that were exerted upon his healing hand by the malignant force of the illness-demon.[18] For the listener, tactile contact with the radio loudspeaker became a prosthetic extension of Roberts's gift of discernment and detection. Thus, as Roberts laid his hand upon the microphone or a physical stand-in within the studio during the "prayer-time" of his famous *Healing Waters Broadcast*, the ailing patient placed hands on the radio loudspeaker to access Roberts's manual sense of detection. This tactile/objectile exercise of faith, in turn, "loosed their faith" and created a physical conduit for the communication of healing virtue.

In *If You Need Healing Do These Things*, Roberts emphasizes the radio as an important point of contact.[19] Of course, Roberts's use of radio contact as a technique of immediacy, "liveness," and audience participation was not new. Early Pentecostal radio pioneers of the late 1920s, such as Sister Aimee McPherson, also encouraged listeners to make tactile contact with the loudspeaker during the prayer.[20] Roberts, however, made radio tactility a centerpiece of his *Healing Waters Broadcast* and explicitly formulated the theologico-technical phrase "radio as a point of contact." Moreover, *If You Need Healing Do These Things*, a how-to manual of faith healing, features an illustration explaining how the point of contact works. At the top of the image sits Roberts himself in front of a large microphone exclaiming, "Rise, the Lord maketh the [thee?] whole." A bedfast and sickly looking man is located in the bottom corner of the illustration, his feeble hand outstretched and touching the radio, while a gigantic divine hand reaches down from heaven to touch his head and thus communicate "healing virtue." Providing a striking example of the disavowal of the material conduit in the moment of healing cure or efficacious divine communication, the radio loudspeaker, placed prominently in front of the prostrate patient, voices the ironic words, "ONLY BELIEVE."[21]

Likewise, a prefiguration or anticipation of the "radio as a point of contact" can be seen in the pictures and descriptions taken from Roberts's massive tent revival campaigns of the 1940s. Inside what was then the

FIGURE 3 Illustration of the "Point of Contact" from the healing treatise

largest tent in the world, sick patients would form a "prayer line" or "healing line" in the front of the sanctuary, to be prayed over, one at a time, by Roberts's hand. This massive tent auditorium depended on a large public announcement system to broadcast the voice of the healer throughout the throngs of faithful and expectant audience members. Roberts's praying voice and his right hand of discernment were therefore already mediated by a technological system of voice amplification that was literally inserted between the body of the healer and the patient (fig. 4). The microphone, or technological extension and amplification of the voice, was already mediating the patient-healer complex; Roberts would often hold the microphone in his left hand, its large steel housing held close to his mouth, while his right hand reached out to both "discern" the illness of the patient and communicate healing virtue. The technology of radio broadcasting allowed Roberts to propose a strange mimicking of the healing technique within the amplified space of the revival tent. Roberts asked listeners to put their hands upon the apparatus in order to gain access to divine healing power. The materialities of the radio, combined with a need to produce a sensation of "liveness" and immediacy for the distant listening audience, initiated a curious reversal or inversion of the tactile healing technique.

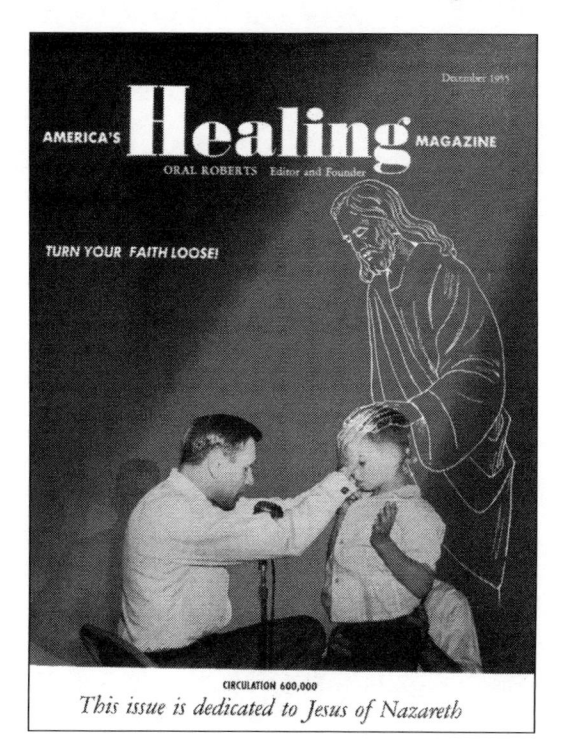

FIGURE 4 Iconic image of the famous healer

In this way, the faithful listeners experienced an artificial or prosthetic embodiment of Roberts's spiritual gift of haptic detection; they experienced the tactile sensations of heat and pressure from the vibrating electric diaphragm of the radio loudspeaker. In terms specifically related to the radio apparatus and the challenges of communication at a distance, the point of contact can be seen as a theatrical production of immediacy or "liveness" through a strategic thematization of an unanticipated or unregistered potential of the radio apparatus. Hearing the prayer issuing from the loudspeaker in an experiential condition of "blindness," the listener-participant laid on hands to "fill in" the disembodied and distanced voice. Deploying two sensory modes—the auditory and the haptic—during the performance of healing prayer created a powerful sense of immediacy with the praying voice. More than this, however, the discontinuity or disjuncture between sounds registered by ear and vibrations felt by hand was likely experienced by many tactile listeners as the miraculous healing power of the Holy Ghost.

To experience sound through the hand, as a deaf person palpating the throat of someone speaking in order to "hear," creates a sense of disjuncture between the body's capacity to register and process sound and the sheer materiality of sound experienced through the hand. This sensation of vibration not only corresponds or co-registers with certain sound-meanings of the radio voice, but the sensitive capacities of the skin are able to register heat, pressure, and vibration that are "unheard" by the ear. Radio tactility thus allows the listener to experience the prayer in a profoundly different sensory mode than is possible in other worship contexts and media environments. Sensations of Holy Ghost power surging through the radio loudspeaker reside in this productive space of the experiential gap between the haptic and the audile. This sensation of excess during the practice of radio tactility informs the healing testimony of Sister Violet and her reliance upon tactile and kinesthetic metaphors to describe the miraculous moment when she feels her radio trembling with divine power. Sister Violet's testimony is a tactile sensation of skein prayer experienced through the hand. Indeed, the tangled excess of noise, percussive pops, and wailing produced through the performance of skein prayer is manually registered through the loudspeaker as a series of warm, trembling vibrations.[22] This particular practice of radio audition seems to emphasize the tactile sensibilities at the expense of aural experience.

Crucial theurgical techniques within the context of charismatic faith healing, such as the tactile "point of contact," were thus developed specifically in relation to the radio apparatus and actively incorporated into the worship styles of the Appalachian faithful. Modes of listening and understandings of faith healing insinuated themselves into the "normal" church context through the mass mediations of the radio apparatus, at least since the early 1930s. Emphasizing the intertwining of charismatic practice and media technologies such as the radio also attests to the thorough modernity of "old-time gospel" and prevents the typical view of religion in Appalachia as "isolated" or "timeless." Charismatic practices such as skein prayer and radio tactility can be seen as performative negotiations of a specific technologically mediated environment, just as much as attempts to influence and instantiate supernatural power. There are crucial moments within the ritual context where the two seemingly discrete phenomena—the performance of prayer and the technical apparatus—become indistinguishable.

Within the charismatic tradition, the phenomenon of radio tactility points to a "prosthesis of prayer" and an "apparatus of belief" supplementing the spiritualized rhetoric of faith healing. Many of the faithful within the charismatic community and beyond emphasize that prayer is unmediated and free from material conduits, claiming "there is no distance in prayer." In academic analysis, many so-called belief-centered theories of ritual efficacy relegate the force of charismatic healing techniques to internal psychological mechanisms and cognitive processes. Both everyday and scholarly understandings of "faith healing" thus take for granted the internal, spiritual, and belief-centered characteristics of this curative technique. Yet the prevalence of material "points of contact" such as the radio apparatus suggest otherwise. Perhaps a reconceptualization of the term "faith" in the ubiquitous phrase "faith healing" would be useful.

The exercise of faith — and its visceral, embodied connotations — seems to be activated in material objects and technological apparati exterior to the religious subject. It is as if faith does not reside in the interior structures of cognition and belief but instead remains hidden within the external object, ready to be "let loose," "unleashed," or "released" through the explosive tactile performance of the "point of contact." Through the machinations of the radio apparatus, the religious subject is able to "reach out and touch faith." Faith therefore seems to make its appearance felt in and through specific processes of objectile and technological mediation.

Yet to conclude by suggesting that faith resides in media radically exterior to the religious subject would be merely to reify what seems to be a peculiar oscillation at work within the term "faith" itself. The precariousness inherent in prayer demands some kind of performance or practice of faith. This performance of faith is not only a spiritual form of volition or belief that would propitiate the precarious contingencies of divine communication. Rather, it is simultaneously a performative revelation and concealment of the material conduits of divine communication. Its power depends on a disavowal of the tangible media of prayer in favor of some spiritualized form of belief. The word "faith," then, encapsulates both the material conduit of prayer and its simultaneous denial. In an instant of self-effacement, the radio loudspeaker voices "ONLY BELIEVE" at the very moment when the ailing patient must make tactile contact with the apparatus in order to receive healing power.

Just as haptic and kinesthetic sensations were restored to the necrosed and benumbed finger of Sister Violet through tactile contact with the radio apparatus, the miraculous presence of the Holy Ghost makes its appearance to the particular sensory registers of the religious subject as a specific effect of technological mediation. The apparatus, as a kind of prosthetic sixth sense, attunes the perceptual faculties to specific somatic experiences of the "transcendent." The material and technological prostheses of prayer extend the perceptual capacities of the subject somewhere else, yet this religious experience of *ecstasis* (literally, talking outside the self) can never be abstracted from the material devotional practices that "stand in" between the everyday and the sacred. The Holy Ghost moves in that ecstatic space between body and apparatus, and thus Sister Violet feels her radio "shakin'" with divine power. To rephrase the passage from the book of Romans (10:17), perhaps it would be more appropriate to conclude that "faith cometh by *touching*."

III. Ritual Resonances of the Radio Voice

The phenomenon of healing radio tactility is a preeminent example of an interfacing of techniques of divine communication and the technology of the radio apparatus. However, many other examples evoked and performed within the charismatic worship space of the live studio suggest the intimate relations between experiences and understandings of prayer and the radio apparatus. This section describes several recurrent motifs within the context of the charismatic radio broadcast to reinforce the phenomenal impact of the radio voice on experiences of divine presence, prayer, and healing efficacy.

A Ritual Procession around the Microphone

ALDIE: I may just have ta preach here in a minute, seems like tha sangin' ain't goin' no where.
Before I do, I'm gonna go ahead and preach here in just a minute, if it be tha Lord's will.
[*In an informal yet imperative voice*] Francis come'ere.
'Fore I do I don't know why, I don't know why
[*Arranging the most efficacious ritual positions*] No give me your other hand . . .
I don't know why. I don't know why.
But before I preach, I need ya ta just walk around this mic here a-time'er-two.
[*Intense, visceral voice*] I need ta walk her around this mic here a-time'er-two!
I don't know why.
Ah' but God does—agh [*Poetics of breath beginning to emerge*]
Ah' God knows what's goin' on—agh
He knows our problems—agh
An' tha troubles that we all have—agh

But I'll tell ya today that we got a God today,
Ah' Francis, that'll reach down—agh
An'll maketh a way when there seemeth to be no way—agh
Ah' praise God
As far as the prayer warriors—agh
It seems like God's takin'em out one at a time—agh
But I got news for Mr. Satan—agh
Honey I got news for'em—agh
Ah' tha same God—agh
That was here with Joe Shelton—agh
The same God here with George Jackson—agh
The same one here with all the others—agh
He's still here today—agh
He's still blessin' today—agh
If you'll believe in tha name of tha Lord.
There's a healin' commin' fer somebody,
I thought it was Gordon, it ain't Gordon—
[*Loud, boisterous voice*] *It's you gonna get that healin' this mornin'!*
It's you!
Thank God, thank God, thank God.
God's gonna heal ya, and ever-thang's gonna be alright.
I don't know what she needs.
I don't know what she needs.
She's gettin' a blessing, or she's gonna get a healin'.
[*Brother Aldie's voice becomes indiscernible amid the claps,
    singing, vocalizations, and glossolalia inundating the space
    of the live studio.*]
[*Speaking once again in close proximity to the microphone,
    with a voice clearly registered*]
Gordon may get a healin', no doubt in my mind that he is.
But right there's the one tha Lord told me gonna get a healin' this
    mornin'.
But didn't tell me 'til right now.
Francis needs a healin' [*Glossolalia clearly audible and forceful
    in the background*]
I told ya I'm gonna preach here in a minute.
Arizona make yerself at home, help pray [*Arizona enters the live
    studio*]

> Come help pray, make yerself at home [*A brief "silence" in which only speaking in tongues is heard filling the studio and resonating from the loudspeaker*]
> Help pray for her.
> The Lord's gonna give'er a healin' this mornin'.
> The doctors are givin' bad reports,
> But we got a God today that don't give no bad reports.
> We got a doctor today, an' his name is Jesus. [*Multiple individuals speaking in tongues, clearly audible*] (October 25, 2009)

Three weeks later (November 15, 2009):

> ALDIE: I feel bad a'doin' this, but I gotta obey tha Lord.
> That was that same service, I believe,
> That the Lord had me ta walk Francis around this podium three times [*The podium holds the microphone*]
> Francis I'm not pickin' on you, but we gotta do it again today.
> And I don't know what it's for.
> But I know One that's got a reason for it.
> [*Several praise reports and testimonies are given, as well as the announcement of prayer requests*]
> Ever-body come on over here, we're gonna pray.
> We're gonna pray an' after we pray I'm gonna walk Francis around;
> Or no, we're gonna do one song first.
> And then we're gonna walk Francis around this podium.
> An' ask ever-body in radioland an' here in tha studio ta help us pray.
> Don't know why, but God does.
> Help us as you will.
> [*Prayer begins, followed by a song*]
> You know Jesus said I'll use the foolish thangs ta confound tha wise.
> An' alotta times I do things like this,
> An' people, I don't know, they don't understand.
> An' seems like if you cain't give'em a name or tell'em what it is about,
> Then they get real quiet to see what's gonna happen.
> But if you're here to serve tha Lord, let God have his way.
> Don't you worry about what God's gonna do,
> Let him do his job, 'cause he knows what it's about.
> I'm gonna take Francis around this altar three times,
> An' I want you people ta pray.
> Somebody . . . is gonna get a miracle.

Whether it's right here in this building,
Or whether it's in radioland,
Somebody is needin' a miracle this mornin'.
An' God is gonna give you that miracle.
It may be me, I don't know.
I had back surgery February this year, ever-thang in there is loose;
   [*Pins, rods, and cage in spine*]
Doctor says it's loose-as-a-goose.
And they gotta do it all over again Tuesday. [*Intense congregation response begins building and continues until prayer cycle commences*]
Landis has gotta have two hips replaced.
It may be him, I don't know.
It may be Brother Henry's eyes, I don't know.
It may be Sister Dixie's feet, I don't know.
It may be one a'ya'll, I don't know.
It may be somebody in radioland, I don't know.
But thar's one thang I do know.
When God says ta do somethin',
If we'll do what he says ta do,
Ever-thang'll be alright.
Pray for us.
[*As the communal prayer commences, Aldie can still be overheard for several lines until his individual articulations are inundated by the charismatic vocalizations, prayers, percussive claps, and the song, "Put Jesus on the Mainline," performed simultaneously by members of the congregation.*]
Father God in tha name a'Jesus,
Lord as we obey you, God.
Ah' Lord you told me ta walk'er around three times,
An' you didn't say why.
You said walk'er three times.
As we walk'er around God.

The commencement of this ritual of divine healing is marked by a sudden compulsion to walk around the in-studio microphone. In this performance of ritualized circumambulation, the bodies of the participants are drawn by some ineluctable force of gravitation to walk around the microphone. This ritual demarcation of a sacred circle produces through bodily techniques and prayer a sacred space encircling the most consecrated point where healing power will be communicated from the sacred to the everyday: the microphone.[23]

The divine guidance driving this ritual procession demonstrates a particular force of attraction to the microphone. As an artificial organ of hearing that is always listening, always registering even the sounds that are unheard and unattended by the "natural" ears of the in-studio congregation, the artificial sensitivities of the microphone become a divinatory apparatus that will soon reveal the locus where the healing efficacy will be instantiated. As the most forceful point of consecration at the center of the sacred circle, the microphone is a divine ear that not only registers the presence of earthly sounds but also "hears" the physical procession of bodies around its electro-mechanical organs. The microphone's capacity to "hear," in turn, both reveals the source of illness and announces the manifestation of healing power to come.

The act of physically demarcating a space around the microphone thematizes the particular sensitivities of this technology of hearing. Performatively revealing the presence of the microphone within the space of worship, as Aldie grasps the hand of Francis and escorts her around the microphone, an audible effect of distance is created for the listener as the voice varies in intensity, clarity, and audibility during this ritual procession. The ritual performatively reveals the organizational capacity of the microphone within the broader infrastructural complex of the radio apparatus (transmitters, receivers, loudspeakers, electricity, and so on). Through the mouth of the loudspeaker, the sensitivities of the artificial ear (microphone) convey this experience of ritual movement in a particularly compelling way. Thus, it is precisely through its emancipation from an everyday perceptual grounding in the visual that the translation of a ritual procession through the radio apparatus produces a compelling aural effect. Through the ear, both the artificial one and "natural" one, the listener gets a sense of the spatial proximity of bodies in the performance of a ritual ambulation around the in-studio microphone. In this way, divine awareness and the artificial hearing capacities of the microphone collapse into indistinction: *"Ah' God knows what's goin' on—agh."*

Hearing Tongues through the Loudspeaker

ALDIE: You know it made me feel good there yesterday.
Ya know we all-time tellin' people, tryin' encourage 'em ta obey tha Lord.

An' it was real good ta see Claude there Friday night.
Hear his witness; an' he's tellin' us about listening to tha [radio]
   program,
An' how he heard Violet on the program here talkin' in tongues.
An' he heard it an' interpreted it, *an' it's fer him.*
I never did hear her interpret it, I guess maybe she did.
But he said he did, *an' it's fer him.* (December 2008, WGTH;
   italics for emphasis)

Name Called over the Radio

ALDIE: Ya know, alotta times God lets us hear thangs that we
   don't do.
Just for the Glory of tha Lord,
One morning I's up here an' I was preachin' so hard.
An' that afternoon we went ta church where we's pastorin' over here.
An' this young lady come out there and told me,
Said, "Aldie," said, "I want ya'll to pray for me."
Said, "You called my name on tha radio program."
Said, "An' I began to shout."
Said, "I's warshin' dishes."
I don't remember now which dishes she had in'er hand
They went flyin' across tha kitchen.
She said, "An' I's a'throwin' water ever-whar, shoutin' ever-whar."
An' said, "You called my name and told me to come out here,
   that I was gonna be healed."
Church, I didn't say it.
She heard my voice but it wasn't me.
I didn't say it—I know I didn't.
They gonna take'er breasts off.
[*Speaking to a member of the studio congregation*] You remember
   Sister Faye?
She come up an' we prayed for'er.

This nonrepresentational force of the radio voice issuing from the loudspeaker actively calls out the listener, as in the next account of the woman who tries to turn her radio apparatus off, and is exemplified through Brother Claude hearing "tongues" through the radio loudspeaker. Once again, the listener is singled out by the radio voice, "an' it's fer him," and this in the face of a sound emerging from the loudspeaker that transcends or exceeds the meaningful articulation of everyday language. In this way, glossolalia sounding from the mouth of the radio apparatus becomes doubly compelling in that the loudspeaker itself compounds a process of possessed "speakers" that are animated by forces from elsewhere. Glossolalia through the mouth of the radio loudspeaker reveals the compelling structure of the radio voice that is, under normal circumstances, the sublimated or habituated experience of a sonic presence that is sensed as immediate, as if coming from within the home, yet communicated from some uncertain elsewhere.

Divine Radio Vision

ALDIE: Let me tell ya somethin', I don't know what none a'you need.
I only know what I need.
But God's got an all-seein' eye.
Had one woman tell me a few years back,
Said, "Can you see through that radio?"
Said she's gonna turn'er off, I's preachin' on'er.
Said, "The Lord turned the radio on, and I turnt it off."
An' I think ya'lls with us when she made that statement [*Addressed to members of the studio congregation*]
Gonna turn the TV off an' turn the radio on.
She said, "I wanna hear what they gotta say."
Lord made'er turn the TV off an' turn'er radio on.
An' said, "You's preachin' on me," an' turned it back off.
The Lord made'er turn it back on.
We went by to visit that day, but wasn't goin' to visit her,
We was goin' ta visit her mother-in-law.
An' the mother-in-law happened ta be at her house.
An' she said, "Can you see through that radio?"
An' I said, "No, but I know one that can."
I know one that can.
She said, "I had ta call a preacher, an' I repented and made thangs right."
Listen, God knows what he's doin', church,
He knows what you've done [*Vehement, growling tone of voice*].

In yet another case of a listener being compellingly called out by the voice issuing from the mouth of the radio loudspeaker, this auditor is so shocked by the experience of being singled out by the radio voice that she attempts to turn off the speaking apparatus. Even this attempt at silencing the direct address, however, is preempted by the compelling force of the divine moving her hand to reach toward the radio once again. In an unanticipated twist that I have heard described several times during my research, this anxiety-provoking experience of being interrupted is also accompanied by a sensation that the radio apparatus facilitates a preternatural capacity of vision. Miraculously extending God's "all-seein' eye," the infrastructure of the radio apparatus becomes a prosthetic augmentation of divine perceptual capacities. Thus, the field of vision of the divine eye is opened through the mechanical mouth of the radio loudspeaker.

Translated into an anxiety in relation to the preternatural sensory capacities of the divine, this account suggests the particular unease experienced by the listener at being addressed by a public voice through a technological infrastructure that extends into the private interiors of the domestic space.[24] It is not merely the explicit content of the religious broadcast that places a specific demand upon the listener in his or her singularity, but the very structure of the listening environment organized through the radio apparatus itself.[25]

After an attempt to silence this calling from the mouth of the loudspeaker proves futile, the member of the audience is compelled not only to keep listening, but to reach out for yet another "disembodied" voice to confess and repent to this infrastructure of voices emancipated from bodies. The disembodied voices of the confessional box have been liberated from the wooden frames and arabesque screens within the space of the church and now reside in the electro-acoustical housings of the wired and wireless mouthpiece: the microphone and its radio.

Sermon 1

Sister Julie's Preachin'

Praise you Lord, Hallelujah, glory to tha lamb of God [*As she approaches mic, these phrases become clearer and more audible*]
    It's good to be here today, an' I need your prayers. So you pray that I'll just min-ster exactly what the Holy Spirit—ah, a'bids me ta min-ster. 'Cause I'm not here for myself, but I'm here that I might be a blessing, that I may be of help—ah
    Ah' ta someone, glory to that lamb of God.
    Maybe someone thanks that they's no hope—ah
    But I want you ta know that hope is in Jesus—ah
    Glory to tha lamb a'God, allota times—ah
    Ah' we go to people for help, we go to people
    Ah' ta have ta tell'em our heart needs help an' things—ah
    But you know the only thing, the only advice we can give—uh
    Is in Jesus Christ—ah
    Ah' the only way—ah
    Ah' glory to God when we're goin' through things—ah
    In our lives is ta trust tha Lord God almighty Hallelujah
    An' I want ya to know he'll never let us down—ah
    He was always thar with his hands outstretched—ah
    Ah' waitin' for his people ta come ta him—ah
    Ah' that he can lif'em up, glory to tha lamb a'God—ah
    An' he will you today—ah
    An' if you'll just give—ah
    Ah' give it over ta him—ah
    An' trust him—ah
    Ah' we've gotta get our minds off—ah
    Ah' the situations that we're goin' through—ah
    Ah' you know the devil want us—ah
    Our minds ta wander on ever-thang—ah

An' get it off-a Jesus—ah
Ah' glory—ah
An' when we start gettin' it off-a Jesus—ah
Ah' we stop—ah
Ah' winnin' our battles—ah
Ah' but tha minute we come back and realize—ah
It's gonna take Jesus—ah
Ah' then he come on tha scene, glory—ah
Unto tha lamb a'God—ah
An' I wanted to minister today—ah
Ah' over in tha fourteenth chapter—ah
Of tha book of Saint Luke—ah
Ah' you know alotta time when tha
Ah' Jesus, this is when Jesus—ah
Ah' before he went to the cross—ah
Ah' when he's goin' through fixin'—ah
Ah' to go—ah
Ah' on a mission, glory—ah
His work was almost finished here on this earth at this time—ah
Ah' but had to get it finished before—ah
Ah' he ascended back ta his father—ah
Ah' 'fore he went to tha cross for you and I—ah
Ah' but when he was teachin' here—ah
Un-ta Israel
Ah' glory to tha lamb of God—ah
Ah' lotta times he used parables—ah
Ah' because—ah
Ah' they could easily—ah
Understand tha parables—ah
Ah' glory to tha lamb—ah
An' sometimes tha parables—ah
Ah' when you interpret they're spiritually interpreted—ah
Ah' glory to tha lamb a'God—ah
Ah' but I wanted you—ah
Ah' to go over'n at sixteenth—ah
Ah' chapter of that great supper—ah
Well glory to tha lamb a'God—ah
Ah' the Lord has that supper prepared today, Hallelujah—ah
Ah' biddin' his people ta come in—ah

Ah' biddin'em ever-whar glory—ah
Ah' ta come in to that supper of tha lamb of God—ah
It said then, said he unto them—ah
Ah' a certain man made a great supper—ah
An' he bade many—ah
An' sent his servant at suppertime—ah
Well glory—ah
Ah' ta say ta them that were bidden come—ah
For all thangs are now ready
Well glory to tha lamb of God
I believe today all things are now ready—ah
Ah' fer tha commin' of tha Lord—ha
Ah' because time is short—ah
It's time we get serious about that work God's called us ta do—ah
It's time glory to tha lamb of God to quit playin' around—ah
Ah' they's no time fer playin' around no longer—ah
Ah' glory to tha lamb of God—ah
It's time for us ta get serious—ah
About our soul's salvation—ah
Ah' ta go before the Lord—ah
An' ask him—ah
If they're anything in our lives—ah
Ah' glory to God that he's not pleased with—ah
An' cleanse us—ah
Ah' totally from ever-thang—ah
Ah' that would hinder us—ah
Ah' from enterin' in to tha kingdom of heaven—ah
Ah' because he's commin' after those—ah
Ah' without spot—ah
An' without wrinkle—ah
A'glory be to tha lamb of God—ah
An' we gotta be that way—ah
If we expect ta see tha kingdom of God
Our heart has got ta be perfect with'em—ah
Hallelujah ta tha lamb a'God—ah
I know we make alotta excuses—ah
Ah' but let me tell ya our hearts gotta be perfect with God
Hallelujah
Hallelujah

Ah' glory to tha lamb—ah
An' we cain't blame others—ah
Ah' glory—ah
Hallelujah I'm just gonna go of the way of the leadin' of tha Holy Spirit—ah
   Ah' you know when Adam'n'Eve—ah
Ah' when they sinned in tha garden—ah
Ah' what was the first thang when
God came to'em—ah
Ah' they were makin' all kinds of excuses—ah
Ah' Eve was blamin' tha serpent—ah
Adam was blamin' his wife—ah
Ah' glory ta God—ah
It's so easy ta blame our neighbor—ah
It's so easy ta blame—ah
Ah' those that goes ta church with us—ah
An' we're gonna stand alone—ah
Ah' we're not gonna be able ta say, Lord—ah
Ah' because of that one—ah
Are because of this'un—ah
Ah' but God is gonna look at your heart—ah
An' he knows—ah
Your record is gonna be fore'em—ah
We cain't make any excuses.
Hallelujah.
Glory to tha lamb and they all
Listen at this—huh
Huh—they were begged ta come ta that supper—ah
An' they all with one consent—ah
They all agreed and they begin to make excuses—ah
Ah' the first verse said unto them—ah
I have bought a piece of ground—ah
An' I must needs go and see it—ah
Well glory—ah
An' I pray thee have me excused—ah
An' another said I have bought five oxen
Yoke of oxen—ah
An' I go ta prove them—ah
An' I pray—ah

Have me excused—ah
Ah' tha firstin'—ah
Ah' was a self-interest—ah
Ah' the second was tha self-will—ah
Well glory, an' another said I have married a wife—ah
An' therefore I cannot come—ah
All these excuses—ah
Ah' glory ta God—ah
An' you know all them—ah
Is not sin—ah
Ah' but it was because—ah
Ah' they were be puttin'em—ah
Ah' before tha Lord Jesus Christ—ah
Ah' this here—ah
Ah' this parable
I know it says a certain man that certain man is God—ah
An' that servant is Jesus Christ
Ah' that tha Lord sent—ah
An' he's prepared a place in tha kingdom a'God
Ah' fer his children
Ah' Jesus said I go away
An' I prepare a place for you
An' I'm a'cummin' again
An' receive you unto myself—ah
An' that where I am you may be also
This is Jesus speakin'
Ah' glory to tha lamb of God
Ah' but excuses are bein' made
Ah' tha Lord didn't come, Jesus didn't come
Ha' ta say what—ah
Ah' can he—ah
Ah' do for tha world—ah
Ah' what can that world do for him
Ah' but he came ta see
Ah' what he could do fer tha world—ah
Well glory
An' that was the love—ah
Ah' that he had in his heart—ah
Hallelujah

What could Jesus do, well glory
An' he come—ah
An' they paid that price at Cal-vry.
Ah' fer you and I
That's what he did
That was love that took'em to tha cross—ah
Hallelujah ta tha lamb of God
It was the love glory—ah
Hallelujah
An' he was reachin' out—ha
Ah' fer his people n' I know—ah
This parable was for
Ah' tha Israelites at that time, I know that—ah
I know—ah
Ah' but its fer tha church today—ah
Hallelujah to tha lamb
Ah' because we're makin' too many excuses—ah
Ah' Sunday mornin'—ah
Ah' we get up—ah
Oh this is tha church world
Hallelujah
So many decide
Huh' they wanna spend time with their family
Ah' the only day of the week—ah
Ah' glory
They are puttin' their family before God
So many—ah
Is makin' excuses 'cause—ah
Ah' they're watchin' others' lives—ah
An' those lives are not linin' up with tha word—ah
An' so they think if they can get by they will too
Ah' well let me tell ya they are not gonna get by
Hallelujah because when they stand before tha Lord
They will also—ah
Glory ta God—ah
Ah' see where they made their mistake at
They're people deceived today—ah
Ah' they've watched others—ah
An' the others got by with thangs—ah

An' they thank they got by
But nobody
Is gonna get by with sin—ah
Ever-body—ah
When you onced accept Jesus as your savior—ah
Ah' you're held responsible
Ah' fer tha sins you commit from then on out
Ah' you'll have ta come
Ah' glory ta God before tha throne a'God
Hallelujah when you sin
And we all make mistakes—ah
An' we'll sin
Ah' but glory ta God we have a advocate—ah
Ah' with tha father
An' he welcomes us in.
Hallelujah
Ah' but ya know tha church—ah
Ah' world today—ah
Is so sad—ah
Ah' that they—ah
God is makin' tha call
An' he's callin' fer those that have back-slid up-on'em
Ah' those—ah
That got hurt—ah
An' have gone away from tha house a'tha Lord—ah
Oh let me tell ye church—ah
It's not tha church that's done you that way—ah [Sung lines]
It's not tha church maybe somebody—ah
Has hurt you—ah
A'glory but it's not tha church—ah
Well glory we hold things again' tha church—ah
Ah' when one person—ah
Ah' will hurt us or somethin'—ah
Ah' but let me tell you today—ah
Ah' God wants you—ah
Ah' ta-be whar he wants you ta-be—ah
Ah glory to tha lamb a'God—ah
He wants you to go to tha church—ah
Ah' whar he wants to place you—ah

Ah' he has a work fer each one of his children—ah
Ah' they've gotta be—ah
A'whar he wants'em ta-be—ah
Well glory to tha lamb a'God—ah
Ah' God—ah
Hallelujah
His word doesn't change—ah
His word will not change fer you—ah
An' it will not change fer me—ah
Hallelujah
An' tha price Jesus paid—ah
Ah' was settled long ago—ah
An' tha word was written—ah
A' glory to God—ah
A' long ago fer us—ah
An' it will not change—ah
An' we gotta line up with'at word—ah
Ah' we got ta let tha love of tha Lord shine out of us—ah
Ah' we got ta let tha light'a tha Lord shine—ah
Oh glory ta God they is no excuse—ah
I remember that song they used ta sing—ah
Ah' there's no excuse today glory ta God—ah
An' God'll not take no excuse from you—ah
An' he'll not take it from me—ah
Hallelujah we're—ah
A'stayin' home—ah
A' because we wanna stay 'ome—ah
Glory ta God we'll answer to tha Lord—ah
If we're not servin' tha Lord—ah
An' walkin' in-at—ah
Call of God—ah
If we're not walkin' in at call-a-God
We'll answer to God—ah
Hallelujah ta tha lamb a'God—ah
Ah' you can make all kinda excuses—ah
Ah' but when you stand that call—ah
Hallelujah it's without repentance—ah
Ah' you will stand before tha Lord—ah
Ah' glory ta God—ah

An' you gonna—ah
Ah' be ashamed—ah
Ah' because you didn't—ah
Ah' go ahead with the work of tha Lord—ah
Ah' that God called you into—ah
Oh glory to tha lamb
Lord is callin' you today
Ah' get back in
Ah' it's not too late yet—ahh
Ah' get back in,
I'm callin' my children today back in
Well Glory ta tha lamb of God
He's callin'—ah
Oh—ah
Heed to his call today
Heed to his call
Well glory—ah
Hallelujah
I know it mighta been a-long time [*Rough, guttural monotone*]
Ago—ah
An' that you—huh
Ah' been outta church—ah
Well now is tha time—ah
Oh it's ready—ah
Time is ready fer ye ta go back—ahh [*Visceral, guttural*]
Hallelujah do yer first works over
Well glory to tha lamb of God—ah [*Forceful intensity in following lines*]
Hal-le-lu-jah
An' because—ah
An' God is biddin' today—ah
Oh God is biddin' today—ah
Well glory—HA-HA [*Brief interruption of laughter followed by clearly audible and forceful inhalation*]
Well glory to tha lamb a'God—ah
An' blessed be tha name of tha Lord—ah [*Like chat of an auctioneer*]
Ah' let me tell you God will not fail you—HA-HA [*Sung line, followed by pronounced inhalation*]
Hallelujah to tha lamb—ah

He's a faithful God—HA-HA
He'll stand by in his word before'em his word—hah
Oh you don't have to worry 'bout God—HA-HA
Because he'll be here on time—ah
Hallelujah . . . —ah
When we face some thangs—ah
An' we think he might be too late, but let me tell ya
He'll come through on time for ya [*Brief pause before commencing next cycle*]
Hallelujah to tha lamb—ah
Oh glory—ah
I know God's speakin' today—ah [*Allusion to anointed speech*]
Hallelujah to tha lamb
I had no idea I's gonna say these thangs—ah
But oh glory—ah
Ah' there's so many stayin' outa the houses of the Lord
Ah' tha houses of tha Lord are getting empty—ah
Oh glory to tha lamb—ah
An' let'em use you for his glory
Hallelujah
Ah' you'll not regret it—ah
Ah' glory he'll bless you goin' an commin'
An' it says here—ah
An' so that servant—ah
Who was Jesus came—ah
An' showed tha Lord these thangs—ah
An' then tha master of tha house bein' angry had said to his servant
Ah' go out quickly into tha streets—ah
An' tha lanes of tha city—ah
An' bring in hither the poor and the maimed—ah
And the [?] and the blind ha-ha
An' the servant said Lord it is done—ah
Thou has commanded yet there is room—ah
Children there is still room—ha
Hallelujah it's not too late—ah
Ah' glory to tha lamb a'God—ah
Ah' just come before'em with um-ble heart—ah
An' a contrite—ah spirit—ah
An' here he was sayin'—ah

How tha master was angry
You know why he was angry
'Cause his chosen people Israel
Had rejected him
Ah' his people Israel—ah
Ah' rejected him—ah
An' at tha time their hope was gone
But now it's opened—ah
It's opened up ta ever-body
It's opened up ta ever-body today—ah
Whosoever will glory to tha lamb at's why Jesus died—ah
Ah' that whosoever will—ah
Ah' glory ta God—ah
An' live by that word—ah
'Ey can have a home in glory
An' you know what, we might face alotta thangs—ah
Ah' but it'll be worth whatever you—ah
Hafta go through in this life ta make it ta heaven—ah
Oh glory it'll be worth it sometime—ah
You might hafta go all alone—ah
Sometime yer mate don't want ta go to tha house of tha Lord
Ah' but you can go-on anyway, Hallelujah
Ah' because it's a person relationship with tha father
An' God'll bless you commin'n'goin'—ah
Ah' glory ta tha lamb a'God
Hallelujah
An' when tha servant said Lord it is done—ah
As thou has commanded, yet there is room
Hallelujah ta tha lamb
There is room for you today—ah
Hallelujah
An' the Lord said unto the servant—ah
Ah' go out in tha highways an' tha hedges—ah
An' compel them ta come in, that my house—ah
Well may be filled—HA-HA
Well he's tellin' you go out in tha highways
He wants tha word ta go out there—ah
In tha highways n'tha by-ways—ah
An compel'em ta come in—ah

Ah' glory to tha lamb—ah
He wants it ta go out ta ever corner of tha earth—ah
Hallelujah
He wants tha word ta touch ever heart—ah
Ah' that ever-body'll
Ah' be able ta hear tha word—ah
An' they have ta make tha decision on their own—ah
Oh glory ta tha lamb a'God
Ah' we've gotta get busy—ah
An' get this word—ah
Out—ah
Ah' glory ta tha lamb a'God
An' they're good preacher's everywhar—ah
A'ministerin' tha word—ah
If people will only heed—ah
An' get in that word and study tha word—ah
So you'll not be deceived—ah
Oh glory ta tha lamb a'God—ah
Hallelujah
Why I said unto you—ah
That none of these men which were bidden shall taste of my supper—ah
Well it already—ah
Time—ah
Had given tha last opportunity—ah
An' glory to them back then that praise tha Lord— HA-HA-HA
[*Massive breath*]
Well glory tha door was open— HA-HA
Through Jesus when he died—ah
Well glory ta tha lamb a'God
An' it's fer ever'body
It's for the Jews—ah
It's fer the Gentile
It's fer all tha prophets—ah
Oh it's fer ever'body today—ah
Heed to his word today—ah
An' come forth—ah
An' in him—ah
An' glory to tha lamb

He said—ah
An' there were great multitudes with him and he turned and said unto them,
Listen—ah
What he was tellin'em—ah
He said if any man come ta me—ah
An' hate not his father'n'mother'n'wife'n'children'n'brethren'n'sisters yea n'his own life—ah
Also he cannot be my disciple—ah
He wasn't meanin' the word hate as we see it—ah
He mean—ah
Ah' you should prefer him above ever-thang—ah
Ah' you gotta put . . .
Well glory—HA-HA
Ah' when we do that I'm gon' tell ya
Ah' glory ta God, God'll bless ya
Ha
Glory to tha lamb, he just wants ta be first
In yer life—ah
Ah' he won't take second place—ah
Ah' but you put'em first an' in your family
You'll even have more love for your family
Well glory—ah
Ah' when ya put Jesus first—ah
Well glory ta tha lamb
'Cause at love—ah
Ah' that you get from the Lord—ah
Ah' will love them that children—ah
Ah' glory ta tha lamb an' that family
Hallelujah
An' whosoever does not bear his cross—ah
An' come after me—ah
He cannot be—ah
Ah' my disciple—ah
Ah' what it's sayin'—ah
Over in the Mark—ah
Tha eighth chapter tha thirty-fourth verse, he said—ah
An' when he had called tha people unto him with his disciples all there he said unto them—ah

Whosoever will come after me—ah
Let him deny himself—ah
An' take up his cross an' follow me—ah
Fer whosoever save his life—ah
Hallelujah
Ah' shall lose it, but whosoever shall lose his life for my sake and the
Gospels tha same shall save it—ah
Fer what shall it profit a man—ah
If he shall gain tha whole world an' lose his soul—ah
Or what shall a man give— HA
Ah' in exchange for his soul
Oh children today—ah
Ah' this means when we—ah
Ah' glory ta God—ah
When we deny ourselves, when we take up tha cross—ah
Ah if we're puttin' our will—ah
Our ambitions an' ever-thang we have—ah
It's God's will—ah
Oh glory ta tha lamb—ah
Ah' God has plans fer ya whole family—ah
He don't leave your family out when you're dedicated ta him—ah
Oh glory ta tha lamb of God—ah
He's there—ah
A'biddin' you Lord ta stay—ah
Ah' but ya got ta put'em first and foremost—ah
Ah' glory ta tha lamb a'God—ah
Ah' it's a straight—ah
An' it's a narra way, glory ta tha lamb a'God—ah
Ah' in Matthew seven
Ah' thirteen he said—ah
Enter you in at this straight gate—ah
Ah' fer wide is tha gate—ah
An' broad is the way that leadeth to destruction—ah
An' many there be which go thereat—ah
Ah' because straight is tha gate—ah
An' narra is tha way which leadeth unto life—ah
An' few be that find it—ah
A'listen at that gate—ah
Ah' that door is Jesus Christ Hallelujah

Ah' that straight gate is through Jesus tha door
Hallelujah ta tha lamb of God—ah
An' that gate is a'narra—HA-HA
An' that's because you can't partake a tha world an' partake of Jesus too—ah
Hallelujah ta tha lamb—ah
Ah' you gotta be separated from the world—ah
Ah' we're in this world but we don't partake a'tha world Hallelujah
Ha' glory ta God that way ta heaven is narra today children
Ha' but that other way—ah
That leadeth ta destruction it's broad—ah
Ah' why is it broad—HA
Because so many are on it—ah
An' it's a broad road—ah
Headin' fer destruction
Ah' but if you'll heed to tha way—ah
Ah' glory ta tha lamb of God—ah
Ah' you won't have ta worry—ah
Hallelujah
Ah' you can lay down at night—ah—HA-HA
Well glory ta tha lamb an' not worry—ah
Ah' glory—Hallelujah
Ah' whar you'll be—ah
Ah' whar you'll be at in eternity—ah
Ah' you'll not have ta worry when you accept Jesus Christ—ah
As your savior—ah
He'll watch over you
He'll meet your needs glory ta tha lamb a'God—ah
He said—ah
For which of you intended ta be a power send us not down first—ah
An' count tha cost—ah
Ah' whether it be sufficient ta finish it—ah
Left happy after he had laid—ah
Ah' tha foundation—ah
An' is not able ta finish it that behold he began ta mock him sayin' this man began ta build
An' was not able ta finish it, children
Tha price was paid at Calvary, Sister Cathy's commin' at this time
But you know that price was paid at Calvary

Uh' fer you and I—ah
Ah' but they's a price of self-denial that we have ta pay ourselves—ah
It don't cost us no money
Hallelujah it's free
Ah' but we've got to
Ah' live by tha word of God that's our requirement today as Cathy—ah
Ah' come forth today, glory may God bless ye
Hallelujah ta tha lamb.

[*As Cathy gets on the studio microphone to sing a song and close the program, Sister Julie is still overheard in the background voicing praises: Hallelujah, Praise ye Jesus, Praise you Lord*]

CHAPTER 2

Prayer Cloths

Remnants of the Holy Ghost and the Texture of Faith

THERE IS A WONDERFULLY suggestive term used in the textile industry to describe our basic experiential relation to fabric:

> HAND, HANDLE: The reaction of the sense of touch, when fabrics are held in the hand. There are many factors which give "character and individuality" to a material observed through handling. A correct judgment may thus be made concerning its capabilities in content, working properties, drapability, feel, elasticity, fineness and softness, launderability, etc.
>
> The term was originally applied to silk filaments, but the importance of a good handle to textiles has caused the term to take on more importance in other phases of this far-reaching industry. (*The Modern Textile Dictionary*, 1954)

With the textile definition of "fabric hand" in mind, this chapter describes the "character and individuality" of a category of devotional objects variously known as prayer cloths, anointed handkerchiefs, blessed cloths, and faith cloths. These materialized prayers are circulated throughout charismatic communities in southern Appalachia and beyond for the purposes of miraculous healing and divine protection. This chapter explores the elementary haptic qualities of a devotional object that has occupied a crucial position within charismatic healing practices since the early twentieth century. This chapter asks, in short: "What is the *hand* of the Holy Ghost?"

A Coincidence Recalled Up on Schoolhouse Hill

The narrow road wound its way up the side of what the locals called "Schoolhouse Hill." As my truck engine began to grumble in a low labored tone, I geared down as the grade steepened. At the crest of the small mountain, the road opened to an entrance paved in gravel and marked by a particle board sign crumbling at the corners from years of exposure to the harsh Appalachian winters in the mountains of southwestern Virginia. The barely discernible letters that formed the words "Pentecostal" and "Holiness" were so faded by the elements that they recalled the dry bones in the desert often described in small church settings such as the one announced by the sign. The weathered condition of the church sign, however, did not match the condition of the Holiness church itself, which wore a bright new coat of white paint and whose entrance was adorned with a large ceramic pot of well-tended flowers. The verdant grass on the well-kept lawn surrounding the church accentuated the white exterior of the worship space. Automobiles pulled into the parking lot in anticipation of the service. The tiny pebbles that paved the lot made a particularly crisp sound as the wheels crunched upon the gravel. One side of the church lot opened to an expansive view of a valley immediately below and a chain of mountains in the distance.

The beautiful vista and homely flowers seen from the church parking lot, however, were tempered by a chain-link fence that separated the well-tended church grounds from the sagging trailer located on the other side. From the debris strewn about the front yard, a bulldog chained to a small tree cast a menacing stare in my direction, as if to reinforce the slight anxiety I always experience upon entering into an intimate worship context as an unannounced stranger. The section of the yard where the dog was chained had been worn down to a perfectly barren circle. To step from the grass onto the dirt in a transgression of that boundary demarcated between the dog and his chain would surely mean danger.

My interest in this church came through what was at that time the sole focus of my ethnographic fieldwork: radio preachers and their audiences in southern Appalachia. Brother Clarence Brown, who has a thirty-minute program every weekday on the local Christian radio station (105.5 FM, WGTH, Richlands, Virginia), had made an announcement during his broadcast, *The Voice of Healing and Deliverance*, that there was going to be an "old-time foot washing" (pronounced waur-shun) at his church on Schoolhouse Hill. Because I had read about the ritual of foot washing in several accounts of religion in Appalachia, I was eager to observe this traditional ablution in person.[1]

To my disappointment, however, shortly after the commencement of the Wednesday night prayer service, an announcement was made that the elder of the church who usually led the foot washing had fallen ill and was unable to attend the service. In deference to this elder, the congregation was unable to perform the foot washing in his absence. Frustrated, I sat there alone in a pew at the back of the small church, contemplating if I should quietly remove myself from the service and go visit the local Christian radio station instead. Not wanting to seem rude in the eyes of the congregation, however, I resolved to sit through the service.

After several brief introductory announcements and reminders about upcoming church services and gatherings, several members of the congregation came to the podium to sing hymns, either solo or duet. After several songs, the entire congregation joined in the singing of four hymns, each requested by different congregation members, who shouted out the page numbers of the songs in the hymnal. As is characteristic of many Holiness-Pentecostal services in this region, after the conclusion of the singing, Sister Bonnie, who was directing the services, opened a rhetorical space of testimony by asking the church, "Has anybody got somethin' to say for the Lord?"

After a brief period of silence, a middle-aged woman seated on a pew to my right on the other side of the aisle stood up and said that she had a "praise report" to share with the congregation. In what followed, the sister recounted, in minute detail, the accidental coincidence of two automobiles careening down the winding "four-lane" at fifty-five miles per hour. Through the narrative windings of her testimony, the details of the accident began to accumulate: descriptive images of her unbelieving husband and two young sons and the shape and configuration of the vehicles as one "T-boned" the other in the moment of impact. Juxtaposed with the sounds and images evoked by her description of the twisted pieces of automobile entangled in the moment of the crash on a dark and winding highway, her story described how all three of the family members emerged from the wreckage with "not hardly a bruise."

In the performative practice of "testifyin'" within the charismatic space of worship, the recounting of the intricate and at times mundane details of the story is a key element within the overall narrative structure of this form of storytelling. These minutiae, and the time it takes to articulate them, "sets up" the congregation of listeners for a particular experience of faith and the miraculous. Thus, it is not until the end of the testimony, when the narrative structure has developed a tangled descriptive inventory of effects, that the hidden lines of force organizing these seemingly random or *merely coincidental* events is forcefully revealed. The testifying sister reveals that, well before the accident, she had placed three prayer cloths—anointed in that very church by the same congregation hearing the story—in the glove compartment of her husband's small automobile. In that moment, several of the congregation members exclaimed "Yes Lord!" and "Praise God!" along with other sounds of surprised affirmation.

By this point in her testimony, the sister began to cry as she expressed her thanks to God for saving her family. In its basic structure, the narrative testimony is a retelling or repetition of a past event. Yet the narrative performed through the testimonial form suggests that this genre of storytelling is not merely a recounting or repetition of past events, but a way of telling a story that elicits certain effects or appearances of faith. In other words, the narrative structure of the testimony facilitates a particular experience of faith for the listening audience. A performance of faith and the compulsion to recount miraculous events thus draw close to one another. In this way, the material movement of the prayer cloth shadows the force of language as the testimony accrues "faith" through progressive retellings. Both the appearance of faith and the prayer cloth make their most forceful appearance after a temporal deferral. Both faith and an experience of the miraculous emerge through the exchange of stories and objects, and thus ironically circulate within spaces outside the subject. Through its performative capacity to narrate a particular structure of temporal deferral, the poetic technique of testifying conjures an experience of faith for the participants in the audience. The testimony often concludes its temporal accumulation of narrative details by revealing, in the end, that a compelling force was operating underneath these seemingly discrete or discontinuous events *from the very beginning*.

Given the particular narrative structure of the testimony, it comes as no surprise that the sister concludes by requesting that the congregation "make" more prayer cloths for herself and the members of the congregation. In this moment, the circulation of faith and the force of testimony comes full circle. Like the spirit of the gift described by ethnologist Marcel Mauss, the cloth returns with newfound efficacy to its point of origin, albeit in the form of a testimony. And as if to demonstrate that their efficacy was not expended in the moment of the automobile accident, there is a call to further replicate the prayer cloth. *Reasserting their automatic efficacy, the cloths continue to replicate themselves.*

Through the promptings of this testimony, Sister Bonnie calls upon the "prayer warriors" in the congregation to come up and help "anoint" some prayer cloths.[2] This process of anointing is also referred to as "praying the cloths," a suggestive phrase that evokes the intertwined relation between the material object and the voice in the performance of prayer. Indeed, the prayer itself appears to bring or materialize the cloth into existence. As individual prayer warriors arise and approach the pulpit at the front of the church, an elderly woman in the front pew pulls a small sack from her handbag filled with cloth fragments that will be "prayed" by the congregation. As is the case within many small churches and charismatic communities, one member is usually in charge of cutting the cloth fragments from larger pieces of fabric. Perhaps mimicking the millions of prayer cloths circulated through the postal system during the late 1940s and early 1950s by large Pentecostal organizations and charismatic faith healers, the sister in this church also uses pinking shears to give the border of the fabric ridged teeth or scallops.[3] The elderly sister removes a small stack of cloth fragments from her bag and hands them to Sister Bonnie, who then pours oil on her fingers from a glass bottle kept at the foot of the podium and smears the textile remnants with the unction dripping from her fingers. By the time of the actual physical unction with oil, I had approached the pulpit to participate in the "praying" of the textiles.

In order to hide the soon-to-be-transformed fabric remnants from the gaze of the congregants, immediately upon anointing these objects, Sister Bonnie conceals the cloths in the tight grip of her fist. As her fingers close around the fabric, the wrinkled folds of her skin become tightly drawn around the bony protrusions of her arthritic knuckles. Like the skin stretched tightly around the wooden frame of a tambourine, the integument drawn around her fist becomes translucent, revealing the colored veins, sinews, and bones underneath. She extends her tightly clenched fist outward, and Brother Clarence, the actual sibling of Sister Bonnie and the principal preacher of this church, superimposes his hand upon her right fist, further veiling the fabric in layers of skin. At this point in the ritual preparation for anointing prayer, eight members of the congregation surround Sister Bonnie: half the prayer warriors extend their hands to touch the fist of hidden fragments or Clarence's superimposed hand with their fingertips, while the others raise their arms upward with palms oriented down so that the surface of the palm faces the hidden fabric. These specific compartments are sacred techniques of the body that help to instantiate the efficacious healing power of the Holy Ghost into the textile remnants. The oral performance of prayer, therefore, is inextricably linked with these sacred gestures and manual techniques. As a technique of sacred manufacture, the anointing of the prayer cloth marks an inversion in the relation between the hand and the fabric. In this case of ritual substitution, it is not the cloth that veils the hand, as in classic sleight-of-hand magic and older forms of the Eucharist where the hand is veiled in the moment of transubstantiation, but the hand itself that "kerchiefs" or veils the cloth.

Each time this sacred cloth remnant is rubbed between the fingers or upon the surface of an ailing body part, it recalls the intertwined sum of tangled tactile experience when layers upon layers of haptic sensation were combined in a performance of prayer. Thus the handle, or texture, of the fabric allows the sick patient to haptically experience the ritual of anointing once again. In this way, the prayer cloth is a kind of supplemental skin or prosthetic dermal layer that grants access to sacred sensations. Because this tactile experience can never be abstracted from the aural aspects of the *prayer* cloth, the experience of texture upon the skin or between the fingers also recalls, or plays back, the tangled voices and sonic force of the communal prayer. The prayer cloth translates an experience of the voice, its grain so to speak, into a tactile register that facilitates miraculous healing and apotropaic efficacy.

The outstretched arms of the prayer warriors and hands that touch the fist of fabric create a kind of sacred wheel: the arms like spokes connected to the point of tactile unity at the fist-become-hub. This wheel of body techniques demarcates a sacred circle wherein the diffuse potentiality of the Holy Ghost becomes focused or rarefied in the hidden recesses of the fist. Surrounding the sacred wheel and creating a field of concentric circles, the other prayer warriors, myself included, who are not directly involved in the sacred wheel stand around this inner circle with hands raised upward, palms oriented downward toward the hub, as if to further focus the efficacious force of the Holy Ghost into the center of the circle.

With all the prayer warriors in place, the assembled congregation begins the practice of communal prayer, wherein each congregant simultaneously prays his or her individual prayer in a loud, urgent voice. This communal prayer performance creates an entangled force of sound that goes beyond everyday articulations of the voice and the capacity to register or discern meaningful sounds. At certain times during the performance, however, word fragments or phrases are discernible above the "numinous" din of the skein prayer, such as the several instances when Brother Brown shouts in a loud emphatic voice, "Anointing go into *this* cloth!"

Again, this manual technique and spatial demarcation cannot be abstracted from the vocalization of prayer that accompanies it. The performance of skein prayer provides an oral counterpoint to the entangled haptic sensation of the warriors' intertwined manual experience within the sacred wheel. The ear is able to experience what is sensed on a tactile register and vice versa. The tactile sensation of the cloth provides a kind of haptic mnemonic device for the "playback" of the skein prayer. As described earlier, skein prayer refers to a traditional theurgical technique wherein all the members of the congregation begin praying their own prayers out loud and simultaneously. This tangle of voices, in addition to the hand clapping, ejaculations (Yes Lord! Amen! Jesus!), and other vocalizations accompanying this enthusiastic communal prayer, creates an auditory effect of a dense nonrepresentational noise. This numinous noise is a pivotal moment in the "anointing" of the prayer cloth. When this tangle of language becomes dense and ecstatic, it signals to the congregation that the power of the Holy Ghost has been successfully "prayed down."

As a crucial theological term within the charismatic worship milieu, the "anointing" slips between the actual physical application of oil and the moment through prayer when Holy Ghost power is instantiated into the fabric. In fact, perhaps it would be more appropriate to say that the two moments are often totally indistinguishable, each having not merely a metaphorical significance, but a fundamentally tangible or palpable presence. In this way, the anointing can never be abstracted from its original connotations with the massaging of animal fats into the skin to facilitate consecration.[4] Moreover, this intimate association between the anointing and the rubbing of oil upon the surface of the body helps to explain the importance of the material qualities of the prayer cloth. The supple "drape" quality of fabric and its accompanying ability to fall upon the contours of the physical form, or "flow" upon the body's surface, put cloth in a similar category of tactility with that of unguents and oils. This bodily sensation residing at the heart of the anointing also sheds light upon the phrase to "pray it," in reference to the performance of skein prayer. As the phrase so forcefully suggests, to "pray it" literally entails a physical manifestation or instantiation of the vocal efficacy of prayer into a physical object.

As the intensity of the skein prayer gradually decreases, finally ending in a short yet profound silence, the sacred wheel breaks apart as the prayer warriors disperse. After the anointing is complete, Sister Bonnie opens her fist to reveal the transformed cloth: from mere remnant to the sacred receptacle of prayer and the concomitant power of the Holy Ghost. Revealed anew, the prayer cloths are distributed to any congregation member who may desire one. While at the front of the church, I obtained one of the cloths, a three-inch by three-inch square of white cotton sheeting cut with pinking shears.

This initial exchange of hands—though the very "praying" of the cloth entails crucial supplementations of the tongue and the hand—often commences a series of hand-to-hand exchanges as the blessed cloths are circulated throughout the community through friends, co-workers, neighbors, and relatives. Thus, the "exchange of hands" is a crucial element in the appearance of belief, not only because it inaugurates a physical circulation of objects that begins to accrue a compelling force, but also because this "exchange of hands" connotes the communication and recollection of mutual experiences of tactility. These haptic encounters, in turn, help to produce the sensory effects that mark the presence of the sacred. Through the palpation of the cloth's texture, its physical properties signal *both* a tactile immediacy for the handler *and* a simultaneous awareness that other hands have also experienced this textured surface of prayer. The moment the handle of the fabric is experienced as a tactile sensation, this feeling of presence becomes even more forceful and compelling, precisely through its doubled structure. That is, the texture of the cloth is intensely present *and yet* somehow communicating or extending to another sensory register *somewhere else*. This sensation of mutual tactility at a distance, then, is also implicated in the physical circulation of the anointed cloths through an "exchange of hands."

What I did not realize as I sat there in the back pew of that Pentecostal-Holiness church, disappointed that no foot-washing would take place during that Wednesday night prayer service on the top of Schoolhouse Hill, was that the force of substitution was already operating within my project. After this service, I was convinced that the phenomenon of the prayer cloth and its concomitant exchange of hands was a crucial materiality of faith that had to be explored during my research. Thus, in an exchange of a hand for a foot, the force of substitution was already circulating within my research. And through the time it has taken to articulate this anointed process of bodily augmentations and substitutions through the texture of a rag metamorphosed into a sacred object, my ethnography has been caught within the currents of narrativity and been compelled to repeat, once again, the miraculous testimony of the prayer cloth.[5]

Devotional Density and the Rosary Bead

How could we begin to describe and theorize the devotional specificities of the prayer cloth? In other words, what is the significance of the *fabric itself* and what could be called the specific *textures of faith* within the charismatic tradition of healing prayer? In order to open a space of comparative leverage to explore the hand or phenomenological texture of the prayer cloth, my analysis will briefly touch upon the density, surface, and shape of another popular material object in the history of Christian material devotions, the Catholic rosary bead.[6]

In his controversial analysis of the underlying forces compelling the widespread popularity of praying the rosary, sociologist Michael Carroll focuses upon "the most immediate and concrete aspects of the devotion."[7] For Carroll, the devotional technique of "fingering the beads"—running the hard beads (traditionally ceramic, wood, glass, or metallic filigree) between the thumb and fingers while reciting repetitive prayers—was a kind of manual simulation of the sensation of defecation. Although I will not recount all the elements of this analysis of a devotional compromise between unconscious desires and conscious prohibitions,[8] what has been particularly useful in this analysis is the author's attempt to explain the popularity of a devotional technique through an inquiry into the basic haptic sensations and manual techniques that characterize this material prayer aid. Working from Sandor Ferenczi's essay on the transformation of anal-erotic desires, Carroll traces a substitutive history of erotic tactility moving from the softness of feces to the density of coinage. The specific tactile sensations of the density, shape, and textured surface of the rosary bead as it is squeezed between the thumb and the index finger replicate on the level of manual gesture both a sensation of defecation and the prohibited desire to play with feces.[9]

Of course, the devotional technique of fingering the hard beads was not only an inextricable aspect of the recitation of the prayer—a classic *aide memoire*—but it functioned within the medieval monastic order as a kind of sacred abacus for the counting of repetitive and incredibly arduous penitential exercises (genuflections).[10] As was characteristic of so many aspects of monastic life (clock, timing, regimentation), the prayer beads, like the clock, were an object that facilitated a rigorous regime of discipline in the name of sanctification and consecration.[11] The hard, cold feel of the beads seems related to the history of a devotional practice characterized by rigid discipline and the repetition of arduous penitential exercises; a rigidity and density that, ironically, according to Carroll, substitutes for a desire to play with something soft. On the level of technique, and intimately related to the machinations of the clock, the rosary could be considered a prayer counting machine designed for single-handed manipulation. More specifically, the spatial alignment of the beads along the string, along with the smooth texture of the beads themselves, allows for the rounded elements to pass easily between the thumb and index finger.[12] Announcing its origins in the knotting of cord and long strips of cloth, the possibility of continuous manipulation and smooth movement of beads through the fingers is made possible by the supple twine that holds them all together. Moreover, this abacus-like manipulation is inseparable from the function of this object within the field of mnemotechnics. The rosary is a kind of silent recording of voice that can be played in a continuous, unbroken chain by the hand: a manual "stand-in" for the voice and the exteriorized mnemonic surface. As a specific mnemotechnical device, the oral performance of praying the rosary is linked to manual gestures and tactile sensations. When played silently, the force of recollection and the movement of thought are located in the progression of the beads through the haptic surfaces of the hand.

As beads arranged along a string, the rosary can be seen as a kind of automatic prayer machine for the repetitive recitation of prayer: an abacus-like apparatus for the counting of extensive penitential exercises. In the case of the rosary, the theme of automaticity or mechanicity entails a kind of habituated or unconscious repetition of the prayer, and as is often the case, the devotional performance is totally abstracted from the oral rite or vocalization, to become a manual-objectile technique of silent playback. As a repetitive act of compulsive manipulation, the pleasurable sensations of these manual gestures and haptic sensations prefigured similar psychological impacts with the operation of modern electrical and ballistic apparati. Thus the compulsive fingering of the sacred prayer machine foreshadows the religious significance of flicking the switch in an age of mechanical reproduction.

Cutting of the Prayer Cloth

What is the significance of the cutting up of the cloth to create a remnant? This image of the cloth fragment recalls the bags and tins that store the scraps used during the transformative process of anointing. These remnant containers are placed on or behind the altar. Receptacles such as these are often kept in the small Pentecostal, Holiness, and Independent churches of southern Appalachia. As I have mentioned earlier, these bags are usually kept by one member of the congregation, who also cuts the fabric into small squares in preparation for the performance of anointing prayer. These bags bear a striking resemblance to what is referred to as a "remnant bag" within the weaving and patchwork community.[13] As the name suggests, remnant bags are filled with scraps, rags, and fragments from cloth that were once "whole" in some other context but that have become worn, tattered, ripped, or threadbare from everyday use. Through creative reuse, the remnant is reincorporated or reformed into another textile surface, thus creating a new unity that is a conglomeration of discrete textile elements: quilts, appliqué motif, clothing repair, or patching.[14]

In the early days of Oral Roberts's healing ministry, before the manufacture of hundreds of thousands of "anointed prayer cloths" was subcontracted to independent factories that produced these sacred fragments on a mass scale, Roberts's wife, Evelyn, along with a small army of secretaries, stenographers, and volunteers from the Ladies Missionary Society, would patiently "cut squares of cloth 2 1/2 inches by 5 inches" from used bed sheets. Evelyn instructed the women to "use old sheets, and be careful to cut them only with pinking shears to prevent raveling, also be sure to keep them in uniform size."[15] In the early years, the late 1940s, of what was to become one of the most influential Christian organizations of the twentieth century, these fragments of cloth were imprinted with a message:

> I prayed over this cloth for God to deliver you—use as a point of contact (Acts 19: 11–12). Oral Roberts, Tulsa 2, Oklahoma. It is not necessary to wear the cloth unless you feel you should. It can be used more than once or for more than one person. If you wish to request more, I will be glad to send them to you. The important thing is to use the cloth as a point of contact for the release of your faith in God, so that when you pray and put the cloth on your body, you will believe the Lord will heal you at that moment. I have prayed over this cloth in the name of Jesus of Nazareth and asked Him to heal you when you apply it to your body.[16]

As if to mimic the automatic efficacy of this fragment of Holy Ghost power materialized in the cloth, the instructions seem to anticipate the future replication and circulation of these objects within the postal network. Thus, the postal service information is printed upon the cloth along with the ritualized healing instructions. Evelyn's insistence on the uniformity of the cloths—the consistency in sacred manufacture—foreshadowed the mass production of these "faith cloths" by machines totally abstracted from the manual process of cutting and printing.[17] This idea of uniformity, moreover, highlights the place of postal relays and economies of exchange as important infrastructures or materialities of the Holy Ghost and divine healing. Thus, the faithful who requested prayer cloths through the mail were instructed not to send their own cloths or handkerchiefs, because the ones manufactured by the healing ministry "are uniform in size and fit nicely into a letter."[18] In this way, the material exigencies of the postal system begin to organize the size and shape of the devotional object. The specificities of the tactile surface of the fabric and the haptic sensations evoked through devotional manipulation are thus intimately related to the mechanized system of the postal network.[19]

Of course, in some circumstances, an entire piece of cloth in its undivided unity is anointed. For example, during a prayer meeting at the home of an elderly sister, one of the participants was inspired to anoint an entire handkerchief he had in his pocket. In this case, the cloth was anointed for a patient suffering from severe gastrointestinal disorders and the "praying" of the entire cloth was necessary so that it could be laid across the surface of the stomach of the patient. In general it seems that the manufacture of the prayer cloth is intimately related to the practice of cutting and thus creating a remnant or fragment from a greater whole. It is perhaps not merely financial exigency, therefore, that old handkerchiefs and used sheets are cut into fragments and stored in the remnant bag.

Even with the production of the prayer cloth on a mass, mechanized scale, there is still an attempt to replicate the semblance of the cloth fragment. Take, for example, the massive contemporary postal circulation of prayer cloths by the Oral Roberts Evangelistic Association, whose anointing machines produce hundreds of thousands of faith cloths with saw-toothed edges, as if they were still hand-cut with pinking shears by Evelyn and her Ladies Missionary Society volunteers.[20] Although Evelyn seems to articulate a merely functional reason for employing a specific type of scissors in the process of anointed cloth manufacture, "to prevent raveling," there are other ways to consider the significance of the ridges that create the border of the prayer cloth. Not only do these ridges, created by the pinking shears—what is termed the "saw-tooth" pattern in the textile industry—maintain the integrity and coherence of the weave, but these edges also create a pronounced tactile effect upon the skin. The name of the tool itself used to cut these ridges, pinking shears, suggests the accompanying tactile sensations of the jagged ridges of a flower and is described in the textile dictionaries using tactile metaphors such as the scalloped ridges of a shell, the jagged and sharp points of saw-teeth, and the raised points of a leaf. As the cloth is rubbed against the skin, held to the ailment, gripped in the palm of the hand, or rubbed between the fingers, these edges further accentuate the sensations of the "hand" of the fabric: density of weave, type of thread fiber, nap, stiffness, drape. Additionally, the teeth of the sacred cloth seem to thematize the process and instrument of cutting itself—on both a visual and a haptic register, signaling once again, albeit on a base perceptual level, the fragmented nature of the object.[21]

Although at first glance the phenomenon of cutting the cloth may seem a mere trivial detail, the cut of the prayer cloth reveals significant aspects of Pentecostal theology on the nature and manifestation of the Holy Ghost. The cuts of these teeth open up a charismatic pneumatology. In most circumstances, the prayer cloth is a fragment or remnant that has been cut, or abstracted, from a larger totality such as a bed sheet or handkerchief. Emancipated from its original unity or utility by the cut, the textile remnant becomes a free-floating piece with a newfound potentiality to be "patched in" to other unanticipated circumstances and surfaces. A patch or rag becomes a kind of floating signifier within the material exigencies of everyday life: literally "standing in" to patch a hole in a miner's coveralls, to soak up bodily fluids, to patch a rip in the screen door, or to become part of a quilt. This textile patch provides a very concrete metaphor for the way in which the power and healing efficacy of the Holy Ghost—itself a kind of diffuse potentiality—is made manifest within the circumstances of everyday life. The percussive pop of hands, acrobatic vocalizations, and the noise of skein prayer act as a kind of theurgical shear: the tongue in prayer carves out a piece of the Holy Ghost like a double-edged sword, cutting a fragment of this power from the diffuse totality and instantiating it into the object. Once instantiated from this totality, the materialized efficacy takes on a life of its own, animated apart from the abstract totality from which it was cut. Thus "prayed down" from the sacred, the transformed rag is once again free to circulate and "stand in" for the needs of everyday life: pain, illness, suffering, danger, evil influences, and financial problems.[22]

The Infrastructure of Healing; or, The Architecture of Cloth

Next to the technical amplification of the voice and the illumination of the electric bulb, the other key infrastructural element in the charismatic healing revivals of the mid-twentieth century was the canvas tent. In everyday parlance, the words "tent" and "revival" seem almost synonymous in that phrase "tent revival." Almost all of the accounts of the rise of major charismatic evangelists of this period feature stories of their desire, indeed the great necessity, to obtain huge tents that would accommodate the masses of expectant faithful. By 1952, for instance, Oral Roberts, the most influential charismatic healer of the twentieth century, had invested over $200,000 in a "Tent Cathedral," which sheltered over 12,500 folding chairs underneath its fireproof canvas roof. "This fine gospel equipment," boasted an article in his popular magazine, *Healing Waters*, "was the largest ever constructed for the gospel ministry."[23]

In significant ways, the rapid spread of the charismatic renewal and the emerging popularity and everyday understanding of faith healing cannot be abstracted from the specific atmosphere or environment created in and through the cloth architecture of the massive tent. The movement and miraculous manifestations of Holy Ghost power cannot be detached from the specific environment created and demarcated within the canvas tent: the heavy, stuffy air heated by the bright electric bulbs, the smell of sweat mingling with grass and sawdust, and the particular resonance of amplified sound. Within this inherently transient space demarcated by the cloth architecture, some of the most important mass crowd phenomena within the United States during the twentieth century took place.[24]

The Tent Cathedral, that basic infrastructural component to the charismatic healing renewal, bears a similarity to the prayer cloth. On a basic level, both objects thematize the notion of portability and itinerancy. This infrastructure of transience so intimately associated with the Tent Cathedral, for example, required a fleet of eight semitrailers to haul the thousands of yards of fireproof cotton canvas as well as a circus-type stake driver from the Lewis Diesel Equipment Company (the same machine, incidentally, used by the Ringling Bros. Circus).[25] The handheld prayer cloth, so crucial an element in the formation and solidification of mass charismatic publics in the middle of the twentieth century, mimics the movement of the canvas healing tent through the infrastructure of the postal system. As if the massive tent were cut into thousands of pieces and circulated through the postal network, the appearance and circulation of faith in the practice of "faith healing" is sustained through hidden infrastructures of stenographers, sorting machines, diesel trucks, envelopes, and storage and relay facilities.

Likewise, both the tent canvas and the prayer cloth have an inherent pliability or flexibility in regard to the necessities of everyday life. Thus, one of the many reasons that Roberts claimed such allegiance to his revival tent was its ability to be pitched in a farmer's field or a vacant space on the outskirts of town when churches or town organizations tried to prevent his healing revival from entering their territory.

This force of attraction between these two textiles presses even closer through the sacred architecture of what was referred to by the Roberts healing campaign as the "prayer tent." This auxiliary tent provided a space of prayer and counseling for attendees at the Tent Cathedral who had just professed their faith to the audience. Compared to the generally orderly and subdued crowds within the main tent, the prayer tent was a liminal space characterized by ecstatic pandemonium and collective effervescence. The cloth architecture of the prayer tent demarcated a sacred circle, thus opening a communicative space for glossolalia, ecstatic prayer, "fallin' out in the Spirit," jerks, and other somatic manifestations of the spirit.

The homology between these two healing textiles was made quite apparent when A. A. Allen, another important figure in the charismatic revival, realized the anointed significance of his old revival tent when God spoke to him: "Don't you know that this tent is saturated and impregnated with My Power? I want you to cut these strips of canvas into little prayer rugs and send them to your friends who are partners in this ministry."[26] Those members of the faithful who were unable to pledge the $100 for the "Power Packed Prayer Rug" could settle for a "Prosperity Blessing Cloth" at a much smaller price.[27]

The Flow of Fabric and the Contagiousness of the Sacred

A song that often resonates within the space of small Pentecostal, Holiness, and Independent churches and radio broadcasts throughout southern Appalachia suggests the transgressive underbelly of the prayer cloth:

> But for the blood, shed on Calvary's tree
> but for the blood, there'd be no hope for you and me
> for all my righteousness was filthy rags
> and that's all I'd ever be
> but for the blood that cleansed and set me free.

Recalling a passage from the Old Testament, the phrase "for all my righteousness was filthy rags" evokes images of the profane antithesis of Christ's cleansing blood, perhaps one of the most ritually dangerous substances in the Judeo-Christian tradition, the *pannus menses* or menses rag. Evoking visceral sensations, both preachers and congregants often invoke these heavily cathected objects with the phrase "and our righteousness is unto filthy rags that raises up a stench in the nostrils of God." This image of the menses rag recalls not only the Levitical proscriptions regarding ritual cleanliness in regard to the menstruating woman, but a long-established ethnological inventory of the magical potential of menstrual blood.[28]

The symbolic horror of the "filthy rag" presses close to the sacred efficacy of the prayer cloth through another biblical reference that provides one of the theological cornerstones for the charismatic practice of faith healing. Thus Mark 5:25–34 recounts the miraculous cure of a woman with an "issue of blood" that had lasted for twelve years, causing her financial ruin and a kind of social death within her community. Current biblical scholarship disagrees on the precise nature and connotation of the transfer of healing virtue in this passage—if it indeed was a kind of ritual transgression or profanation inflicted upon Jesus through the tactile communication with the sick woman according to Levitical proscriptions. These accounts focus on several small details, such as the way the author of the book of Mark describes the "issue of blood." Whatever the case, it is hard to ignore the expression of surprise or shock expressed by Jesus upon registering the tactile contact from the woman. The particularities of this contact seem suggestive of a kind of transgressive communication, specific to a gesture of profane tactility.

After pushing her way through the noisy throng, the ailing woman reaches out to "but touch the hem of his garment" and is instantly healed in the moment of touch and the transfer of healing virtue. This account from the book of Mark, along with numerous references to the filthy rag, suggests that there is a dangerous element of profanation and transgression inherent in the textile of healing. At the very least, it suggests an intimacy between the communication of healing power, bodily fluids, and the anointed cloth. Of course, this force of attraction is clearly evident in the other crucial passages for the Pentecostal justification of prayer cloths, such as the account from Acts 19 when "handkerchiefs or aprons" are taken from the body of Apostle Paul and used to heal the sick. The Greek connotation of this word had specific meaning in the ancient world as a piece of fabric used to wipe sweat and other fluids from the face (*sudarium*).

Contemporary practices of healing through this materialized prayer perform this intimacy between cloth and bodily fluid in very literal ways. Thus the manufacture of the prayer cloth often includes an "anointing" with oil. In this way, the other common term, "anointed handkerchief," is very appropriate because it suggests the place of bodily fluids and a literal flow of force in the practice of faith healing. When I participated in the anointing of prayer cloths in southern Appalachia, I was always struck by the way ordinary vegetable oil was generously applied to the white fragments of cloth. The yellow oil would leave a prominent stain upon the white surface of the fabric, mimicking the sullying of the fabric with bodily fluid (spit, mucus, tears, sweat, and so on).

Once again, the healing ritual of the prayer cloth emphasizes the material characteristics of the sacred object. The absorbent properties of woven plant fiber enable the cloth to become a medium for the communication of sacred fluid. And this notion of fluidity, in turn, so crucial to this healing practice, and an "elementary" quality of the sacred itself, seems to be an inherent physical property of the cloth. Cloth envelops the form that it touches, and in this way becomes an intimate metaphor for skin and tactility. Likewise, cloth blows in the wind, drapes around forms, flows like water, and "fits" the body like an extension of skin and therefore has strong connotations with fluidity. Rendering these basic material properties of fabric in a sacred mode, the prayer cloth reveals the details of an object that would otherwise remain too proximate, intimate, and habituated to be noticed.

Hanky-Panky of the Voice

The charismatic healing revivals of the twentieth century used early Christian accounts of healing power transmitted through tactile contact as a touchstone for their modern curative performances. Accounts of the healing force released through touching the hem of Jesus's garment or the sweat-soaked "aprons" of the Apostle Paul, for example, were constantly invoked to support contemporary charismatic healing techniques. These healing practices of manual contact, however, were not merely part of a lineage of tactile healing techniques uninterrupted from early Christianity and ancient Greek sources; the very sense of touch itself, as well as experiences of "communication," took on specifically modern orientations and organizations in an age of electronic modes of communication, such as the radio, and mechanized networks, such as the postal system.[29] Through new modes of technological reproduction and transmission, the Christian hand of healing and discernment employed a thoroughly modern *haptic* gift extended and attuned by prosthetic extensions of the body.

Though the origins of the prayer cloth, also known as the anointed handkerchief, were traced by the practitioners of charismatic healing back to early Christian sources, the popularity of the prayer handkerchief as a devotional object in the twentieth century had much to do with its symbolic textures and resonances within a specifically modern context. Thus, when the prayer handkerchief emerged as one of the most influential devotional objects in the history of Pentecostalism, the handkerchief, as a ubiquitous utilitarian object, already carried within its woven texture a specific social history and meaning.[30] Tracing some of the specifically modern resonances in the weave of the handkerchief, this section suggests that there were significant forces of attraction between the practice of charismatic faith healing and the modern piece of pocket fabric known as the handkerchief.

The etymology of the word "handkerchief" will help to uncover some of the significant modern resonances residing within this everyday object. Even from the outset, the word carries within itself a curious displacement. Thus the *Comprehensive Etymological Dictionary of the English Language* elaborates on the curiously disjointed or out-of-place character of this word:

> *Handkerchief*: n.—Compounded of *hand* and *kerchief*. Etymologically the word contains a contradiction, since *kerchief* denotes a covering for the *head*, fr. OF. *couvrechef, couvrechief*, lit. "cover-head."

As if to usurp the sovereignty of the head, this displaced hand seems already to be hiding itself under a veil of secrecy—a tricky hand indeed!

This *sleight of hand* at the heart of the word signals important modern associations with the handkerchief as a standard implement within the magician's bag of tricks. Behind the veil of the handkerchief, objects disappear and adroit hands move undetected by the distracted senses of the audience. Though it is difficult to give the precise time period of the widespread use of the handkerchief as an indispensable prop in the magic show, by the time Pentecostal healers were anointing them for the purposes of miraculous cures early in the twentieth century, these objects would have had a strong association, albeit at times implicitly, with shows of magical entertainment.[31]

By the 1920s, the contradiction inherent in the word "handkerchief" announced itself in another way through the popular phrase "hanky-panky." At that time, this phrase took on its contemporary connotation as a secret sexual liaison or erotic encounter. By then, the thoroughly utilitarian object known as the handkerchief had been shortened to "hanky." This playful truncating of the term attests to its pervasive and ubiquitous presence in everyday life. Before the "hanky" took on the libidinal resonance we understand today, it was saturated with the residues of older magical meanings:

> *Hanky-panky.* A synonym for trickery, hanky-panky may have been coined, with the help of reduplication, from the magician's handkerchief, or *hanky*, under which so many things have mysteriously appeared and disappeared through clever sleight of hand. Probably related to *hocus pocus*, it is first recorded in *Punch* (1841).

> *Hanky-panky*, adroit substitution, palming, sleight-of-hand in legerdemain. (*A Dictionary of Slang, Jargon, and Cant*, vol. 1, 1889)

> *Hanky-panky* goes back more than a hundred years and originated in the jargon of fairs and carnivals. It's a variation on the much older "hocus-pocus"—a term used by shysters and magicians while performing tricks. Since there was always something underhanded about such activities, *hanky-panky* has come to mean doubledealing or devious trickery. (*Morris Dictionary of Word and Phrase Origins*, 1962)

> *Hanky-panky* (trickery, deception). The attractive phrase might suggest a sort of conjuring trick done with the aid of a handkerchief ("hanky"), as magicians often do. It is probably, however, an alteration of "hocus-pocus." (*Dictionary of True Etymologies*, 1986)

> *Hocus-pocus.* Sham L. of quack. The fact that *hocuspokusfiliokus* is still used in Norw. & Sw. [Norway and Sweden] suggests that there may be something in the old theory of a blasphemous perversion of the sacramental blessing, *hoc est corpus (filii)*. Hence *hocus*, to hoax (q.v.); later, to drug one's liquor for swindling purposes. (*A Concise Etymological Dictionary of Modern English*, 1952)

The word "hocus-pocus" is now a common designation (at least in the English language) for "a cheat or impostor" and refers originally to the conjurer who by legerdemain deceives the people and pretends to work miracles. In German, the word is used mainly in the sense of "sleight of hand," designating not the performer but the deception by which a trick is done, and this seems to be the more original meaning of the term.

The word is probably a corruption of the Latin words *Hoc est corpus meum*, which is the formula spoken by the priest over the sacramental bread and wine, which thereby is claimed to be transformed into the body and blood of Christ.

In its modern sense, the word can be traced back to the seventeenth century, but the use of the formula *hoc est corpus meum* in the sense of jugglery is mentioned as early as 1579 in Fischart's *Beehive*.

Johann Fischart, the famous German satirist and reformer who lived in the middle of the sixteenth century and died about 1590, speaks of the sacramental transubstantiation as "bread jugglery" (*brotvergaukelung*), and compares the power of the five words to the magic word which Satan uttered when creating monks. . . . Tillotson (1630–1694) in one of his sermons (XXVI) accepts the etymology of the word, saying:

"In all probability those common juggling words of hocus pocus are nothing else but a corruption of hoc est corpus, by way of ridiculous imitation of the priests of the Church of Rome in their trick of Transubstantiation."

We need not assume with Tillotson that jugglers actually intended to ridicule the sacrament. When pretending to transform anything, they simply imitated the process of transformation and naturally used the same words as the priests did, merely because the people believed them to be potent charms, and since the audience did not consist of Latin scholars, they naturally corrupted the words into a formula that was easier pronounced.

The verb "to hocus-pocus" thus acquires the meaning, "to transform, to metamorphose," or "to disguise a change." ("Natural Magic and Prestidigitation," 1903)

As if the tricky hand hidden in the word "handkerchief" was once again reasserting itself as sui generis or automatic efficacy, our tracing of the etymological associations with this word have taken us back to the miraculous transformations and communications of early Christianity. That the modern handkerchief still maintained residual traces of past Eucharistic rites of transubstantiation is once again suggested by the word itself. Thus the *kerchiefing* of the hand bears a striking similarity to the Eucharistic rites of the Middle Ages that veiled the right hand holding the soon-to-be-transformed bread with a sacred liturgical vestment known as the maniple. Once again, standard magical practices can be seen as a kind of profanation of ritual performances within the church.

Through its employment as a prop in the performance of prestidigitation, the handkerchief is the middle term or medium between the aural distraction of the voice and the skillful movements of the hand. In this way, the technique of magical substitution thematizes the voice and the concomitant power of words—*hocus pocus!*—precisely to usurp the place of the ear/voice though quick manual gestures that, so to speak, move behind the back of the sense of hearing. The moment of prestidigitation is precisely that moment of *distraction and sensory disjuncture* when the sound of the voice draws attention away from the movements of the hand.

With these connections and historical linkages of the handkerchief taking us back to the Eucharistic elements and its magical profanations, we come to a problem of the prayer cloth. Through its historical and etymological vicissitudes, the prayer cloth seems to evoke a particular anxiety around the *representational* status of the devotional object. Like the always already exteriorized resonance of the voice outside the speaking subject, the prayer handkerchief, as a materialized instantiation of the voice, marks a particular anxiety around the exteriorities of faith and the force of automaticity.

It is not a coincidence, therefore, that even a cursory reading of the proposed origins of the term "hanky-panky" in the etymological dictionaries reveals this oscillation and anxiety in compelling ways.[32] Thus there are vehement debates among the etymological dictionaries themselves as to whether or not the term "hanky-panky" is *really* a profane derivation or slippage of the sacred Latin phrase *hoc est corpus meum*. Thus the possible origins of the phrase not only signal a profanation, but also suggest the potential of language, as a particular force of exteriority, to take on an unanticipated force outside the subject through a series of reduplications, mispronunciations, and mumblings.

This brief description of some of the historical residues woven into the handkerchief help to shed light on the compelling nature of the Pentecostal prayer cloth as a specific modern devotional object associated with experiences of miraculous healing and divine presence. Thus, the earlier resonances of the handkerchief with performances of distraction and sensory disjuncture between sight and sound in the moment of prestidigitation suggest the way that the "prayer handkerchief,"[a] as a miraculous coupling of *voice and object*, marks a curious antinomy. On the one hand, this devotional object is explicitly described in terms of faith and the aural vocalizations of prayer. On the other (perhaps the left) hand, the prayer cloth embodies an experience of tactile immediacy that seems to operate with a force of automaticity that goes behind the back of "faith." Just like earlier practices of magical sleight of hand, the prayer cloth is an *adroit* substitution of a manual experience for the voice.

Silent Voice: Pantomime

One particular performance of trickery associated with the phrase "hanky-panky" in the nineteenth century was the art of pantomime. The popular treatise on parlor magic, *The Art of Amusing: Being a Collection of Graceful Arts, Merry Games, Odd Tricks, Curious Puzzles, and New Charades* (1866), for instance, dedicates a short chapter to the tricky phrase in question:

> HANKY-PANKY is the name of a certain art practiced by pantomimists of the clown and harlequin school, and is the subject of no little study and practice. We do not think it within our power to define hanky-panky, composed as it is of fictitious whackings and kickings and smackings, unless, indeed, that be a definition. We can, however, give a couple of illustrations of the art as it may be practiced in the family circle. We may look further into the matter at some future day, and possibly a volume of Parlor hanky-panky, beautifully illustrated by the author.[33]

The author goes on to describe several performances of pantomimic hanky-panky wherein, through rapid movements of the hands and fingers, the audience is tricked into perceiving that some portion of the body (knuckles, head, ears, and so on) has been pummeled violently against a dense object such as a wooden door. I cannot resist including one of these pantomimic instructions in its entirety:

> The first example we shall now give is how to knock your knuckles on the edge of a marble mantel-piece or other hard substance without hurting them. It is done thus: You raise your clenched fist high in the air, hold it poised there some seconds for all the audience to see, and then bring it swiftly down; but just before your hand reaches the object, open your fingers quickly, so they will strike the object with a sharp slap, then close them quickly; if this is neatly done, it will appear as if you had struck your knuckles a violent blow. This will make the ladies scream, and every one else thrill of horror. (135)

In order to produce this special effect or "thrill of horror," each pantomime technique outlined in this chapter describes a disjuncture between

FIGURE 5
Hanky-Panky, 1886

> THE ART OF AMUSING. 135
>
> seconds for all the audience to see, and then bring it swiftly down; but just before your hand reaches the object, open your fingers quickly, so they will
>
> strike the object with a sharp slap, then close them quickly; if this is neatly done, it will appear as if you had struck your knuckles a violent blow. This will make the ladies scream, and every one else thrill of horror.
>
> The second feat of hanky-panky consists in knocking your head against the edge of a door with such apparent force as to break your skull, provided it be anything under an inch thick.
>
> This you do by holding your hand which is farthest from the audience on a level with your face,

bodily gestures and the production of sound. In this way, the absence of the speaking voice sets up the viewing audience to focus attention upon the silent gestures, so that the unanticipated irruption of sound, somewhere else, exterior to the mouth of the speaking subject, produces a kind of perceptual surprise-effect or moment of sensory disjuncture. In the moment of hanky-panky, the hands usurp the function of the mouth and announce themselves through a percussive noise. This pantomime thematizes or performs the displacement of traditional orientations or locations of sound and bodily movement to produce shocking effects. In this way, the hanky-panky art of pantomime has important similarities to another tricky art of voice displacement and mouths usurped by hidden hands: ventriloquism. Displaced sound generated outside "normal" regions of vocalization "sets up" yet another significant instance of sensory displacement in the technique of the trick.

Ectoplasmic Textile Tongues; or, The Spiritualist Prayer Cloth

Coinciding with the communicative link-up between Washington and Baltimore through the electrical wires of Samuel Morse's recent invention, in 1848, the Fox sisters from the "burned-over-district" of New York state began interpreting the rap-tap-tappings of spirit communiqués from a spectral beyond. Known as "modern spiritualism," this telegraphic necromancy spread rapidly throughout the United States and Europe during the middle of the nineteenth century. During the séance or sitting, the medium was able to bridge the chasm between the living and the dead, facilitating the appearance of spectral forms, ghostly voices, and other hollow sounds from the afterlife.[34]

Toward the end of the nineteenth century, skillful mediums began channeling not only the traditional immaterial voices and spectral images from the realm of the shades, but *actual* physical substances. Usually extruded through the mouth of the medium, this phenomenon of materialization was termed "ectoplasmic substance."[35] One of the most renowned investigators into the phenomenon of spiritualist materialization, Albert Schrenck-Notzing, described this substance as a "membranous veil, like a cobweb," composed of "compact organic fabrics."[36] Also referred to as "ideoplasty" or "teleplastics," Schrenck-Notzing proposed that spectral fabrics were not actually communications from the realm of the dead, but instead materializations exuding from the memory surface of the medium's "subliminal consciousness." Many incredulous opponents of the spiritualist movement were able to scrutinize high-quality photographs of these so-called ectoplasmic materializations and were surprised that these oral extrusions "closely resembled everyday materials such as wool, cotton, fur and paper."[37] Both mediums and séance participants, on the other hand, believed these ectoplasmic emanations to be a kind of fleshly incarnation from the spirit world—a grotesque parody of the Eucharistic metamorphosis of spirit made flesh.

Even upon cursory inspection, the photographs of manifestations of teleplastic phenomena from the mouth do indeed have a striking resemblance to fabrics woven of delicate thread, or, in other circumstances, fluffy or downy material such as cotton. Yet despite the fact that the spiritual manifestation seems clearly identifiable through the photographic lens as some type of textile, the image of this material exuding from the mouth of the medium still strikes the viewer with a particularly unnerving force.[38] Arousing sensations of horror and disgust, it is as if the tongue of the medium has elongated to monstrous proportions, oozing out of the moist darkness of the oral cavity.

The uncanny effects produced by these specific types of spirit manifestations could be related precisely to the fact that the ectoplasmic substance bears a strange resemblance to cloth. As one of the most ubiquitous and utilitarian objects in everyday life, cloth plays a constitutive role in the unacknowledged demarcation of the boundaries of the subject. Cloth is a kind of extension or boundary between the subject and the exterior world. The ectoplasmic manifestation inverts this everyday demarcation so that the exterior surface ends up oozing excessively from the interior of the body: a regurgitated externality from the dark recesses of the interior.

Despite its disconcerting force, there is something quite apposite about this specific ectoplasmic extension of the tongue within the modern spiritualist tradition. After all, the power in the medium, that spiritual telegraphist, resides precisely in the ability to "get out of the way" and allow the spirits to animate the faculties of vocalization like an instrument. The mouth of the medium was made to speak in both foreign and unknown tongues through the animating force of the spirit. The spiritual manifestation of the ectoplasmic cloth tongue thematizes a basic spiritualist practice on a visual and tactile register.

In an age of communication extended by the electrical telegraph wires, forces from the realm of the dead were able to animate and extend the tongue to horrifying and grotesque proportions. As if to embody the anxieties articulated by Ferdinand de Saussure in his lectures given at the same time as these spiritualist manifestations, the teratological tongue of the medium signaled the exteriority of language by grotesquely rendering its forgotten materialities: tongues, teeth, electrical wires, and inscriptive surfaces.

Not only did these spiritualist manifestations provide a kind of implicit commentary on the changing nature of human subjectivity and the possibility of articulation in an age of technological mediation, but their tongues also portended the emergence of glossolalia on a scale never before heard through the Pentecostal revivals of the early twentieth century. The ectoplasmic tongue of the medium foreshadows the Pentecostal em-

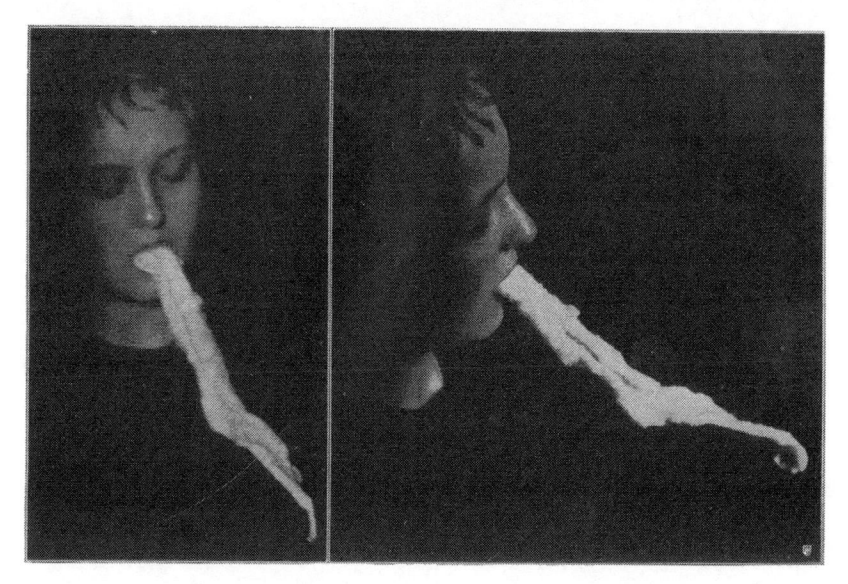

FIGURE 6 Ecotoplasmic materialization from Baron von Schrenck-Notzing's *Phenomena of Materialization*

phasis on glossolalia, a wonderfully descriptive term that emphasizes the movement of the tongue muscle in and of itself, as the preeminent sign of sanctification and the baptism of Holy Ghost power.[39] More than this, however, can we not see in the grotesque textile tongue of the medium a foreshadowing of the pervasive circulation of the prayer cloth beginning in the second half of the twentieth century? And does not the Pentecostal prayer cloth bear a curious resemblance to an exteriorized or severed tongue, flapping in the pneumatic wind of the Holy Ghost and surrounded by a border of teeth cut by the pinking shears? Indeed, one could debate whether the size of the prayer cloth was in order to fit economically within the space of a small envelope or to suggest the glossolalic tongue animated through the ecstatic performance of healing prayer. Thus, the ectoplasmic tongue in an age of the spiritual telegraph foretold of the postal circulation of the severed tongues of the prayer cloth in the ventriloquistic age of the "wireless" loudspeaker.

The Prayer Cloth Testimony of Sister Francis (WGTH, December 2010)

I wanted to tell everybody about the little girls that we've been talkin'
  about for the past three weeks.
Well I wasn't here last week.

But the past three weeks, this little girl in North Car-lina, she had
   anorexia real bad.
And she was really, really in bad shape.
She was eleven years old and her friend also had it.
I don't know what her age was but she . . .
Her mother asked my sister if we would send some prayer cloths.
And we sent a couple of handkerchiefs—anointed handkerchiefs.
And last week we heard, well, I'm gettin' ahead of myself.
The little girl she wrote her friend a letter that she was in the
   hospital.
She was so bad they put her in the hospital and they thought they
   were gonna have to put this little girl in the hospital too.
But thank God they didn't.
She was just so bad and she wrote her a letter, and if you could
   just read that letter, you would never believe that it come from a
   eleven year old girl.
I mean that letter was just, just wonderful.
You'd thank it come from somebody that was in college, the way that
   she wrote that little girl a letter.
And she started tellin' her about God.
And what God could do for her.
And how God could bring both of 'em out of that.
And thank God, the little girl's home.
She came home last week.
And from what I can understand, she's doin' better.
And the little girl that wrote her the letter, she's eating better and
   she's doin' better.
They're not outta the woods, they still need prayer.
But I just thank God for what he has did for these little girls.
And ya know, the mother she told my sister the other day, she said,
   "Will you please ask your sister and her husband if they would
   send me another prayer cloth?"
She says, "They work."
She says, "Those prayer cloths work!" [*At this point in the narrative,
   more robust affirmation from the congregation*]
And you know, and I thought, well how wonderful.
It's the faith, you know.
And I's tellin' my sister, I said, she had the faith that everything was
   gonna be okay with her little girl.

And it just thrilled me when she said that they work.
And we did send another one, but it was for another woman that had cancer and she needs prayer also.
I think that she had surgery, but I don't know how that surgery came out, but I'm praying that everything will work out okay for'er.

The testimony of Sister Francis highlights several significant features of both the narrative form of testimony and the prayer cloth. Like the physical circulation of objects through a system of postal exchange, the opening remarks of her testimony call attention to the temporal dimension of the narrative. Through progressive updates and retellings of the young anorexic girls, the testimony builds and accumulates compelling force. The phrase "we've been talkin'" instantiates a narrative history of talk and prayer and announces that the potential energy of faith is *already* in circulation. This particular testimony marks an immediacy within a temporal framework of "storyin' on thangs" of the spirit. This gesture to the continuous compulsion to narrate the movement of the miraculous performatively instantiates the listener into the continuing circulation and temporal progression of faith.

As a crucial aspect both within the structure of the narrative testimony and the generation or appearance of faith, the temporal themes of displacement and deferral emerge through a brief recounting of the provenance of this particular devotional object: "Her mother asked my sister if we would send some prayer cloths. And we sent a couple of handkerchiefs—anointed handkerchiefs." Faith makes its appearance in and through an originary displacement . Through the intermediary of the sister, the mother of the sick girl asks Sister Francis to anoint a cloth. Even at its supposed origin, faith begins to gain force, like the deadly power of the spirit (*hau*) in the gift exchange process described by Mauss, through progressive displacements and deferrals. The force of faith emerges through its unplaceability, or the perpetual deferral of its permanent and fixed location. And just as the anointed handkerchief is a materialized instantiation of the fleeting vocalization of prayer, the actual physical movement of the sacred cloth remnant between hands and through the post office gives tangible, tactile presence to this perpetual deferral of faith as that which is always about to arrive or make its appearance *somewhere else*. In this way as well, the circulation of talk about the potential efficacy of the devotional object among mother, intermediary, and Francis coincides on a material dimension through the movement of the cloth through a system of exchange.

The circulation of the materialized prayer through the postal system is thus the shadowy material underbelly of the compulsive spirit of talk. As the textile tongue moves, so the tongue itself wags. In this way, a sustaining element of faith—deferral and displacement—is intimately linked to hidden networks of scanning, sorting, and transporting machines. Thus the postal service is an essential material infrastructure of prayer, an apparatus of belief.

In the next movement of the narrative, Sister Francis performs what could be called a "testimonial parapraxis": "And last week we heard, well, I'm gettin' ahead of myself." This momentary slip in the narrative flow is rife with meaning, not only for what it reveals about the particular structure of narrativity organizing the poetic effect of the story, but in its evocation of a *rupture* between the speaking subject and the movement of the story. "Getting' ahead of oneself," especially in this context, heralds the appearance of divinely inspired poetic styles such as anointed preaching and the ecstatic sounds of glossolalia. In a similar way, Sister Francis's testimonial parapraxis, "I'm gettin' ahead of myself," challenges us to begin to think of the ways in which the performance of faith is always somehow *ahead* of or slightly off-kilter from the "believer." Conceived in this way, faith is perpetually moving just beyond full perceptual grasp of the subject through postal networks, narrative circulations, and the compelling force of talk. Thus it is precisely in this deferred or disjointed space of *getting ahead of the self* that faith lives and moves and has its being, so to speak.

This slip within the testimonial form also suggests useful insights into the particular narrative structure of this mode of faith-talk. Thus, on a basic structural level, to reveal the wonderful news of the testimony too early in the narrative form would be to short-circuit the poetic effect that is garnered and released through the performative enactment of the story. Once again, the poetic force of the testimonial form in southern Appalachia is unleashed through a particular structure of narrativity and is not merely a recounting of the "informational" content of a miraculous occurrence. The particular structure of the retelling brings the ears of the listener within its sphere of poetic operation, calling the audience to participate in the instantiation or performance of faith. The revelatory movement of the testimony releases its full poetic force only after the enactment of the story has passed the time and embraced the listener into its operations of expectancy and suspense. And what does the listener get in lieu of this immediate divulging of the stark informational content of the illness, but a performative calling for us to imagine the penning and circulation of a wonderful letter from one frail hand to another.

After moving through the details of the narrative, we arrive at the miraculous coincidence that releases the full force of faith in the very moment that it signals its further displacement. Just before the moment of revelation, the deferral of faith is narrated once again:

> And ya know, the mother she told my sister the other day, she said, "Will you please ask your sister and her husband if they would send me another prayer cloth?"
> She says, "They work."
> She says, "Those prayer cloths work!"

Replicating the initial occasion for the sacred anointing of the prayer cloth, the conversation mediated by a middle person (Francis's sister) generates yet another call for an anointed object. The mother, therefore, could be commenting upon both the miraculous healing efficacy inherent in the cloth *and* this object's capacity to generate the compelling appearance of faith. In almost every instance of testifying upon the miraculous power of the prayer cloth, a repetition of the story has signaled the further replication of the sacred object. Once again, the force of talk and the circulation of the devotional object go hand in hand. In this way, the return to the origin always occasions further replication and deferral.

The next narrative turn is characteristic not only of this specific practice of storytelling but of talk on miraculous healing more generally. As if to wrest the efficacy from the autonomous and automatic circulation of the object from the space of exteriority and thus recuperate faith to the bounded interiors of the subject, Sister Francis emphasizes or attempts to locate "faith" in a definite source: "It's the faith, you know. And I's tellin' my sister, I said, she had the faith that everything was gonna be okay with her little girl."

This subtle disavowal, or distancing from the automatic exteriorities of faith, is a recurrent theme in the narration of faith healing throughout the twentieth century. However, even this attempt to locate the source of faith in the caring mother marks yet another displacement of belief. After all, was it not the mother who initially looked to Sister Francis and her husband as the supposed bearers of faith?

And finally, where is faith to be located when its supposed bearer or guarantor displays a great sense of surprise when talk of the efficacy of the sacred cloth returns to its apparent point of origin: "And you know, it just thrilled me when she said that they work." This revelatory thrill points to the appearance and accumulation of the force of faith through material infrastructures of circulation and the exchange of hands. Faith was not present in the same way at the origin as it was at the "end," but it gained compelling force though its progressive displacements and temporal articulations in exterior networks of exchange. In anticipation of an even greater thrill, and even greater accumulation of efficacy, at the very moment when wandering faith seems to have found its resting place yet another space of storying, anticipation, and circulation is opened within the space of the narrative. Where, then, can faith be located at the end of this miraculous testimony? *It's in the mail.*

> *And we did send another one*, but it was for another woman that had cancer and she needs prayer also.
> I think that she had surgery, but I don't know how that surgery came out, but I'm praying that everything will work out okay for'er.

An Apotropaic Device

Another unanticipated appearance of the prayer cloth occurred while I was interviewing an elderly sister about her practice of listening to live charismatic radio broadcasts. This conversation took place at her apartment in a public housing complex for low-income senior citizens. In a high-pitched voice that labored for breath and trembled like her hands, the stream of spiritual storyin'[40] meandered around the theme of the miraculous until it came across this devilish encounter:

> SISTER DIXIE: You know that lady come helps me, her little grandson, he's five years old. His mommy and daddy is separated, and he's got *angry* in 'im. And she said she had whipped him and whipped 'im. I said, "Get 'im in prayer line!" And I told Ruth, I said, "Ya'll better be gettin' little John in prayer line." [*With nonchalant and dismissive tone*] "Ahh, he'll be alright." I said, "We'll see." Cause see, I could see. And Sue was settin' in the floor one day a'playin'; he just walked over hit that little thang and said, "*Sissy, I hate you!*" I said, "No you don't John, no you don't." And I got him up on my lap and I laid my hands on 'im. And I said, "Devil, now you's well go on away from this baby, 'cause he ain't gonna be raised up to work for you!" And he got out of 'im. And

Ruth, she got a prayer cloth and pinned on 'im. And now there ain't no better young'in.

After casting out the devil through a technique of manual imposition and verbal command, a prayer cloth is immediately employed to ward off any further influences of the devil and his dark principalities upon the helpless child. Used in this way, the prayer cloth embodies yet another function as an apotropaic device.

Typical of these narrative testimonies about the power of the materialized Holy Ghost, Sister Dixie concludes her story, after a brief period of conversation, with a standard qualifying phrase: "If you don't b'lieve there ain't no use ax-kin'." In almost every testimony or spiritual "storyin' on thangs" I have witnessed in southern Appalachia, there is a kind of formalized disclaimer or subtle renunciation of the automatic force of the objectile as a parting qualification to the miraculous narrative. This disclaimer or qualification points to an underlying tension within the circulation of the prayer cloth. Just as the devotional object shifts between hands through the process of exchange, it perpetually oscillates in that gap between the material and the spiritual, between the fleeting sound of the prayer and the material textures of the cloth.

This fleeting nature of faith, and the inability to fully "pin it down" for more than an instant, is shown through the details of Sister Dixie's narrative. Within the relationships between the angry toddler and his caregivers, for example, where is this all-important practice of belief to be located? Does little John believe in the efficacious force of the prayer cloth? Or perhaps the belief of Sister Dixie becomes a kind of supplementary stand-in for a child who is too young to understand the dynamics and meaning of belief itself. The helper Ruth, in turn, could be the locus of belief, as she was the figure in possession of the anointed cloth and she actually pinned it upon the suffering child. Moreover, is it possible that the prayer cloth mechanically performs its apotropaic function outside this apparent field of belief and, through this autonomous and automatic efficacy, becomes a magical object, as defined by classic ethnological sources such as Mauss's *A General Theory of Magic*?[41]

In order to help map the locus of belief, perhaps it will be useful to track the circulation of the cloth itself as it "changes hands," so to speak. As indicated further in the conversation on prayer cloths, Sister Dixie had requested that Brother and Sister Allen, who were also present during the interview, manufacture some of the anointed cloth fragments.

ANDY: And she [Ruth] had prayed on that, or the church had prayed on it?

SISTER DIXIE: Well I had some anointed by Brother Allen 'n' Dorothy, and I gave her one.

After the cloth is anointed through the verbal prayers and manual techniques of an initial community of believers, it enters an economy of circulation, which moves it into the hands of Sister Dixie, who then gives the anointed fabric to Ruth. Based on the testimony of Sister Dixie, we might add that Ruth's lack of faith ("Ahh, he'll be alright") may have been a concern for Dixie, and thus arose the need for the gifting of the cloth in the first place. And finally, within this initial cycle of circulation (one foresees, for example, many other potential exchanges of the cloth after it serves its purpose for the child), belief once again makes its appearance through the affixing of the cloth to the young child as an apotropaic device to repel the efforts of the devil.

The other crucial element in this system of exchange, perhaps the most motivating and contagious force of all, is that of the narrative testimony upon the miraculous movements of the object. In and through the performance of the testimony, the cloth comes full circle by returning to its initial owner. Albeit in the guise of an account of the efficacy of the anointed cloth, the object returns to the original source (Brother and Sister Allen), who were also present during the interview. In this way, the narrative testimony further reinforces and solidifies communal bonds and the power of belief.

There is one overarching question. In what way does this system of anointing, exchange, and narrative circulation temporally articulate belief through moments of deferral and delay? In and through this kind of temporalization, belief emerges and seems to gain momentum or, perhaps we should say, becomes more compelling, as it marks an ever-increasing change of hands. Belief itself, like the *hau* of the gift described by Mauss, gains momentum and force of compulsion in and through this economy of circulation. As the object literally moves between hands, the force of belief, and thus the powerful efficacy of the Holy Ghost, builds to such intensity that this tiny rag, this mere fragment or piece of textile detritus, is able to repel the devil himself. Belief, therefore, makes its appearance not in one single person or practice but in this manifold network and deferred "exchange of hands." In this way, what is at first glance the strongest seat of belief, that of the initial anointing by the Allens, seems to be eclipsed by the process of circulation itself. This circulation, in turn, generates another, more powerful, gravitation of belief—what could be called a spirit of compulsion. As emphasized by Michel de Certeau, belief subsists in and through a temporal articulation that moves through a series of deferrals, substitutions, and temporal lags. Thus, there is always someone else, another potential story, some alterity *elsewhere*, that drives the appearance of faith in and through the promise of its return.[42]

The Sound of the Mechanism: Materialized Prayer

Further asserting the force of repetition compelled through the prayer cloth, Sister Dixie's testimony of diabolical influence and the power of the sacred object precipitated yet another miraculous chain of narrativity. After Sister Dixie responded to my questions as to the process of anointing, Brother Aldie announced another story with a question directed to me: "You do believe in prayer cloths, don't ya?"

> ALDIE: Did we tell you 'bout the man that had artificial hips'n'knees? He came out church, well in fact I mentioned it last week on the radio. He was Presbyterian and he wasn't used to Pentecostal ways. They brought his mother-n-law down there. I know we told you about her comin' outta the wheel chair, runnin' the aisles and so forth. But anyway, *par* [power] got on him, and he come out and ran up and down the aisles. And went back and told 'em that they better b'lieve in it because it was real. "The power of God is real." But anyway, the Lord had spoke to me one day out thar prayin', and told me to have Dorothy go to Dollar Store 'n buy a white sheet. Lay it down in the floor at church, get everybody, you know, anoint it and pray over it. And then fold the sheet in half and cut it: make two sheets instead of one. Then take one section of that sheet, and fold it and cut it again, so it be a total of three pieces.
>
> ANDY: You just prayed over it once?
>
> ALDIE: Yea. Everybody got down, prayed over the whole sheet. And then we cut it, and sent it to Christiansburg [Virginia] to that couple. I coulda sworn that he told me that she had a bad back and he too. They called us, they were so happy. But then, I found out later, like I said I coulda swore they told me she had a bad back. But they called, she said she wrapped that half-a-sheet

around her, and he wrapped the two little ones around his legs; and they shouted and praised the Lord all evenin'. Even slept in 'em. Next day, she went ta get her a shower. When she came out, he had his hand behind his back. And she didn't know what he had—he's a big man, used to be a biker. And she kept askin' him what he had. They was gettin' ready to replace his knees and hips again—he didn't wanna go through it—said he'd rather be dead as to do it. He was a real jealous man, and said he had somethin' behind his back. And she kept askin' im what it was, he wouldn't tell her. Finally she run, started to get by him. When she did he pulled out a gun, and as she run she wrapped the cloth around her and took off runnin' to go out the side door to her son's house. And he snapped the gun, but it didn't go off. He turnt it on hisself and killed hisself. And she said she knew, last time we saw her, she still says she knew, that God sent that prayer cloth to protect her back. 'Cause that's where he tried to shoot her was in the back, and said there was nothin' wrong with her back. She had a perfect back. I'd misunderstood someway er another; said whatin' nothin' wrong with her back. But said she know God used that prayer cloth to protect her back. He'd put the prayer cloths around his legs, but he shot hisself in his head. God can do it. See, he was gonna kill 'em both, but God used a prayer cloth to save her life. She's still alive today.

ANDY: So the cloth carries the . . .

ALDIE: Anointin' of God. Uh-huh. Sure does. Like Dixie said when she had that cloth there, it had the anointin' of God on it, and God honors that! If you pray from the heart, he honors it! Sure does.

Announcing the theme of mechanicity yet again, Brother Aldie's story of the prayer cloth opens with a strikingly visceral image "'bout the man that had artificial hips'n'knees." As if to prefigure the process of the manufacture of the anointed cloth, the theme of substitution and bodily extension is present at the beginning of the narrative. The material "stand-in" or patch that supplements the broken-down contingencies of the everyday is announced as an overarching testimonial motif within the story. Early in the story, the power of the Holy Ghost and the mechanical prosthesis display striking similarities in their mutual ability to assert the force of mechanicity in the practice of bodily movement. The possessing power of the Holy Ghost enables the lame to "run the aisles," while the biomedical replacement of atrophied and defective bone sockets allows the crippled to walk once again. In both instances, therefore, the prosthetic supplement enables the movement of lame bodies.

Another remarkable feature of this story is its descriptions of the transformation of a quotidian object into a sacred receptacle of power. Brother Aldie is divinely inspired to "buy a white sheet" from the place that seems to be the embodiment of cheap everyday commodities, the Dollar Store.[43] Through a process of prayer, techniques of the body, and ritualized cutting of the fabric, the cheap utilitarian object from the Dollar Store will be transformed into a sacred cloth.

The practice of folding and cutting the sheet, which is described in careful detail by the narrator, evokes the classic ethnological descriptions of the part that is equivalent to the whole. Thus, despite the process of dividing the cloth, it still maintains the efficacy that was instantiated into the entirety of the sheet through the initial prayer of anointing. Yet because Brother Aldie invokes this process of folding and cutting with such performative care, and because this theme of the cutting of the prayer cloth is a recurrent practice in the overall phenomenon of this devotional object, it seems likely that the "cut" is not merely a secondary process to allow for a greater distribution of the initially anointed object, but like the incision made by the sacrificial knife, the cut of circumcision, or the fleshly inscriptions of scarification, the act of cutting itself instantiates efficacious force into the object.[44] Just as the percussive pops of hand clapping and loud vocalizations in the performance of skein prayer open a space of divine communication, the cutting or ripping of the fabric is a destructive gesture that completes the materialization of Holy Ghost power.

Additionally, the physical process of cutting the fabric to divide its surface mimics, on a basic material level, the process of narrativity. It is this performance of storying, in turn, that generates the compulsion to repeat stories of the miraculous efficacy of the prayer cloth. The force of belief makes its appearance and accrues force in and through these narrative replications. The actual cutting of the fabric is also a symbolic "cuttin' loose" of storying tongues that will recount, repeatedly, the miraculous movements of the sacred object. The prayer cloth is a textile tongue, cut loose and set free to flap in the winds of narrativity.

This technique of prayer and concomitant rending of the fabric also makes an implicit commentary on the nature and movement of the Holy Ghost within the space of worship and the everyday lives of the charismatic faithful. Just as a scrap or remnant of fabric can be cut from its original totality to be patched in to another textile surface or context, the cutting of the cloth mirrors on a material level the capacity of prayer to cut out, wrest, or excise power from the diffuse totality of Holy Ghost potentiality and materialize it into an object. In turn, this materialized trace of Holy Ghost power begins to circulate autonomously and can be patched in, like a floating signifier, into the exigencies, gaps, and threadbare surfaces of everyday life.

Another recurring theme that is reinforced through Brother Aldie's story is the efficacious transfer of force through tactile contact. Thus parts of the body are literally "wrapped" in the anointed cloth. This devotional technique of tightly wrapping the cloth around the body or afflicted body part creates a kind of sacred supplemental skin that channels efficacious power into the body. Indeed, when Aldie invokes the phrase "they shouted and praised the Lord all evenin'," it is in the context of divine inspiration through possession by the Holy Ghost. An analogous phrase would be "shouted in the Lord." Within this narrative, therefore, tactile contact with the devotional object initiates a physical transfer of power and an ecstatic form of possession in the spirit. In addition, we should notice that the situation seems to be going well for the couple until the wife sheds this sacred skin in order to perform her daily ablutions: "Next day, she went ta get her a shower. When she came out, he had his hand behind his back." The body unclothed in this materialized prayer becomes vulnerable to the forces of evil.

Helping to precipitate the moment of violent crisis, the theme of the prosthetic reappears at the crux of the narrative: "They was gettin' ready to replace his knees and hips again—he didn't wanna go through it—said he'd rather be dead as to do it. He was a real jealous man, and said he had somethin' behind his back." It is precisely within this space of mechanicity that the miraculous moment of coincidence unleashes all its narrative force. The snapping sound of mechanicity as the hammer of the revolver automatically collides with the firing pin in response to the pull of the trigger marks the moment of coincidence between a naked body, jealous rage, and a materialized prayer. Several seemingly random or unrelated elements are collapsed into a shocking moment of the miraculous through the snapping sound of the machine. In this miraculous collision, however, the force of divine automaticity inherent in the sacred cloth inserts itself between the machinations of the firing pin and the explosive charge of the projectile. Reaffirming the force of automaticity, the materialized efficacy of the prayer cloth derails the machine, causing a "misfire." Ironically, however, the failure of the mechanism only acts to reassert or reaffirm the force of automaticity with newfound intensity. In this way, ideas of luck, quintessence, and chance, which are made to appear through the mechanical operations of the revolver, are translated or organized by the materialized efficacy of prayer and Holy Ghost power.[45]

Like the clicking of the revolver's hammer, the movement of the narrative, the very narrative structure formed through the miraculous testimony, unleashes the force of belief through a temporal deferral or delay. It is not until the end of the narrative progression, when the story has built tension and accumulated an inventory of at times seemingly random details, that the story tracks back to the beginning to reveal that the forces of divine organization were *already working* upon events within the narrative. A misunderstanding or confusion at the beginning of the narrative thus turns out to be divinely guided: "I'd misunderstood someway er another; said whatin' nothin' wrong with her back. She had a perfect back." A disjointed experience of temporal lag is effected through the narrative progression, and just as the listener is drawn into the performative movement of the story, the force of belief has *already* made its surreptitious appearance.

Yet in the very moment that belief makes its tricky appearance through the temporal progression of narrativity and the circulation of material objects, a gesture is made to mitigate the autonomous externalities of faith that seem to have moved on their own through the story. True to the narrative form of testimony, Brother Aldie does not leave the automatic efficacy of the prayer cloth in free circulation but attempts to recover it within the stable interior of the "believing" subject. In the final words of his story, we are left with the sound of prayer resonating within the bounded interiors of the heart instead of emerging through the mechanical "click" of the trigger.

Mentioning the Prayer Cloth

Both detailed testimonies and brief references are made during worship services in regard to the prayer cloth. These recurrent appearances within the performative dialogue of the charismatic milieu attest to the prevalent use and circulation of these materialized prayers within the community. A brief mention of an anointed cloth by Brother Aldie provides a representative example:

ALDIE: An' I'd like ta tell Brother Kenny, I thank ye for tha prayer cloth. I wanna thank Kenny and Darleen, they sent me a prayer cloth th'other night, and it's been on me, still is. [*Aldie laughs*] *I've been wearin' it religiously*, so, we thank you for it. (WGTH, November 8, 2009; italics for emphasis)

Brief descriptions of prayer cloths such as this are often given over the radio, within the context of the *Jackson Memorial Hour* broadcast and on many other live charismatic radio programs. Brother Allen's specific descriptions of this practice of devotion demonstrates that the blessed cloths are often worn for prolonged amounts of time: "It's been on me, still is. I've been wearin' it religiously." An important aspect of the prayer cloth, therefore, is its habitual or prolonged use.

Accounts such as these contradict one of the few published descriptions of the use and manufacture of prayer cloths within the Pentecostal tradition. In an interview that has been published online, historian of religion R. Marie Griffith claims that "since they're [prayer cloths] used in times of crisis, the prayer power that they had may not be active six months later if something else comes up. They are immediate objects."[46]

As we have seen in other accounts of the materialized prayer, however, it is precisely through habituation and perpetual use of the prayer cloth that this object makes its (re)appearance with the most compelling force of faith. As in the miraculous incident of the mother who placed three anointed handkerchiefs in the glove compartment of her husband's automobile, the compelling gravitation of the devotional object achieves its most powerful effects though a structure of deferral, habituation, and forgetting. Moreover, Griffith's insistence on the immediacy of the prayer cloth belies its crucial importance as an apotropaic device against the devil and his dark principalities, such as in the case of Sister Dixie and the pinning on of a prayer cloth to an afflicted child. To be sure, the efficacy of the prayer cloth takes on a force of immediacy, yet this temporal instantiation of force in the here and now emerges through a process of temporal articulation characterized by deferral. This temporal lag is articulated through both the movement of the testimony *and* the physical circulation of the devotional object.[47]

Sacred Automaticity: Prayer Cloths, Machines, Accidents

The slightly uneven and disproportionate black lettering on the hand-painted sign reads "The Independent Bible Church of God at Red Ash." As if to mimic the images evoked by that singular name, "Red Ash," piles of brick lie strewn about the ground on one side of the grey and dilapidated church: red bone remainders of prosperities past. When the coal still poured from the tipple of the Red Ash Coal Company, this structure was once a filling station, and the bricks, now detritus, formed a mechanics' automotive garage. The name Red Ash was taken from the streaks of iron that occur in the various coal seams located in this region of southern Appalachia; when this type of high-grade anthracite is burned, it leaves behind ash tinted with a reddish hue.[48] This eponym, moreover, seems to suggest both a traumatic history of industrial mining accidents and a disquieting portent of disastrous events to come.[49] Indeed, haunted like the rusted skeletal remains of the iron tipple scaffolding that once conveyed the coal from the dark bowels of the mine into the connected machinery of the railway, the name recalls that catastrophic explosion in the year 1900 that snuffed out the lives of forty-six miners employed by the Red Ash Coal Company.[50]

As is characteristic of a mining company town, the church in Red Ash, Virginia, is perched precariously close to a road that winds through the narrow holler, to more efficiently convey the human labor to the dark subterranean face of the coal seam. The gears and belts of the industrial extraction system move out into daily life, impinging upon the domestic space.[51] Across the road are railway tracks, which still transport coal from a functioning mine at the mouth of the holler. A steep embankment behind the church leads to the recently expanded Route 460, connecting Richlands and Grundy, Virginia, with its sharp curves and tiny guardrails that barely separate the asphalt from precipitous descents into ravines and hollers below.

Inside the church, brightly colored tapestries of the Last Supper and images of Holy Spirit Doves and massive praying hands adorn the walls. The hum of engines that once must have resounded in this space have now been replaced with the fatigued crackling of an air conditioner and the slightly out-of-tune and static-filled whir of a vintage electric organ.

What follows is an account of the manufacture of anointed prayer cloths that occurred during one of my several visits to the Independent Bible Church of God at Red Ash. This particular Monday evening church service

FIGURE 7 Advertisement for the Red Ash Coal Company, ca. 1900

was the occasion of a funeral eulogy for the older brother of the pastor. Somewhere in his seventies, Pastor Arnold is tall and lanky in stature. There is a high-pitched hollowness to the timbre of his voice, as if his vocal chords have been worn thin and his jaw made stiff from so many years of anointed preaching. In this moment of anointed rhetorical style, the power of the Holy Ghost takes command of the organs of vocalization and plays them like an instrument. The particular quality of the brother's voice, however, does not detract from the poetic force of his preaching but in fact gives his rhythmic delivery an added intensity:

> I've got some prayer cloths here
> We're gonna pray for here just in a little while.
> I think a brother wants one right there, don't he, Glory to God.
> Amen, these prayer cloths,
> Amen, is Bible.
> Ah, if you want one, ah, to put in your shirt pocket, put in yer wallet'n carry with ye.
> Amen, 'cause we're gonna anoint'em with oil,
> Amen, and pray the prayer of faith over'em, amen.
> And let that prayer cloth be with ye, amen.
> 'Pos-tle Paul, amen, he said, amen, Glory to God,
> He cut up his apron strangs, can ya say amen?
> He was a tent maker, so he wore an apron.
> He cut it up after wearin' that apron, amen, preachin'.
> He sweated on it, the anointin' got on it, can ya say amen.
> And the cloths went out from his body:

And the lame were healed,
The deaf were healed.
The blind were healed, glory to God.
So the prayer cloth, amen, is very important to you,
Amen, for *safety*.
Can ya say amen, glory to God,
Up on the highways.
And the Lord knows everybody needs God out thar,
Can ya say amen,
On the highways.

Several minutes after this initial announcement that the congregation was going to "pray for" and "anoint" the prayer cloths, the pastor's wife, Sister Eva, reached behind the podium and brought out a clear plastic bag full of small squares of cloth (roughly three inches by three inches). These squares were cut from mass-produced bandanas, bright yellow and orange in color; the jagged cuts that formed the squares left tiny pieces of thread hanging from the sides, so that the textile fragments seemed to be rags or pieces of detritus rather than the soon-to-be receptacles of the Holy Ghost. Several of these cloth fragments were removed from the bag and then "anointed" with an ordinary bottle of vegetable oil, which is kept in a wicker basket in front of the podium.

After the unction of the scraps, Brother Arnold gripped them tightly in a fist and called the elders of the church to come up and pray. Eight congregation members (six older men and two older women) gathered around Brother Arnold, reaching out their hands to touch the top of Brother Arnold's fist. As if to focus the diffuse power and potentiality of the Holy Ghost that will be instantiated during the prayer, the congregants' arms formed a kind of sacred wheel whose spokes met at the hub of the fist gripping the cloths. The techniques of bodily comportment and manual gesture that are associated with this specific anointing prayer demarcate a sacred space for the instantiation and focus of sacred force. These anointed techniques of the body open a space of entry for the healing efficacy of the Holy Ghost.[52]

The anointing of the scraps can be thought of as a ritual process of manufacture, taking quite literally the etymology of the word "manufacture" as the combination of *manus* (hand) and *facere* (to make). Between this sacred technique of manufacture and the force of an object that seems to automatically or mechanically move on its own is a suggestive group of terms mingling manual dexterity with magical secrecy. One thinks, for example, of the wonderfully revealing words "legerdemain" (*leger*, light; *main*, hand), sleight of hand, hanky-panky, underhanded, and prestidigitation (*presto*, quick; *digitus*, finger). The theme of magical substitution is thus related to the technical notion of a manual "knack," *habilité*, and adroitness. The prayer cloth itself, also referred to as the prayer handkerchief or anointed handkerchief, suggests a logic of hand-kerchiefing: the crafty gestures of the hand and fingers are veiled by a pocket-sized piece of fabric. In the ritual anointing of the prayer cloth, however, the techniques of substitution are ironically inverted: the hand itself veils the cloth in skin during its metamorphosis from rag to sacred devotional cloth. The popular term "anointed handkerchief" suggests an element of secrecy and substitution residing within the sacred object.

In this manifold experience of tactility, hands layered upon hands, techniques of manufacture are inextricably linked to the oral performance of prayer. Brother Arnold begins praying out loud in a forceful voice, and the other *hapticly enmeshed* members quickly follow, each praying his or her individual exhortation out loud, at the same time. This cacophonous tangle of voices, this skein prayer, sonically mirrors the tactile experience of the sacred hub of hands. The importunate voice of Brother Arnold at times emerges clearly from this dense atmosphere of noise, as he describes several situations "out on the highways" and commands the prayer cloths to be efficacious apotropaic devices in these circumstances. After the prayer reaches a climax of sonic force, this numinous noise, dense with the tangle of language, begins to lessen in intensity until all the congregants have ceased praying. In the strikingly quiet moment after the prayer is finished, the brother opens his hand to reveal the objects, which have undergone a miraculous metamorphosis from mere rag to sacred cloth. Through this haptic ritual, prayer itself and the concomitant power of the Holy Ghost that has been invoked through this performance has been instantiated into the physical object—a materialization of the spirit.

What is particularly revealing in this process of sacred manufacture is that moment during the initial description of the prayer cloth in which Brother Arnold makes a seamless transition from the theme of miraculous healing to that of *safety*. Let us recall the words of Brother Arnold:

And the cloths went out from his body:
And the lame were healed.
The deaf were healed.

The blind were healed, glory to God.
So the prayer cloths, amen, is very important to you,
Amen, for *safety*,
Can ya say amen, glory to God,
Up on the highways.

Healing and safety occupy similar positions within Brother Arnold's classification of the types of efficacy inherent in the prayer cloth. Once again, that curious name "Red Ash" seems to resonate with this theme of safety in a particularly compelling way. After all, the word "safety" in this context recalls early mining accident prevention campaigns from about 1900 that were initiated to stem the rising tide of mining disasters precipitated by increased automation and mechanization in the coal extraction process. During these early (and largely ineffective) campaigns, slogans such as "Safety First!" and "Be Careful!" became the watchwords of the time. Even today, many residents of this region in southern Appalachia employ the early mining phrase "Be Careful!" as an ominous farewell. Sedimented into this invocation of safety at the Independent Bible Church of God at Red Ash, therefore, is a long history of mechanized coal extraction and the catastrophic dangers associated with this industrial process.

Announcing the themes of automaticity and mechanicity, the equation of safety on the highway, and thus with *automobility*, further solidifies this genealogy. The theme of the *automatic* acts as a kind of middle term, bringing these two seemingly uncoincidental objects, the prayer cloth and the *auto*mobile, together under one field of gravitation. That the automobile is related to some notion of automaticity seems self-apparent; yet how is the prayer cloth, an object so intimately associated with *faith*, related to the perhaps more sui generis associations of the automatic?

Recall the moment during the rite of healing prayer when Brother Arnold can be overheard commanding the prayer cloths to be efficacious safety devices "out on the highways." Though early in the service, the brother describes how the congregation will "pray the prayer of faith over'em," and it is as if during the heightened emotional intensity of the prayer, Brother Arnold is speaking incantations into the cloth. In this way, crucial aspects of the process of anointed manufacture of the prayer cloth seem to circulate outside a logic that would otherwise be beholden to the precarious contingencies of the Holy Ghost for the communication of efficacious force. In this moment, the precarious nature of faith and the sacred communicative relay between the sacred and the everyday is short-circuited or circumvented by the sui generis force of the brother's words, *in and of themselves*. It is as if at the very heart of the ritual of anointing resides the specter of a renegade or traitor who renounces the contract of belief in favor of some more immediate form of power, thus yielding to the ineluctable call of the automatic.[53]

Moreover, after the cloth's metamorphosis from mere rag to sacred object, the curative and evil-repelling efficacy of the fabric circulates freely, unencumbered by any precarious dependence upon the abstracted and autonomous Holy Ghost. Indeed, in what seems to be a classic moment of magical profanation, the autonomous and diffuse power of the Holy Ghost has become instantiated into an object that begins to circulate freely in the everyday world. The prayer cloth does not need a communicative link to the sacred, or even faith for that matter; it carries within its weave a sui generis efficacy unbeholden to the typical or self-apparent demand of faith. Thus the brother's instructions to "put it in your shirt pocket, put in yer wallet'n carry with ye." Through the process of prayer and manual gesture, what was once the autonomous and contingent force of the sacred, has, quite literally, become *portable*.

What is important to note is the way this materialization of the spirit carries with it an antinomy or double bind. At one moment, faith seems to reside within a religious subject dependent upon the precarious whims of the divine; at other moments, it is as if belief itself has been *exteriorized*, taking on a life of its own within the object. In that moment of anointed objectification, stable notions of human subjectivity become troubled by a constant oscillation between interiority and exteriority, subjectivity and objectivity, magic and religion.

Likewise, this force of attraction manifests itself in the narrative form of testimonies that seem particularly compelled to repeat stories of the miraculous *coincidence* between the prayer cloth, the body, and the machine in the shocking moment of accident. Recall for instance, that my first encounter with the prayer cloth during fieldwork was through the testimony of a mother whose two young sons and husband had emerged miraculously unscathed from the twisted wreckage of a violent automobile accident. After recounting the wreck itself in painstaking detail and marveling at the fact that no injuries were sustained by the members of her family, she revealed that she had placed three prayer cloths in the glove compartment of their automobile.

Like sacrifice, faith often finds its most powerful manifestation in a moment of violent coincidence. In this shocking moment, the faith object that had been forgotten, unremarked, or neglected—merely stowed away in the glove compartment—reemerges with unanticipated force and intensity. This is a moment of *both* revelation *and* consternation: on the one hand, a newfound faith in the forgotten object: *"My God, prayer cloths really work!"* On the other, a sense of the efficacious operation of the object totally exterior to any subjective exercise of faith. That which was used as an apotropaic device to temporarily ward off the dangerous specter of automaticity ends up reinstating it in unanticipated ways. True, the deadly repercussions of the accidental coincidence seem to have been averted, if only for a moment; yet the force of the automatic not only persists, but seems to manifest a newfound intensity in the compulsion to repeat the shocking events. Like the circulation of a prayer cloth, narrative testimonies take on a life of their own: compelled to repeat, almost automatically, the story of the accidental encounter.

With the explosive resonances of Red Ash still ringing in our ears, perhaps it would be appropriate to conclude this fragment of analysis with a word of *caution*. That is, before we safely demarcate these metaphysical subtleties of the materialized Holy Ghost to some otherwise arcane and isolated practice down in southern Appalachia, perhaps it would be useful to recall that over 56 percent of our nation's electrical infrastructure is powered by the combustion of coal extracted from regions surrounding the Independent Bible Church of God at Red Ash. It is quite likely that the very electric bulbs in the room where you are currently reading this page are directly connected to these mines through a massive machine ensemble of belts, tracks, and wires. In this way, the illuminated environment that is allowing you to read the words printed on this page is intimately related to the subterranean darkness of the mine. Perhaps the oft-forgotten or repressed infrastructural organization of everyday life helps to explain that strange and foreboding sense of unease that is aroused the moment the lights flicker.[54] In the contemporary genres of the uncanny, for instance, the unexpected flicker of the electric bulb signals or portends the irruptive presence of the horrible thing into the intimate and homely space of the domestic interior. This classic contemporary moment of the uncanny recalls the spectral logics and explosive coincidences that lie hidden underneath the homely environments of everyday life. The flicker of the bulb, the sudden twitch in the functioning of the electrical infrastructure, brings to the surface, if only for an instant, an awareness of the massive chain of electrical infrastructures that connects the interior of the home directly to the railway tracks inside the mine. In this way,

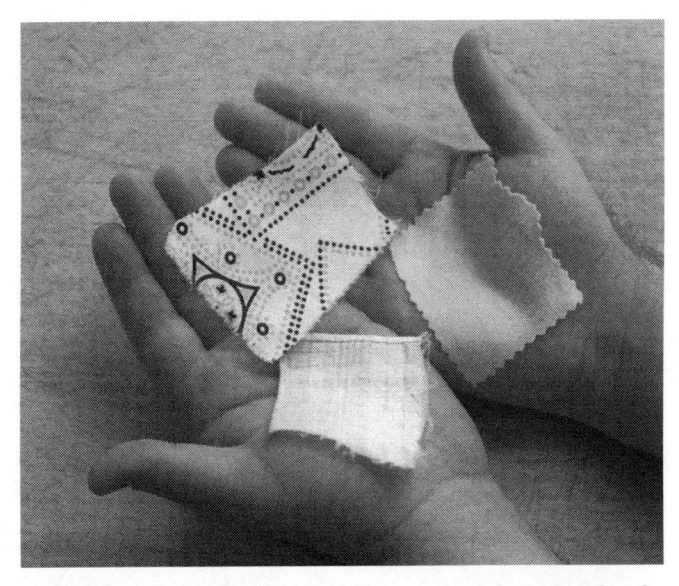

FIGURE 8 Prayer cloths, clockwise from upper left: anointed at the Independent Bible Church of God at Red Ash; a materialized prayer from the Pentecostal-Holiness Church at Schoolhouse Hill; a faith cloth anointed by Brother and Sister Allen at the Radio Station (Photo by Sarah E. Blanton)

the flicker of the light on that dreary and foreboding night is that vague awareness that yet another explosion has occurred within the mine, and that the miner, transformed into a strange acephalous creature by the percussive force of the explosion, still retains his grip upon the machine. I leave you then, with that compelling Appalachian farewell that simultaneously recalls the industrial shocks of the past and portends of disastrous coincidences to come: *Be Careful!*

Excursus: Holy Ghost Bumps

There is a phrase often invoked within the charismatic worship spaces of southern Appalachia that gets to the heart of the basic experiential character of so-called old-time religion: "I want somethin' I can feel!" And yet this emphasis on embodied experiences of tactility and kinesthesis is ironically in relation to a presence that cannot be experienced or enframed through everyday faculties of sensation and perception. This nondescript "somethin'" is the spectral presence of the Holy Ghost that manifests itself in and through the charismatic practitioner's *quickened* flesh and augmented perceptual faculties. Perhaps there is no better example of this particular embodiment and registration of the presence of the Holy Ghost than the mark made by the spirit upon the surface of the skin:

> DOROTHY: They ain't no feelin' no better'n tha Holy Ghost chills, are they?
>
> VIOLET: Linda said, "Eeew, I feel somethin'!" [*Laughter from both women*] She knew, when them tongues started rollin' she started feelin' it, you know. She knew, said, "Eeew, I feel it." See, when that genuine tongues comes out, and I tell you what, you feel it too! You can feel it (Violet interview, March 8, 2009).

Although the Holy Ghost chills are often precipitated through the force of images and memory traces evoked during ritual performance, there are certain aspects to the experience of Holy Ghost chills that not only fall outside the enframements of narrative and ritual structure, but seem to register precisely that which persists outside or beyond the particular enframements of perceptual awareness.[55] In this way, the epidermal layer itself seems to be registering a presence that remains inaccessible to conscious layers of sensory awareness. The most forceful experiences of the Holy Ghost chills described are those that literally erupt from the dermal boundaries of the subject outside of contexts of worship such as church, prayer meetings, or gospel broadcasts. Within the profane spaces of the everyday, the chills announce an irruptive presence that moves behind the back of everyday perceptual faculties and structures of awareness. In this moment of sacred chills, the very integument of the subject becomes doubled, at once "detecting" a presence that is intimately proximate and yet somehow outside or exterior to the subject's normal frames of orientation in the world.[56] It is this involuntary or automatic aspect that adds compelling force to the experience of Holy Ghost chills.

> ALDIE: But you asked also 'bout what inspired Dorothy. She's told me, an' her daddy has too, he told me he had watched her, without her knowin'. But she's told it in the past, how that as a little girl she'd set in the car, an' watch his arms when he's drivin'. Watch the chillbumps—ya know how ya get anointin' sometimes ya get chill bumps on ya—an' he'd be meditating on what he's gonna preach or whatever, an' the chill bumps come on his arms, an' how she'd set an' watch. And she told me tha same thang over-tha past, that she used-ta watch'em get tha chill bumps; watch tha *par* a'God

get on'em. And ya know, she wanted that feelin' as just a little small child.

DOROTHY: [*Interjecting*] That's what we're tryin' ta stress to that people now. Unless you been there an' know it an' feel it, you cain't 'splain it [explain it], you know, ta people. They've got ta get it on their own. But I mean *it's real*. It's real as nowadays as it was in tha Bible days.

ANDY: Ya'll talkin' about the anointin'?

DOROTHY: Yea, the anointing. But people are just so dried up now. I mean, it's like they're too lazy ta move an' they don't want ta throw they hands up and praise tha Lord. *An' he inhabits our praises; he wants our praise.* An' he don't want us to be ashamed of it. (Interview, February 10, 2009, Berwind, West Virginia; italics for emphasis)

The anointing, that ritual technique of consecration intimately associated with the rubbing or massaging of oil or other unguents upon the surface of the body, finds its most powerful manifestation upon the dermal surface that itself *secretes* the presence of the sacred.[57]

An "altar call" voiced with imperative urgency into the studio microphone at the end of a Sunday broadcast from the WGTH radio station also describes this particular flesh of the spirit:

BURT: If ya don't have it fixed up, by all means get ya sins under tha blood.
An' Brother Mike, we don't do this just ta miss Hell;
Look at the blessin's we got outta this.
Ya know I was standin' over thar awhile ago,
An' the preacher was sangin' that song 'bout "bow down."
I could feel the Holy Ghost bumps goin' up-an'-down my spine,
Up-an'-down my arms.
One blessin' that you get from servin' the Lord! (July 1, 2007, WGTH)

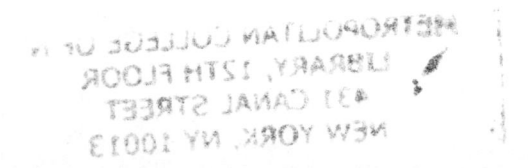

The Holy Ghost bump is a crucial haptic sensation of what I have elsewhere called the "texture of faith." In fact, the somatic "bumps" of the Holy Ghost seem to be woven into the same experiential surface as the prayer cloth. Recalling the particular sensations of fabric "hand" (associated with the type of thread, density of weave, drape, pliability, and so on) and the scalloped ridges often bordering the anointed fabric, the Holy Ghost bumps are literal embodiments of an otherwise tactile experience of prayer as the hand rubs the fabric between the fingers and upon the skin. Rubbing the faith cloth, moreover, not only recalls the feelings associated with the "tongues a'rollin'," as described by Sister Violet, but helps to precipitate, once again, the manifestation of sacred bumps upon the skin. In this ecstatic sensation of Holy Ghost bumps, the very integument of the subject becomes like a prayer cloth, and the dermal surface that once demarcated the boundaries of the subject become the manifestation of a holy texture that persists in spaces radically exterior to the supposed boundaries of the subject. Once again, we have a complex interplay between the texture of the prayer cloth and the movements of the tongue in performances of intercessory prayer and glossolalia.[58]

In terms of the specific relations between the surface of sacralized fabric and the raised dermal surface of the Holy Ghost chills, the irruption of the presence of the Holy Ghost from the epidermal layer sheds light upon the importance of manifold tactile experiences during the process of anointing and the sacred manufacture of the prayer cloth. Recall that the process of consecration of the fabric consists of a tight grip around the cloth remnant, which is covered by multiple hands wrapped around, touching, or superimposed upon the fist gripping the cloths. This surplus of tactile stimulation in the moment of sacralization mimics the suprasensory manifestations and haptic capacities of the Holy Ghost bumps.

Like a blind man reading the bumps of language though his fingertips, the Holy Ghost makes itself manifest in ridges on the skin for those who do not have eyes to see the presence of the spirit. Yet the meaning of these somatic bumps is not articulated through a symbolic or representational mode, but instead in the opening up or breaking of the surface of skin itself. In this way, Holy Ghost bumps rising from the epidermis are like ellipses upon the surface of the printed page or the somatic equivalent of the percussive clapping made during the performance of ecstatic healing prayer. The sacred bump announces a break or a dissolution of the everyday boundaries of subjectivity and meaning.

As the somatic clap upon the surface of the skin, the Holy Ghost bump signals the point of indistinction between spirit and flesh. Reiterating the force of tactility within charismatic experience, the Holy Ghost enlivens the papillary ridges of the dermis, becoming a supernatural organ or prosthesis of the subject's "natural" cutaneous sense. Yet this divine sensation of tactility is never fully "linked" or organized with the everyday perceptual capacities, but it persists, somehow, outside the conscious structures of awareness while nonetheless announcing a compelling presence of something that lies just beyond the frames or capacities of everyday experience. In the moment of Holy Ghost bumps, the subject is no longer in his or her own skin, so to speak, but is clothed in the sacred fabric of the spirit.

Warsh the Chill Bumps Off

DOROTHY: And ya know I got a little great nephew.

You know that ever-body's, been on ever prayer board ever-whar, ever-church. [This line makes reference to the prayer boards that are located in the main halls of many churches in this region. These boards often contain written prayer requests, photograph pictures of people in need of prayer, and prayer cloths penned upon the corkboard.]

An' ya know, last week they was another thang comin' on his throat that

they woulda hada took him ta Col-a-rod-a.

Ta have removed again after havin' forty surge-ries.

They called a pastor down North Care-lina.

An' he prayed fer J. J.

An' he said, "That first prayer didn't go through; put that baby back on the phone again!"

An' he told'em, he said, "Open his mouth."

Said, "Look an' see if it's gone."

An' they watched it, Francis, right before their eyes [*Loud percussive claps*]

They watched that thang—it went away—it went away.

Whoo-Glory!

Oh we praise-ya mighty God!

Ya know tha daddy was cryin'.

An' my sister had chill bumps all over'er.

She said it wutin' but a few minutes—ahh [*Audible secondary inhalation*].

An' ya know I'm not makin' fun in no way, no shape or form,

I'm just tellin' you what J. J. did.

An' it watin' but a few minutes—

ALDIE: [*Interjecting*] He's only six years old.

DOROTHY: He's only six.

An' said he come through the house an' he goes, "*Whooo-agh, Whooo-agh.*"
An' said his whole body was a'shakin' and a'tremblin'.
Linda said, "Can you get tha Holy Ghost at that age, an' that young?"
I said, "*You sure can.*"
John the Baptist—ah [*Audible inhalation*].
Before he was ever brought inta this world
He leaped in his mother's womb,
An' 'at was with the Holy Ghost—ah.
An' ya know tha Lord, there's nothin' impossible with God.
An' Linda said his whole count-ance [countenance] changed—ah.
As he was goin' backwards—ah.
Said his daddy grabbed'em, ya know, as he was *goin' out in tha spirit* as sure as I'm a'standin' here today.
An' I told Linda, I said, "How much more; how much more,
Is the Lord gonna show ya'll,
Ta get you involved in tha church an' tha house of God?!"
Ya know that little fella's workin' overtime
Tryin' ta let ya'll know, there's a God out thar that loves ya!
That your household needs to be saved today [*Rapid percussive clapping*].
An' she's in tha bathtub tryin' to *warsh* the chill bumps off.
You cain't warsh tha par a'God off!
You can not—ah.
I don't care how long—ah.
You stay in a tub a'water!
How long you may run or where you may go ta hide,
You cain't hide from God,
He knows whar you're at—ahh.
An' he's gonna know where you're at on Judgment Day.
An' you'll wish you had not-a-run.
You'll wish you had-a-stayed.
You'll wish you had-a-prayed.
And ya know, Oh God, I love'em today.
An' I told Francis, I said, "You gonna try ta come to tha program tomorrow?"
She said, "Yes, I've got alotta people ta pray about."
She said, "We got alotta good thangs to tell about too, don't we."
    [*Laughter in the studio*]

An' ya know, it's good ta be able ta tell about good thangs that God has done.
An' ya know I'm just grateful from tha bottom of my heart.
An' Aldie's gonna have to say a few words
An' let me get my breath.

INTERLUDE

Sermon 2

Sister June's Bulldog Preachin'

We gonna be a'readin' in Proverbs today, and you be much in prayer for us.

In the sixteenth chapter of Proverbs, praise tha Lord and glory to God,

We just wanna read a little bit-cheer, a'praise God.

Speak as God would help us, praise God today.

Glory to God, he said the preparation of the heart in man and the answer of the tongue is from the Lord.

All the ways of a man are clean in his own eyes, but the Lord weigheth the spirit.

Commit thy ways unto the Lord and thy thoughts shall be established, praise God.

You get your mind upon the Lord,

and you walk for him and talk for him,

An' ever-thang else'll fall in place.

I b'lieve I read over, glory ta God.

Over in the New Testament whar it said seek first the kingdom of God,

And all these other thangs a'be added unto ya, praise tha Lord.

He said in the fourth verse, it said, in the third verse it said,

Commit thy works unto the Lord and thy thoughts shall be established—ahh.

And the Lord hath made all thangs fer himself.

Yea—ahh

Even the wicked for the day of evil.

Everyone that is proud in his heart is an abomination unto the Lord—huh

Though hands join in hand he shall not be unpunished—ahh

Ah' glory ta God, praise the Lord today—ahh

By mercy and truth iniquity is purged—ahh

And by tha fear of the Lord men depart from evil, praise God—ahh

Ah' glory ta God when you get down and pray and get your [*Audible breath*]

Ah' sins under tha blood, ask the Lord to forgive ya of ever-thang—hah [*Audible breath*]

Ah' glory ta God today—huh

And Jesus comes inta your life, glory ta God—huh

You wanna depart from all them evil thangs that men does—ahh

Ah' glory to God—huh

He said that when a man's ways please the Lord—huh

He maketh even his enemies to be at peace with him—huh

He said better is a little right-us-nuss than great revenge—ahh

Without right—ahh

Ah' glory ta God—ahh

I'd 'trather be a little bit right with God as a whole lot right with tha devil, praise God—ahh

Ah' glory to God, he said a man's heart devises his ways—huh

But the Lord directeth his steps, praise God—ahh

A divine sentin [sentence] is in the lips of the king

Ah' but his transgressions—ahh

Not in judgment, praise God—ahh

He said a just wayeth—ahh

A just way and a balance are the Lord's—ahh

And all the weights of the bag are his work—ahh

Ah' glory ta God, and it is abomination ta kings—ahh

Ah' ta commit wickedness—ahh

For the throne is established by right-us-ness—huh

Ah' righteous lips are the light of kings—ahh

Ah' glory ta God are the delight of kings—ahh

And they love him that speaketh right, praise God—ahh

Ah' glory to God, God wants you ta speak tha truth—huh

Ah' glory ta God it don't make no difference who it hurts—ahh

Ah' people'll say well—huh

I told just a little white lie to keep from hurtin' somebody's feelin's—huh

Ah' honey let me tell you somethin'—huh

I'd ruther hurt somebody's feelin's as see them lost-n-die-lost-n-go-down to a devil's hell—huh
>Ah' praise the Lord
>Glory ta God, he said the wrath of a king is a messenger of death—huh
>But a wise man will pacify it, praise the Lord—huh
>In the light of the king's countenance is life—huh
>And his favor is as a cloud of the latter rain—huh
>How much better is it ta get—huh
>Ah' wisdom than gold—huh
>An' a great understandin' rather to be chose than silver, praise the lamb of God—huh
>Ah' glory ta God I'd ruther be a poor paw-per—ehh
>As rich in this world—huh
>And be lost without God—huh
>And die'n'go-down to a devil's hell—huh
>Ah' glory ta God whar I cain't take a penny with me. [*Pause*]
>A highway of the upright is to depart from evil—huh
>Ah' glory ta God, he that keepeth his ways—huh
>Preserveth his soul, glory ta God—huh
>Tha highway of the upright—ahh
>Is to depart from evil—huh
>And he that keepeth his ways preserveth his soul—huh
>Ah' glory ta God, you got some work [*Two hand claps*] ta do ya-self—huh
>It's not all in God's hands—huh
>Ah' glory ta God,
>Once he saves you honey, you gotta work yerself—ahh.
>[*Pause, silence*]
>He said pride goeth before destruction—huh
>And a haughty spirit before a fall—huh
>Ah' better is it to be of a humble spirit—huh
>With tha lowly—huh
>Ah' than ta divide the souls' spoils with the proud—huh
>Ah' glory ta God—huh
>Ah' Hallelujah, he that handleth—ahh
>Ah' matter wisely shall find good—huh
>Ah' glory ta God, praise the Lord—huh [*June's voice beginning to develop gritty, rasping voice and aggressive, intense timbre*]

Ah' Hallelujah today—huh
An' who-so-ever—huh
A'trusteth in the Lord happy is he—huh
If we keep our mind on God—huh
An' ever-thang we in need of—huh
We ask God ta move'n'bless it—huh
And God—huh
If you want me ta have it you give it ta me—huh
An' if it's not your will Lord—huh
Ah' don't let me get it, praise God—huh
Ah' glory ta God let God have control of all'a'that—huh
Ah' praise tha Lord—huh
And we'll be a-happy people praise God—huh. [*Pause*]
He said he that handleth a matter is wisely—huh
Ah' shall find good—huh
And whosoever trusteth in tha Lord happy is he—huh
Tha wise—huh
The wise in heart shall be called prudent—huh
An' tha sweet-nuss—huh
Of the lips increase learning—huh
Understanding—huh
Is a wellspring of life—huh
Unta him that hath it—huh
But tha instructions of fools is folly—huh
Ah' glory ta God today—huh
Ah' hallelujah to Jesus—hah
The heart of a wise teacher—huh
Ah' glory ta God—huh
Ah' praise God—hah
The heart of tha wise teaches his mouth—huh
And addeth learning to his lips, praise God—huh
Honey we gotta learn ta keep our tongue under control—huh
An' say God—huh
Ah' you put me on, I've often said this—
Put me on that potter's wheel—huh
An' turn it an' turn it—huh
An' make me ta what you'd hav-me-ta-be—huh
Ah' glory to God, praise tha Lord—huh
He said pleasant words are as a honeycomb—huh

Ah' sweet ta tha soul—hah
An' health to tha bones [*Hand clap*]
Praise God—huh
Ah' tha words of God are sweet—huh
Ah' glory ta God today—huh
Ah' they're like a honeycomb—huh
He said thar is a way that seemeth right unto man—huh
But the end thereof are the ways of death—huh
Now they's alotta people said, well—huh
I'm-a'walkin' fer God—huh
I'm a'livin' fer tha Lord, praise God—huh
Ah' glory ta God—huh
Ah' praise tha lamb-a-God, I've been livin' fer'em fer thirty or forty year—huh
An' still you don't have—huh
Ah' glory ta God no more right-us-ness than what ya started out with—huh
You've not growd a lick in tha Lord—huh
Ah' glory ta God, praise tha Lord—huh
He said—huh
Thar is a way that seemeth right unto man—huh
But the end thereof are the ways of death—huh
He that—huh
Ah' laboreth labor fer himself—huh
For his mouth craveth it of him—huh
An ungodly man diggeth up evil—huh
An' his lips thar is as a burnin' far [fire], praise tha Lord—huh
Honey, that old tongue is a deadly thang—huh
Ah' glory ta God, praise tha Lord—huh
An' you get out here—huh [*Commotion in background, child falls and begins screaming loudly*]
In tha summertime you get a rattlesnake or a copperhead bites you
Ah' praise tha Lord—huh
An' glory ta God, ah'praise God
If you don't go to tha doctor an' get help—huh
Ah' praise God—huh
Ah' you'll die—hah
An' that's the same way with that old lyin' tongue—huh
Hit's-as-poison-as-a-rattlesnake-bite—huh

Ah' glory ta God it's out thar a'tryin' ta stir up strife—huh
An' hurtfulness'n'trouble—huh
Ah' glory ta God, praise tha Lord—huh
Hit's all-time tryin' ta do somethin' mean—hah
A'tattlin' on people, tellin' lies—hah
A'talkin' 'bout somebody—huh
Ah' praise God—huh
Ah' but let me tell you—huh
He said an ungodly man diggeth tha people an' his lips there is as a burnin' *far*—huh
He said a forward man's soul strives, an'a whisper separates ye friends—hah
A violent man entices his neighbor—huh
An' leadeth him unto the way that is not good—huh
Ah' glory ta God—huh
He shutteth his eyes—huh
Ah' ta devise forward thangs—hah
A'movin' his lips—hah
He bringeth evil ta pass—huh
Ah' glory ta God—hah
Ah' praise tha Lord—hah
We better watch out—huh
Of tha thangs we do—huh
Ah' Hallelujah ta God—huh
Ah' keep ourself under correction—huh
He said a horny head—huh
Is a crown—huh
Is a crown a'glory!—hah
And it is to be found in the way of the righteous—hah
Ah' glory ta God—huh
He said he that is slow ta anger—huh
Is better than the mighty—huh
And he that ruleth his spirit—huh
Ah' than he that taketh tha city—huh
Ah' glory ta God—huh
I'd ruther have a good spirit wit God—huh
Than own all the world—huh
Ah' Hallelujah ta God—huh
He said the light is cast inta tha lap—hah

Of the hole disposed thereof—huh
Is of the Lord's—huh
Ah' glory ta God honey—huh
We might thank, well—huh
We're doin' alright—huh
Ah' glory ta God, but today—huh
We better open up our eyes an' know—huh
Ah' who we're servin'—huh
Ah' glory ta God—huh
He said an ungodly diggeths up evil—huh
An' his lips—huh
Ah' thar is a'burnin' *far*—huh
Oh my God—huh
My God is able ta keep us—huh
He's able ta keep us, praise God—huh
An' let us live fer him—huh
An' walk in his love—huh
An' talk in his love—hah
Ah' praise God today—huh
Ah' what a mighty God we're servin' today—huh
Ah' glory ta God, tha old highway—huh
Ah' highway of tha upright—huh
Is ta depart from evil—huh
An' he that keepeth his—ahh
Ah' way preserveth his soul [*Pause*]

Honey, if we live fer God, He'll hep us. [*Voice noticeably raw, grating, and gruff here*]

He'll hep us.

God will hep us when we thank we got nobody—hah

Oh praise the Lord

He said I'll be thar and I'll stick closer than a brother—hah

Ah' praise tha Lord today—huh

I'm glad we got somebody we can depend on—ahh

I'm glad we got somebody, we can take hold-a that big nail-scarred hand.

Ah' glory ta God—huh

He said when a man's ways please the Lord—huh

He maketh his enemies—hah

Ah' ta be at peace with him—huh

Ah' honey you serve God—huh
Ah' glory ta God praise tha Lord—huh
An' God'll make a way fer you—huh
He'll make your enemies be at peace with you—huh
Ah' glory ta God—huh
Ah' praise tha lamb of peace with you—huh
Ah' God is a merciful God—huh
An' he's able to keep us—huh
He's able to heal us, he's able ta
Ah' glory ta God, to feed us, put food on our table—huh
Ah' give us an automobile ta ride—huh [*Intense*]
Ah' home ta live in—huh
Ah' healthy kids—huh
Ah' God is able ta do anything today.
[*Quietly; a gentle calmness in the next six lines*] What a mighty God we serve.
He said pleasant words are as a honeycomb,
Sweet to tha soul and health to tha bones, praise tha Lord—huh
Oh glory ta God—huh
Ah' God can hep you—huh
Ah' praise tha Lord—huh
I've talked ta people before—huh
Ah' glory ta God and they seem like they in tha-awfullest shape at ever was—huh
So down'n'out, n'don't know where ta turn to—huh
Ah' glory to God, set down'n'talk with'em fer maybe thirty or forty minutes, 'er har [or an hour]—hah
Ah' glory ta God, n'they'll say, "I'm shore glad you come by my way"—huh
"I'm shore glad"—huh
"I found somebody ta talk to"—huh
I said, Well honey you can talk ta the Lord anytime—huh
Ah' just find you a place some-whar—huh
An' cry out ta him—huh
An' he'll be thar, he said, I'll—huh
Ah' be closer than a brother to ye.
He'll hep you.
Oh he'll comfort your heart, he'll be thar for ye.
Glory ta God, I'm glad today—huh

That we got somebody—huh
We got somebody that can comfort us and keep us—uh
In tha time—ah-need and in tha midnight ar [hour]—huh
When you thank, well I don't have a friend in tha world—huh
You ken have somebody in Jesus praise God.
He said, I'll be thar.
And I'll stick closer than a brother.
He said, I'll go all the way with ye.
Ain't nobody else can go all tha way with ye.
Nobody.
Eh your brothers'n'sisters, your mommie'n'daddy, your children, your husband, your wife;
They can just go so far.
And then they'll stop right thar.
'At's far as they can go.
Ah' glory ta God, I'm glad, praise God,
When it comes down fer me ta die—huh
My family might go to tha graveside—huh
Ah' glory ta God.
An' 'at's as fer as they can go—huh
'Ay can look down in 'at hole on me—
They cain't go no further—hah
Ah' but I got a man 'at can go right down in'ere with me—huh
An' when resurrection day come he can rise outta thar with me.
Ah' glory ta God
They ain't nothin' too big 'at my God cain't handle it.
Glory ta God.
He'll be right thar.
Now he's not no little ol' bitty thang—huh
Ah' glory ta God
But I am glad he is so little he can get in my heart—huh
Ah' glory ta God
Get right down in'ere n'make me clean'n'wholed—huh
And pure, praise tha Lord
People say oh you cain't live holy.
[*Emphatically*] Oh yes you can live holy—huh
And you'd better live holy—huh
If you don't live holy you're never gettin'-in where he's at—huh
He said to be ye holy, for I am holy

Ah' glory ta God—huh
And people'll tell ya they cain't live holy—ahh
I cain't live pure—huh
I cain't live clean—huh
Ah' glory ta God he said without holiness—huh
Ah' no man's gonna see tha Lord—huh
Ah' so honey if you're not holy—huh
You're not gonna see him today,
When you leave 'his world
I see our times come'n'gone.

We trust today we've said some'in ta hep you. We want ya ta know that we love ya, an' Jesus love ya. He gave his life that you could have life, and have it more abundant. An' we be back next week if it's tha Lord's will, preachin' you the good news of the gospel. An' we love ya in the Lord. An' we turn it back to the radio announcer at this time.

CHAPTER 3

Preaching
The Anointed Poetics of Breath

The absence of visible persons makes the "radio voice" appear more objective and infallible than a live voice; and the mystery of a machine which can speak may be felt in the atavistic layers of our psychical life.
—THEODOR ADORNO, *Elements of a Radio Theory*

In the same way the Spirit also helps our weakness; for we do not know how to pray as we should, but the Spirit Himself intercedes for us with groanings too deep for words.
—Romans 8:27

AFTER THE INTRODUCTORY REMARKS and a series of songs, testimonies, and healing prayers, Brother Aldie approaches the microphone stand in the live studio of radio station WGTH in Richlands, Virginia, to begin his sermon. Before he begins, however, a curious sound is registered and translated through the radio apparatus. In preparation for the delivery of the word to the faithful listeners out in radioland, the brother must open his leather-bound Bible, which is clenched in the teeth of a metal zipper. As his hands slowly and methodically unzip the stained and well-worn leather covers of the Holy Scriptures in preparation for preaching, the radio microphone clearly registers the unclasping of each of the metallic teeth as the mechanical slider is slowly pulled down the clenched zipper chain. Registered through the sensitivities of the ear of the studio microphone and voiced through the mouth of the radio loudspeaker, this normally inaudible and unremarked noise is sounded through the apparatus as if it were some massive machine giving access to a large object. The apparatus of radio grants this aural access to an acoustic unconscious that renders hidden resonances disconcertingly and shockingly present in ways hitherto not heard in the space of worship. Like the magnification of the pores in the skin of a human face seen through the lens of the camera, the microphone/loudspeaker complex renders the metallic teeth of the zipper

115

monstrous, enlarged, and amplified to a striking degree. Before the sacred word is channeled through the mouth of the preacher, the apparatus voices the word—the material sound of the good book itself. It is as if the mouth of the preacher will begin to repeat what is *already* moving through the mouth of the radio loudspeaker or public announcement system. With the sacred word open before him, Brother Aldie begins the sermon:

> In tha book Ezekiel in tha thirty-seventh chapter, I preached on this allot. But not what tha Lord gave me this mornin', an' if he anoints me I'll preach. If he don't, I'll sit down like I always say. Because we realize today that tha word a'God is anointed, this Bible right here, the words that's on the inside, those words are anointed. But if the individual gettin'em out is not anointed we can't help nobody. Without tha anointing a'God we cannot bring these words out; we can hurt people but we can't help'em. So y'all pray that God will anoint me this mornin' an' it be his will, that I bring forth anything from these words today.

The "anointing" is a crucial theological motif in the Pentecostal-Holiness sermonic traditions of southern Appalachia. As suggested by the words of Brother Aldie, the anointing connotes a divinely inspired form of speech that is characterized by prosodic elements such as the rapid chanting and sung intonation of words, as well as percussive respirations that punctuate the end of the preached sermonic line. When the anointing "falls" upon the preacher, his or her mouth is literally filled with the power of the Holy Ghost. This power, in turn, grants the orator a linguistic fluency and bodily comportment that transcends the stylistic boundaries of everyday speech. This chapter explores some of the inspired poetic styles that characterize this region of Appalachia, paying close attention to the relationship between the anointed mouth of the preacher and the mechanical voice of the radio loudspeaker.

Just before Brother Aldie approaches the studio microphone to preach, his wife, Sister Dorothy, prays a special prayer in preparation for his sermonic delivery:

> Jesus God touch Aldie today God. Lord *give'em the breath*, God, ta bring your word forth today God. Lord help us all Jesus! Oh Yes! Hallelujah, Hallelujah! Praise God. [*Percussive clapping*] Whooo, Glory!

Sister Dorothy's prayer is revealing because it suggests the importance of breath within the practice of anointed preaching. Her prayer for anointing could be taken quite literally as a desire for the *inspiration* of the Holy Ghost. The anointed style of preaching has a specific relation to breath and the practice of breathing. Midway through the sermon, Brother Aldie gives further description of the "anointing":

I just open my mouth—agh.
And usually I'm 'bout fifteen or twenty words behind what tha
    Holy Ghost gives me—agh.
Ah—praise God.

Characterized by an abrupt exhalation of air at the end of the sermonic line, the practice of anointed breathing is a key poetic element in the performance of preaching. Like the dry bones in the book of Ezekiel, this particular type of respiration forms the skeletal structure upon which the rest of the poetic form is enlivened. Generated through the undulation of the entire upper body, a percussive respiration is produced through a particular bodily gesture, or what could be considered a technique of dance that visibly rocks the torso back and forth.[1] The first moment of respiration is characterized by the convulsive and abrupt tightening of the abdominal muscles. Through a total evacuation of air from the lungs, this abrupt tightening of the diaphragm generates a percussive "grunt." The first time I heard the term "grunt" used to describe this particular charismatic preaching style in Appalachia was while putting up hay with Baptist ministers, who inflected the word with a slightly pejorative timbre, but I have since heard practitioners of the percussive breath themselves refer to this key prosodic element as a "grunt." Moreover, there is a special expression associated with this anointed breath as being "grunted in the spirit." This word evokes the visceral, abrupt, and urgent nature of this sound and is invoked by the anointed practitioners of this sermonic style; therefore I employ the term "grunt" throughout the chapter.[2]

This sudden constriction of the abdominal muscles draws the chest and head forward, as the shoulders shrug upward. After this total expenditure of breath through the percussive grunt, the chest is immediately plunged out and upward. The shoulders as well are shot back as the lungs are rapidly filled with air through the second movement or inhalation of this breathing technique. At the same time, the head moves upward with the rapid rising of the chest. Upon the secondary inhalation, this respiratory dance of the upper body is also accompanied by visible flexing of the neck muscles.

Demonstrating what Marcel Jousse, founder of orality/literacy studies and student of Marcel Mauss, calls the "laryngo-buccal gesticulation," the vocalization of the percussive grunt cannot be detached from the techniques of dance that help to generate and, in turn, are generated by it.[3] This anointed poetics of breath, therefore, presses close to what many Holiness and Pentecostal preachers in this region refer to as "being danced in the spirit."[4] This technique of danced breath places extreme physical demands upon the body of the inspired orator, evinced by the beads of sweat that appear upon the brow of the preacher; here these sacred beads gather, rolling down the face to soak a ring around the collar. By the end of this performance, the fatigue generated is evident as the respiratory capacities of the body are stretched to the limit, pushing the lungs to the brink of hyperventilation. After the anointed poetics of breath leaves the body, the orator seems literally "out of wind," as if he or she has just run a footrace or completed an extreme feat of manual labor. With flushed-red face and sweat-bedraggled brow, the exhausted preacher laboriously pants, trying to "catch one's breath" after the inspiration of the Holy Ghost has departed.

The first forward movement that generates the percussive exhalation can be thought of as the setting of a respiratory "spring." This convulsive tightening of the abdomen and total evacuation of breath through the grunt builds momentum for the following deep inhalation, which fills the lungs with a reserve of wind for the next sung or chanted poetic line. Linguists employ the term "breath-unit" to connote this standing reserve of wind, which will be expended in the process of articulation. This grunt not only punctuates the poetic line, sounding out a kind of vocalic marker or aural period, but it also creates an overall rhythmic structure to the performance. Moreover, it can be seen as a strategic technique of breath that enables the deepest inhalation in preparation for the next sung line. Like a bucket thumping the bottom of the well, the momentum of the grunt reaches to the depths of the respiratory organs, allowing the mouth to draw from a deep source of inspiration. The grunt is both a key rhythmic device and a respiratory spring that sets the diaphragm for the following inhalation.

This poetics of breath dramatizes the very act of breathing itself, an action, moreover, that usually remains beneath the surface of awareness as one of the body's autonomic processes. In this dance of sacred breath, the act of respiration is itself doubled. Like bellows manipulated by hands unseen, the chest cavity heaves with convulsive undulations. The sound of the breath and its accompanying movements signal to the congregation that the anointing has "fallen" upon the preacher, filling his faculties of vocalization with a rushing mighty wind from some divine elsewhere.[5] Gradually moving upward from the belly to announce a tongue that moves on its own, we hear the noise of the diaphragm, lungs, larynx, and velum rustling in winds blown from beyond.

Closely related to the particular grain of voice that is evoked through the percussive grunt, the chanted and rhythmic lines that fill the space between breaths are often characterized by a particularly abrasive or raspy timbre. For many preachers in southern Appalachia, the texture of the anointed voice takes on a rough, *almost growling quality*. Translating the voice into a tactile mode, the rough timbre of the inspired voice invokes the chips of pocked and rusted iron flaking from the skeletal remains of abandoned mining tipples, the rusted indentations of a machinists' file, and the abrasive surface of tar paper that covers the space between pine boards on the small company homes of coal mining towns. There is an intense aggression to this grain of voice, as if the anointing force of the Holy Ghost has pushed the musculature and viscera of the throat almost to the point of breakdown.[6]

At strategic points in the sermonic line, this visceral grain of voice is suddenly rendered smooth and flowing through the transition from chant to song.[7] A particularly striking poetic effect is created when the raspy rhythmic sound of the sermon suddenly soars into intoned sung lines. In these poetic moments, the sermonic words are melded together in an undulating melodic line. For many of the preachers that I heard in the space of the radio station and over the airways, the transition from the raspy chanted mode into sung lines announced a new level of affective intensity for both the orator and the congregation. In terms of the overall structure of the delivery, the abrupt and visceral grunt of the percussive breath always continues to mark the end of the sung line, even when the sermon has taken on a particularly melodic and mellifluous character.

As an intermediate form between the growling truculence and sung importunateness of the voice, the chanted words of the sermon find a monotone tonal center that closely resembles the rapid articulations of the southern tobacco or livestock auctioneer. The persistence of this warm monotone of the voice also sets up the listener for a particularly striking effect when a sung line, elongated "Whoop," or other sound is suddenly woven into the prosodic line.[8] When young or inexperienced preachers from this region imitate the more established poetic techniques of seasoned preachers, the difficulty in acquiring the embodied knack or habitus of this poetics of breath is revealed. Some young preachers, for instance, give out shallow grunts at the ends of their sentences. Because this superficial grunt does not open a space of breath that prepares for the next chanted line, it clashes with the overall sermonic architecture and actually impedes the rapid rhythmic delivery characteristic of the anointing. When this anointed technique becomes a total poetics of breath, establishing the basic architecture of the sermonic form, the percussive force of the grunt becomes off-kilter in the strictest sense of the term. When this deep poetics of breath inspires the preacher, a sense of doubling or displacement emerges between the rhythmic and intoned words of the sermon and the very vocalic-clap that makes way for the next sermonic line. To put this another way, there seems to be a rupture between the force of articulation and the visceral organs of the body that are voicing these words. The percussive grunt, therefore, can be defined as the sound that is produced when the gap between the sacred and the everyday is suddenly closed through a pneumatic gesture.

The Sacred Belly Laugh

During an interview early in my fieldwork at the Allens' home in Berwind, West Virginia, Sister Dorothy was showing me pictures taken at the Wilderness Chapel, where they had once ministered. We flipped through an album of Polaroid photos covered by translucent cellophane sheets as it rested atop a small cigarette-scarred table holding cups of coffee and an ashtray for the remnants of the generic menthols that they so frequently enjoyed. As Sister Dorothy casually turned the pages, narrating the photos of worship and fellowship at the Wilderness, my attention was suddenly drawn to an image of several congregants lying upon the floor. Gathered around these prone worshippers were other church members whose faces radiated an ecstatic joy. They seemed to almost rock from the page in paroxysms of belly laughter. The caption at the bottom of the Polaroid, now slightly yellowed from age, read: "The day the church got the laughing spirit." After inquiring about the meaning of these ecstatic faces and postures, Sister Dorothy explained that during this particular church meeting, the power of the Holy Ghost fell upon the entire congregation in the form of the "laughing spirit." This divine power brought with it an uncontrollable self-effacing laughter that also initiated a "fallin' out in the spirit," wherein several members of the congregation fell violently to the floor and lay prone from several minutes to several hours.

The inundation of the worship space by the force of the laughing spirit is an extreme example of the importance of laughter within the charismatic worship milieu. Far from being a somber and cautious environment, the space of contact between the sacred and the everyday is permeated with a playful levity. This joviality, moreover, seems to complement the spontaneous, improvisatory nature of charismatic worship styles and performances of prayer. Throughout the service, the participants are making subtle jokes, telling humorous stories, and kidding with one another. In fact, there are key moments within this worship context when the force of laughter and the sacred sounds of ecstatic prayer and other anointed performances become indistinguishable.

The phenomenon of belly laughter also bears important similarities to other poetic techniques and performative exclamations within the enthusiastic environment. For example, the percussive breath that punctuates the chanted sermon could be seen as an intermediate form of anointing, or "baptism in the spirit," en route to what some would call a more enraptured form of divine speech. As the mighty hand of the Holy Ghost penetrates deeper and deeper into the organs of vocalization, it reaches the pit of the stomach and begins to pound the diaphragm like a drum.

In terms of the basic technique of breath, both the percussive grunt and deep laughter emerge from the recesses of the stomach. Similarly, in both techniques there is a force of automaticity at play animating respiration through convulsive movements of the abdominal muscles. The visual rocking and heaving of the torso of the preacher's chest during inspired performance closely resembles that of a belly-laughing congregant. When the power reaches ecstatic intensity, the sermon abandons many of its everyday representational vehicles, yet maintains the percussive skeleton of the poetic form. This percussive architecture includes not only the engastrimythic (literally, divine speech emerging from the belly) "agh" and the disjointed punctuations of sacred laughter, but also the anointed flappings of the tongue.

Other enthusiastic techniques of the body are intimately related to the percussive beats of laughter as well. The rapid yet disjointed clapping that accompanies skein prayer and other emotional moments can be seen as a manual technique of sacred communication corresponding to the convulsive flexing of the muscles of the diaphragm—both percussive techniques at once invoke *and* announce the powerful efficacy of the Holy Ghost.[9] Both the grunt of the preacher and the staccato rhythm of laughter signal that the participant is animated by forces from *elsewhere*. On the material-visceral level of language itself, these ecstatic beats "sound" the muscles of the lower abdomen, the lining of the throat, the warmth of saliva, and the density of the teeth in and of themselves, in a nonrepresentational noise that finds its force outside the everyday structures of symbolic articulation. The telltale twitch that signals the classic moment of spirit possession is thus expressed or "sounded" in and through the organs of vocalization.

Contagious Laughter and the Force of Narrativity

The testimony of Sister Z, who had been recently released from prison, precipitated Brother Aldie's telling of this humorous story. As Sister Z testified into the microphone of the live studio, she described her conversion experience as "God dealin' with'er heart" while listening to the *Jackson Memorial Hour* worship service over the radio.[10] At the time of her conversion, this sister was incarcerated in a Virginia penitentiary, and she listened to the charismatic radio broadcast on a small receiver located in a communal recreation area. After this conversion narrative, Sister Dorothy announced that Sister Z, along with several others, would be baptized at Sandy Bottom, and she invited the radio audience to come and participate. Sandy Bottom is the local name for a popular swimming hole and is a traditional site for baptizing that is located near a pull-out from a gravel road outside the city limits of Richlands, Virginia. The water in this baptizing hole is about waist deep and the spot is shaded by massive oak and walnut trees. The depth of the water allows the presiding preacher and participating elders the freedom to forcefully immerse new converts into the chilly water.[11] After the invitation to the listeners out in radioland, Sister Dorothy said a few more words that seemed to open the space of narrativity around the themes of sacred transformation and the power of the Holy Ghost:

> DOROTHY: We're prayin' that God'll warsh them afflictions right
> down the river.
> We've seen so many people go in'at water ain't we.
> And we seen 'em come out healed and refreshed and renewed today.
> When she goes in'er, we know God can.

"Floppin' Fish"

ALDIE: [*Softly chuckling in his deep voice*] Just real fast 'fore we pray, I thank this is so cute. She's talkin' 'bout goin' in tha water, n'Dorothy sayin' we seen so many thangs at tha water. But we saw somethin' one time at tha water, and I think it is . . . hilarious myself. But her nephew by marriage came over'n, you know, Z's family I thank's gonna video or film or take pictures or somethin' over thar today. But it just so happened her niece-'n-nephew come over to see us one Sunday to the radio program, n'his truck broke down'n some of tha guys from tha radio program'n myself went out thar to help'em fix it. Didn't have the parts, had to get tha parts'n by then we had to go to church. And we asked'em could he wait 'til afterwards, n'he said yes. Dorothy said, "There's somebody ta run tha video; we'll get this on camera." [*Laughing under his breath*] So we went out there ta tha riverbank an' God bless his heart, we love'em dearly. He's still not saved, but he'd never been in church. He'd never seen, or been around, anybody go out under the *par* a'God. They was forty-nine, that we put forty-nine times, that we dunked people under'tha water 'at day—an'at was a perty good little job! [*Chuckling*] But I tell ya what, he got out thar and he started videoin', an laid that camera down'n got in tha car. An' we asked'em afterwards, why? And he told his mother-in-law, my wife's sister, he said, "They have no compassion fer nobody." [*At this point in the narrative, Aldie's pace and intensity of delivery quickens, with the sound of the congregation members laughing throughout this second portion of the account*] Said, "They was people started goin' out in'at water," an' said, "started floatin' down tha water," said, "Aldie'd run grab'em, and somebody'd hep'em over'n they'd lay'em up on tha bank," said, "they's flippin'em up'er like ol floppin-fish!" Said, "They didn't offer no CPR, they didn't call no 911." He said, "I got in tha car and closed tha windas'n set there in tha sun." He said, "Now they art'ta have more love about them than that if they gonna be Christians." But he'd never been around the *par* of God. I thought that was so cute. [*Laughing*] But ya know today, God still loves'em, and now he has been around the *par* of God. God's dealin' with'em, and I b'lieve one day he will be saved. [*At this point the communal prayer begins*][12]

Within this space of worship, laughter emerges from within the most holy of circumstances: the rite of baptism and the transforming power of the Holy Ghost. Stories such as these not only signal the sacred element inherent in the phenomenon of laughter but also suggest the immanence of so-called Holy Ghost power to circulate in the everyday lives of the charismatic faithful. More specifically, the loss of agency and the precarious blurring of subjective boundaries that is often the focal point of humorous stories such as the Floppin' Fish are not characterized by the extreme horror or unease of an unplaceable presence such as the epileptic fit described by Freud in his essay on the uncanny. These humorous narratives of the spirit point to the playfulness and ease with which these congregations interact with forces of possession, singularity, and the miraculous. Once again, this levity and playfulness is the very antithesis of nonchalance or frivolity; it suggests the particular character of practices of divine communication and the efficacious circulation of sacred force within the spaces of the everyday.

Even ritual preparations for healing prayer are interspersed with moments of jocular banter and humorous play:

> ALDIE: I couldn't help but laugh a few minutes ago. [*Chuckling*] I love my little woman. And we pick at each other. She's settin' over there a minute ago on tha piana, n'she said: "Just a minute now we're gonna turn little ole Aldie loose." An I thought, "I'm not tied up I don't reckon!" [*Robust congregation laughter*] I thought if I looked around see'd if I was chained up'er in tha corner or somethin'. But anyhow we like to pick at each other, and we thank God for this opportunity to be here. (WGTH, December 2010)[13]

"Runnin' in the Spirit"

> ALDIE: And I've never forgot, when we lived, like I said, over'n the valley. I'd stand behind Dorothy—I'll try to make this short—a bunch of singers, you know, would get around tha piana, and I's behind'em with my bass. Had a new bass that Dorothy had bought me, collector's edition: they whatin' but five of 'em made to begin with. Made by Fender. Loved 'at guitar. An I'd stand back'er a'playin' it, n'tha par-a-God get on me, and I wouldn't lay my guitar down. I's afraid it'd get broke or whatever, ya'know. He [George Jackson] told me, he said, "If-a God cain't take care of that guitar, you don't need it; throw it down and do what God'd

have ya ta do!" Well tha *par's* common' on me to actually run; I mean my feet'be makin' ninety, an' I wouldn't go nowhere. I'd brace my feet, ya know; I wouldn't run. So he told me, he said, "The Lord will chastise you Aldie if you don't." So one night I made my mind up, I'm gonna obey tha Lord. That's why I'm a'goin' to church to obey tha Lord, not people. And they were all gathered up around Dorothy at one side, right in fronta me, a'singin' an old song that you mighta heard before: says, "I shall not be moved." I thank that's tha name of it. Now they up'er singin' that, and tha par-a-God hit me and I slung'at collector's edition down and away I went. An' so help me, Andy, they parted like tha Red Sea—all 'cept fer one old lady. She musta been seventy year old: looked like she played for the Pittsburg Steelers. I mean she was real wide-'n'-narra down, but she was old, you know. An she's standin' there with her hands in tha air, a'singin' "I shall not be moved." Well 'bout time she said, "I shall not be moved," I couldn't stop, and I knocked her down, jumped'er, went to tha door, her friend grabber'er. She couldn't move'er. An' I hit that door an' I come back, an' it was like some-un' had a'holt-a-me, I couldn't quit runnin'. I come flyin' back an' they drug her up in tha seat— an' I felt like dyin'. Really to God I felt like this couldn't a'been tha Lord—I done kilt this lady. But she went out in tha spirit there, during that period of time, an' I didn't know that then. I's still young in tha Lord.

So anyhow, they drug'er up in a seat and Brother Jackson began to preach, an' he preached a long time. I's sittin' thar thankin', "What am I gonna do?!" She had a lady went to church with'er, and drove'er, or rode with'er rather. Ah, she's kindly mental I guess, or something, and she had trouble with her speech. An she kep lookin' at me like, you know, you come toward my friend I'm gonna hurt'ye! But she couldn't talk plain. And I was bothered so badly, an she finally woke up and her friend helped'er to tha back row, back to tha back seat 'stead of tha front. An' Brother George got through preachin', he asked her, "Is there any thang you'd like to say for tha Lord?" She said, "Yes," said, "Whooo-Honey," she said, "Whar I been I cain't tell ye." Said, "I b'lieve I been by the river Ezekial." She said, "I don't know what hit me," she said, "But I never had such a great feelin' in all my life." And for years she started commin' to tha radio program and our church, a'beggin' me to do that again, and I said I couldn't, I'd hurt you. She's always beggin' me ta do it again. I told'er, said I'd hurt you if I did—I didn't know what I was doin'! But George told me, he said, "Your guitar's fine." It didn't even knock it outta tune and I slung it down in tha floor. Didn't even knock it outta tune, didn't scratch it, nothin', you know. God knows what he's doin'. But then, you know, we all got a big laugh—I still laugh when I thank about it. (Interview, February 10, 2009)

As evinced by the particular prosodic style of the delivery of this narrative, this next story made its appearance during the course of one of Brother Aldie's anointed sermons on live radio, 105.5 FM (WGTH), in Richlands, Virginia.

"Heavyset Woman"

Ah' praise God but listen ta me [*Words are drawn out in a husky growl*]
I want ya to know—ahh.
I knew a woman one time—ah.
It was several years back—ah.
Ah' down near Bradshaw—uh.
An' I won't call her name or anything.
She's dead-'n'-gone now—uh
Ah' but she was a heavyset woman—ah
Ah' she was huge I guess ya could say
Weight-wise for'er size—ah.
She was real short'n heavy—uh
And she went down ta tha PTL Club—uh [*Praise the Lord, the Evangelical empire of Jim Baker*]
An' she went down thar she'd had cancer [*Drawn-out last word*]
An' the doctor said—uh
That she only had a few days left—uh.
An' she went to church—uh
She was a Christian
An' she went down to tha PTL Club—ah
Ah' praise God
An' she went down'n they prayed fer her—huh
An' she come back—ah
An' she went back to tha docter—ah

An' he searched her—ah
I mean he done ever test—ah
That could be done—ah [*Intensity and viscerality of voice beginning to build*]
Ah' known to man—ah
An' he said, "Your cancer is gone"—huh
"What happened ta you!?" [*Loud clapping and vocal affirmations from congregation*]
An' she said I went down—ah [*Very gruff growl, importunate timbre of voice*]
Ah' ta tha PTL Club—ah
An' said, "They prayed for me"—ah
An' I was made whole—ah
An' he got angry—ah
An' he said, "Go back"—uh
An' hav'em pray 'bout 300 pound off of ya—ah! (WGTH, April 19, 2009)

Toward the end of this story, a tension builds between the audience's desire to respond to the humorous features of the narrative on the one hand, and its disapproval of the attitude of the medical professional on the other. This tension seems to add to the force of the laughter circulating throughout the story. Because Pastor Allen was under the power of the anointing while recounting the story, its implications seemed to fall upon the more sedate and disapproving aspects of the acerbic unbelief and caustic consternation of the doctor. However, in several other circumstances, Brother Aldie has told this story with an emphasis upon the humorous side, and with a particularly laugh-inducing effect. Within this particular context, laughter comes not from the figure of the "heavyset woman" but from the consternation displayed by a representative of Western biomedicine in the presence of the miraculous.

Another humorous space of storying on the spirit is opened through Brother Allen's phrase, "If you ain't got'em, you can't feel'em—you've left'em!" during a moment of heightened emotional intensity in the broadcast studio. The following account is instructive in the place of ironic humor within the sacred milieu, and also in the essential role that visceral, somatic sensations play in the charismatic religious experience. This story accentuates the palpable pneumatic force of the Holy Ghost with a humorous air:

Holy Ghost Lingerin'

ALDIE: I've never forgot, one night we stopped to pick Walter'n'Dixie up ta take'em to church. An' I asked'er, could I go to tha bathroom. An' I went in thar and tha chillbumps come, n'tha *par*-a-God eat me up. [*With guttural gusto*] An' I said, "Somebody been in this bathroom a'prayin'!" [*Congregation laughter*] They went ta laughin'. Dixie told me later, said, "It was my prayer room, Aldie, it's my prayer room." [*Energetic voice*] Well she just left that prayer room, 'cause she shore left the Lord, an' tha presence right behind. But ya know the presence a'God is with us no matter whar we at. You may leave the church today, but tha presence a'God will not leave instantly. He'll hang around. [*Opens space for another story*] (November 15, 2009)

An indissociable technique of breath *and* emotional state, laughter circulates within the space of worship in ways similar to the quickening power of the Holy Ghost through the anointed poetics of preaching, ecstatic vocalizations, and glossolalia. The force of narrativity and the concomitant compulsion to retell opened through the associative chain of meaning moves through the congregation like the contagious force of the sacred. Just as the poetics of anointed breath facilitates the accumulation of emotional intensity among the congregation members, the humorous narrative opens the space for the contagious breath of laughter. When the rocking breath of laughter irrupts within the space of charismatic worship, the force of automaticity has already begun to make its appearance.[14]

The Story of the Smile

DOROTHY: And then Brother Henry got a good doctor's report
He says somebody got a prayer through fer him.
So let's give tha Lord a great big hand, Hallelujah [*Sound of hand clapping*]
The Lord surely is a'movin'.
He surely is a'workin'.
You know 'fore I finish givin'-in the prayer requests,
I seen this lady on TV, an' it was called extraordinary healin's.
She was settin' on tha couch an' she was readin'.
I don't know if she was readin' her Bible or what she was readin'.
But this big dog was there, an' it was a friendly lookin' dog.

And he didn't mean to, but he jumped up on tha couch an' when
    he did, he took out part-a-her lip.
'Cause his tooth came down on it, ya know.
An' they said that they was gonna have ta do nineteen surgeries
    on her.
An' she said, "No."
She said, "I'll have *one*."
An' he said, "I wanna show you."
Said, "They's gonna glue her lip, what they did put back on, to
    her gum."
An' she'd never open her mouth, you know, and then she would never
    smile again.
She'd never smile again.
An' she said, her smile, she loved her smile because she was a
    preacher.
An' she said, "Lord I just cain't do this."
She said, "I'm a preacher."
An' she said, "I don't want your nineteen surgeries."
And he said, "Well, just look at my book."
An' she said, "No."
She said, "I've got my book that I look at."
[*With a tone of condescension*] An' he said, "Well what book do you
    look at?"
She said, "I look at tha Bible."
She said, "I look at tha Bible."
She said, "I trust in tha Bible."
She said, " I trust in tha Lord."
She said, "I went home an' I put ever *pitcher* I could find that I had a
    smile on my face."
She said, "I put it up on tha wall."
An' ever time I walked by those *pitchers* I said, "Lord I'm gonna smile
    again." [*Audible breath*]
"You gonna fix me an' I'm not gonna have ta have all those
    surge-ries—ahh"
An' she went ta her church at'night an' [*Audible breath*]
Oh you could tell those people was believin' with ever-thang they had
    in'em.
An' they was prayin' [*Audible inhalation*]

> An' she turned her back, she said, "You go ahead an' look at me."
> She said, "'Cause this is fer my first surge-rie—an' it'll be my last."
> An' she said, "An' it don't look good."
> She said, "But God's gonna touch me."
> An' after they prayed an' she turned her back ta tha people like this an' [*Audible breath*]
> She raised her hands and she kept ast-in' God ta heal'er.
> An' when she turned back around,
> That bruise was gone.
> That bloody look was gone.
> She was back.
> An' she had a smile.
> I mean she smiled like you, Betty! [*Raucous laughter*]
> *She was smilin' like crazy!*
> An' you know, God can do any-thang if we allow him to. [*Betty is a member of the studio congregation. At this moment, Sister Dorothy lets out a burst of laughter so intense that it overwhelms the sensitive capacities of the microphone and is translated through the loudspeaker as a fuzz or grain outlining the percussive force of her laughter.*]

This story provides further evidence as to the centrality and compelling force of laughter within the charismatic space of worship, and it also performatively reveals important elements of narrative structure within the testimony. The particularities of this form, in turn, help to invoke laughter and other emotional experiences. The affective force that is unleashed through the poetics of testimony is, of course, not made possible through the mere recounting of the "informational" aspects of a TV show. The force generated through the particular structure of narrativity characteristic of the testimony is in this poetic form's ability to *perform the event itself*, or bring the listener into the gravitation of storied events. The story of the miraculous smile does not merely recount the narrative form of the television program; the elements of the story are creatively recombined and performed to enable a specific experience or effect. In this way, the poetic force of the testimony and its very narrative structure is not so much about *re*-presentation as it is about performatively instantiating a specific emotional experience of faith in the here and now.

Often the appearance of the testimonial seems to be characterized by a sudden irruption into the worship context. Associative chains sometimes trigger the retelling of a faith story, while in other instances, the storyteller seems abruptly moved by divine inspiration to testify. This divinely inspired process of narration seems to be suggested just before the opening of the story on the miraculous smile:

> The Lord surely is a'movin'.
> He surely is a'workin'.
> You know 'fore I finish givin'-in the prayer requests.

A compulsion to enact the narrative seems to interrupt the normal course of events, placing a kind of call or demand on both the storyteller and the audience. The gravitational pull of narrativity is already organizing the worship milieu through the particular force of language.

Typical of this narrative poetics, the testimony describes in vivid detail the visceral elements of the story. Through a specific technique of storying, the imagination of the listener is focused upon a lip dangling from the mouth, and a slow-motion shot of a massive canine tooth sinking into the ruddy surface of the lower lip. In a surrealist montage, the listener hears of glue and gums and the benumbed sagging gape of a dumb mouth. This narrative close-up of the carnal details of a body "got down" creates a sense of empathy for the sick and opens a space of vulnerability in the listener by cultivating a heightened awareness of the fragility and precarious boundaries of the fleshly body.[15]

After generating this sense of urgent empathy with the listener, the testimonial often stages a dialogue between the "patient" or protagonist of the story and a representative of Western medicine. Heavy with power dynamics, the miraculous potentiality of the Holy Ghost opens a space of "back talk" in regard to bureaucratic conceptual frameworks and biomedical conceptions of health and disease. As we also heard in the story of the "heavyset woman," the doctor makes implicit commentary upon the faith of the protagonist with a tone of condescension that is literally performed through the vocalizations of the storyteller. In these testimonials of faith, the figure of the doctor becomes the caricature of educated unbelief and rigid bureaucracy. This gesture of unbelief on the part of the medical bureaucrat, however, is always met with an obstinately defiant call of faith and openness to the irruptive potential of the miraculous.

At this point in the testimony, the force of narrativity has built so much momentum that a subtle poetics of breath begins to emerge. The tone of Sister Dorothy's voice has now gained an importunate quality, and she begins to make clearly audible inhalations at the ends of some testimonial lines. There is often an arbitrary line of demarcation between the performance of the testimony and the anointed poetics of preaching. This intensity of tone and breath coincides with a mounting sense of tension and expectancy within the listening audience. The narrative technique of testifyin' instantiates the experience of the listener into the movements of the story. Or to put this another way, the poetic structure forges an experiential link between the characters in the testimony and the listening audience. Through this performative intertwining of audience and story, the listener no longer hears the account as a distanced or abstracted observer but is actually brought into the storied events:

> An' she went to her church at night an' [*Audible breath*]
> Oh you could tell those people was believin' with ever-thang they had in'em.
> An' they was prayin'. [*Audible inhalation*]

As this moment in the progression of the faith narrative, it is not some abstracted church that has mobilized "ever-thang they had in'em" to help instantiate the miraculous power, but the listening audience itself that experiences a kind of self-referential account of individual experience within the movements of the story. The story becomes a mirror image through which the audience is able to recognize faith on a basic experiential level. Through this performance, a palpable expectancy is released and is thus a performative enactment of faith in and through the temporal articulation of the narrative. Through the storied performance of a healing prayer, the tense expectancy of the audience is released through the image of a smile that unleashes the visceral laughter of the storyteller. And through the temporal articulations of the narrative, we are able, if only for a moment, to fill that silent space of the gaping mouth with laughter.

The Anointed Laughter of Sister Julie

On the level of the techniques of breath, there is a similarity between the percussive exhalations that mark the end of the sermonic line and the belly laugh. The sermonic style of Sister Julie, one of the most performatively gifted preachers I have heard in southern Appalachia, demonstrates this structural homology. One of the hallmarks of Sister Julie's sermonic style is a chanted, rhythmic form that periodically breaks into rising intonations of sung and elongated words. Juxtaposed with the chanted monotony of her voice, which occasionally reaches such a low and extremely guttural timbre as to totally shed any feminine vocal marker, is a smooth weaving together of intoned sung words that creates a particularly striking poetic effect within the overall sermonic structure. As the emotional intensity of her sermon increases, the chanted monotone and accompanying hyperventilated grunt punctuating the line yields to a deeper form of breath that opens the performance into sung phrases that rise and fall in intonation. Sister Julie's audience is well aware that the emergence of sung lines from the monotonous chant signals a deeper anointing; as she breaks into song, the studio audience acknowledges this performative power with vociferous affirmations: "Yes, Lord!" "Amen." "Whoooo!"

During sequences of heightened charisma, the piercing punctuations of the percussive grunt give way to what I can only describe as brief moments of low, guttural laughter. In this moment of sacred respiration, the percussive grunt and the guttural laugh seem at times distinguishable only by the break or silent pause that briefly separates them. Laughter is a kind of repeated grunt followed by a deep and more pronounced inhalation in preparation for the delivery of the next sermonic line. Indeed, this laughter seems to throw the loose rhythmic structure of the poetic form off-kilter—if only for an instant. There is a brief slippage or interruption, like the skipping of a phonograph, between the immediate coincidence of the mouth of the preacher and the anointing power of the Holy Ghost:

Oh glory to the lamb of God
Lord is callin' you today
Ah' get back in
Ah' it's not too late yet—ahh
Ah' get back in,
I'm callin' my children today back in
Well glory ta tha lamb of God
He's callin'—ah
Oh—ah
Heed to his call today
Heed to his call
Well, glory—ah
Hallelujah
I know it mighta been a-long time [*Rough, guttural monotone*]
Ago—ah
An' that you—huh
Ah' been outta church—ah

Well now is tha time—ah
Oh, it's ready—ah
Time is ready fer ye ta go back—ahh [*Throaty, guttural*]
Hallelujah, do yer first works over
Well glory to tha lamb of God—ah [*Forceful intensity in following lines*]
Hal-le-lu-jah
An' because—ah
An' God is biddin' today—ah
Oh God is biddin' today—ah
Well glory—HA-HA [*Brief interruption of laughter followed by clearly audible and forceful inhalation*]
Well glory to tha lamb a'God—ah
An' blessed be tha name of tha Lord—ah [*Like chant of an auctioneer*]
Ah' let me tell you God will not fail you—HA-HA [*Sung line, followed by pronounced inhalation*]
Hallelujah to tha lamb—ah
He's a faithful God—HA-HA
He'll stand by in his word before'em his word—hah
Oh you don't have to worry 'bout God—HA-HA
Because he'll be here on time—ah
Hallelujah—ah
When we face some thangs—ah
An' we think he might be too late, but let me tell ya
He'll come through on time for ya [*Brief pause before commencing next cycle*]
Hallelujah to tha lamb—ah
Oh glory—ah
I know God's speakin' today—ah [*Allusion to anointed speech*]
Hallelujah to tha lamb
I had no idea I's gonna say these thangs—ah
But oh glory—ah
. . .
An' they're good preachers everywhar—ah
A'ministerin' tha word—ah
If people will only heed—ah
An' get in that word and study tha word—ah
So you'll not be deceived—ah

Oh glory ta tha lamb a'God—ah
Hallelujah
Why I say unto you—ah
That none of these men which were bidden shall taste of my supper—ah
Well it already—ah
Time—ah
Had given tha last opportunity—ah
An' glory to them back then that praise tha Lord—HA-HA-HA
[*Massive breath*]
Well glory, tha door was open—HA-HA
Through Jesus when he died—ah
Well Glory ta tha lamb a'God
An' it's fer ever'body
It's for the Jews—ah
It's fer the Gentile
It's fer all tha prophets—ah
Oh it's fer ever'body today—ah
Heed to his word today—ah
An' come forth—ah
An' in him—ah
An' glory to tha lamb.[16]

Sister June's Bulldog Preachin'

With her long grey hair pulled tightly back in a ponytail, Sister June Sweeny's outward appearance seems to mirror the timbre and grain of her voice: austere, strict, and slightly foreboding. Like Sister Julie, Sister June is among the most poetically gifted preachers who have weekly programs on radio station WGTH in Richlands, Virginia. Unlike many of the other worship broadcasts, however, Sister June rarely has a studio audience, other than the grandchildren whom she often watches during her thirty minutes of preaching on Saturday afternoon: "I got my grandson with me, he's almost two years old, an' I'm kindly keepin' an eye on him. So praise the Lord, you pray for me today."[17] The presence of Sister June's grandchildren in the live studio is often registered by the microphone as their little voices mimic her singing and talk with each other. Once again, the presence of young children, along with the periodic disruption and vocal intrusions into the sermon that they cause, attest to the informal environment of many of the live preaching broadcasts. In the previous sermonic interlude, for instance, Sister June's two-year-old grandson can be overheard making an abrupt "thumping" noise in the background, followed by piercing cries of distress. The child presumably fell and hit his head, and thus cries loudly for several minutes. Though this incident took place during a crucial emotional section of the sermonic form, Sister June's poetic performance barely misses a beat, despite the fact that she does stray from the microphone for a moment to make sure that no serious harm has befallen the child.

Despite the subtle harshness and stridency in the grain of Sister June's voice, there is an attractiveness to the character of her speech; her voice is like the hard oak handle of a tool polished smooth by years of contact with the grip and sweat of the hand whose burnished surface beckons hands to touch its surface once again. During her anointed preaching, this stark sincerity becomes more pronounced, and at times her voice breaks into the harsh raspy timbre that is characteristic of other sermonic styles in this area. And although Sister June's sermonic line is often punctuated by the poetics of the anointed grunt, what seems to differentiate her style from the others is her seamless fusion of passages from the King James Bible, with stories, colloquialisms, and words that characterize everyday modes of talk in southern Appalachia.

A poetic force is released through Sister June's particular linguistic capacity to fuse the mellifluous style of the King James Bible with motifs and turns of phrase from everyday life in southern Appalachia. There are times within her sermonic delivery when it is difficult to recognize the biblical passages and phrases, so seamlessly are they woven into the fabric of the sermonic form. This poetic *charismata* to weave together different forms also points to a prodigious mnemonic capacity that is opened through the anointed sermonic technique of gesture, breath, and story. Her capacity to recall countless biblical passages with such fluidity and ease, as well as to seamlessly patch them into the overall sermonic structure, is so large that the listener often does not realize in the immediacy of the anointed performance that he has just heard a Bible verse.

Enlivening the sermon to make concepts such as sin, gossip, and hatred resonate with palpable force, her anointed poetics melds the flowering prose of the King James Bible with striking everyday images that grab hold of the listener:

SISTER JUNE: So if you in Jesus,
You're in a safe haven today.
If you in Jesus,
You in tha arc of safety.
If you're in Jesus you got a hedge built up around you. [*Intense vocalization*]
I read over'n the Old Bible whar he said,
He'd take down the hedge an' let tha devil in.
Let me tell you honey,
You keep prayin' and standin' fer Jesus,
An' he'll keep 'at hedge built up around'ye.
Glory to God.
You take a big pond a'water,
Glory ta God,
If it's got a little bitty crack in it,
Or a little small needle-hole in it,
'At water'll go ta seepin' through thar.
An' after-awhile it keep drippin'-drippin'-drippin',
After-awhile it'll have a little spew about it.
[*Vocal intensity quickly building*] After-awhile it'll gush open and be a'runnin' ever-whars—ahh
That's tha same way, praise God,
You let sin get in your life a little bit,
After-awhile—ahh [*Audible inhalation*]
It'll take aholt!
Glory ta God—ahh
It'll be worser than a bulldog aholt on ya!
And won't turn-a-loose of ya!
Glory ta God.
[*In a voice of markedly gentler and softer tone*] It'll clamp down, that sin will.[18]

. . .

The heart of tha wise teaches his mouth—huh
And addeth learning to his lips, praise God—huh
Honey we gotta learn ta keep our tongue under control—huh
An' say God—huh
Ah' you put me on, I've often said this—
Put me on that potter's wheel—huh

An' turn it an' turn it—huh
An' make me ta what you'd hav-me-ta-be—huh
Ah' glory to God, praise tha Lord—huh
He said pleasant words are as a honeycomb—huh
Ah' sweet ta tha soul—hah
An' health to tha bones [*Hand clap*]
Praise God—huh
. . .
An ungodly man diggeth up evil—huh
An' his lips thar is as a burnin' far [fire], praise tha Lord—huh
Honey that old tongue is a deadly thang—huh
Ah' glory ta God, praise tha Lord—huh
An' you get out here—huh [*Commotion in background as child falls and begins screaming loudly*]
In tha summertime you get a rattlesnake or a copperhead bites you
Ah' praise tha Lord—huh
An' glory ta God, ah'praise God
If you don't go to tha doctor an' get help—huh
Ah' praise God—huh
Ah' you'll die—hah
An' that's the same way with that old lyin' tongue—huh
Hit's-as-poison-as-a-rattlesnake-bite—huh
Ah' glory ta God it's out thar a'tryin' ta stir up strife—huh
An' hurtfulness'n'trouble—huh
Ah' glory ta God, praise tha Lord—huh
Hit's all-time tryin' ta do somethin' mean—hah
A'tattlin' on people tellin' lies—hah
A'talkin' 'bout somebody—huh
Ah' praise God—huh.

These arresting images of the everyday press close to another recurrent theme in Sister June's preaching, what she sometimes refers to as the "Holy Ghost'n'far [fire]." More often, however, this force is referred to through a unique pronunciation of the word "power": *par*. This *par* circulates in the world like some diffuse potentiality or efficacious potential, ready to be instantiated into the operations of the everyday. This theme of *par*, even when not explicitly mentioned, metaphorically and physically saturates the worship milieu:

SISTER JUNE: Because Jesus has more *par* than the devil has.
That ole devil's got alot a'*par*, don't get me wrong.
They's sa-many people lettin'em have it.
Ah' glory ta God.
People that used to walk upright before God and live good fer tha Lord—huh
They've turned thar *par* right over to him—ahh
Ah' glory ta God,
They right back out in sin doin' tha thangs of tha devil—ahh
Ah' praise God, an' that give him more *par*—hah
Ah' praise tha Lord—ahh [*Begins building in forceful intensity*]
Ah' but I'm servin' one, glory ta God [*Full visceral force, begins beating podium in rhythm*]
I don't care if you backslide today on Jesus—ahh
He still retains his *par*—ahh
He never loses no *par*—ahh
He's still got the same *par*, praise God
[*Soft, intimate voice*] But that ole devil just has what *par* you give'em.
An' I'm glad today, that we don't have to depend on a God, that his *par* is limited.
Because all *par* is given unta Jesus in heaven and in earth.
And he give his *par* unta us—ahh
Ah' glory ta God, if we'll serve him and walk in tha way that he has fer us ta go.

Prayer and its accompanying techniques of manual gesture help to instantiate this diffuse heterogeneous potentiality of Holy Ghost *par*:

SISTER JUNE: Almighty God, reach down and send forth your divine healin' *par*—ahh
We know, God, they's nothin' too big that you cain't take care of it—ahh
Ah' today dear God—ahh
Ah Lord we ast ya ta move an' touch each and ever-one Lord—ahh
That's in need of prayer out thar in radioland, maybe got their hand—ahh
Upon the radio by a point-a-contact—ahh
Ah' touch'em today Jesus, and heal their bodies today—ahh
Anoint us today ta speak what you'd have us ta speak—ahh

>An' we'll not fail ta give you the praise for it all—ahh
>In Jesus's wonderful name we do pray,
>An' amen, an' amen.

Gandy Dancin'

The percussive technique of anointed breath resonates with a tradition of work songs and chants used primarily by black labor crews in railroad-related industries such as timber extraction and coal mining. These section crews, eponymously known as "Gandy dancers," from the Gandy Manufacturing Company, which fabricated the mauls, pry bars, rail-dogs, and other tools necessary for railroad track maintenance, were responsible for realigning sections of railway track after they were displaced by the massive weight of the passing coal trains.[19] This task, known as "lining track," required the coordinated movement of many laborers in order to move the entire track ensemble, which consisted of wooden cross ties, gravel, and steel rails, back into alignment. Failure to synchronize the laborers' movements would result not only in the inability to move the massive rail ensemble, but also severe injury, such as the crushing of limbs under the weight of heavy wooden cross-ties and long sections of steel railing.

Each maintenance crew had a "straw boss," who would sing or chant calls that were crafted to facilitate the rhythmic demands of the specific task of railway work at hand. The special track lining calls, for example, synchronized each crew member's exertion of force upon the twenty-pound steel pry bars used to move the tracks. With all the pry bars pulling in unison, enough force was mustered to move the entire track ensemble back into alignment. The task of track lining required a special technique of the body in which the feet and arms were moved in rhythmic coordination with the steel bar to facilitate the heaving of the track back into place. This interrelated system of bodies and objects, in turn, was organized and actuated in and through the force of song. This movement of body, tool, and track was often actuated through the percussive "hah" or other abrupt exhalations at the end of the rhythmic song phrase. This "dance," or technique of the body, was inextricably linked to the tool-rail complex. "Coordination and timing of each man's exertion was critical. One member of the gang, the caller, synchronized the group's physical movements with his voice, ensuring safety and pacing, while *spiritually uplifting* the men at their work." The following is an excerpt from a Gandy dancing song that was "called" by the straw boss:

[*Singing*] I don't know but I believe I will,
Make my home in Jacksonville.
Oh boys, throw it over—henh!
Oh boys, throw it over—henh![20]

Another example of the coordination of physical labor through chant and percussive breath can be heard in the well-known recordings made by Alan and John A. Lomax in the penitentiary work farms of Tennessee. The song "Katy Left Memphis," for instance, is a collection of stanzas taken from several work songs that coordinated the swinging of axes or the moving of heavy railway hardware during forced labor operations in southern prison systems.[21] Once again, the end of the poetic line is punctuated with a percussive exhalation of air that closely resembles that sonic emanation from the anointed mouth of many preachers in southern Appalachia. This breath, moreover, is simultaneously inflected with the chopping sound of the ax "bit" as it bites into the trunk of the tree. In this moment of coordinated movement, it is as if the deep exhalation of air at the end of the line "sounds" the swinging of the tool—singing the tool's movement—"hah." As one retired section crewman describes it, the song enlivens the movement of the tool: "So Gandy dancing goes in with the music. That's the way it's been since way back. In the beginning of the railroad, you had to line it up. That's where the gandy dances come in. And you even Gandy dance behind a maul. Even spiking, you make the spike maul talk; you sing to it. Like when you're driving a spike down."[22]

Here again, what I want to emphasize is the way that the percussive end-line demarcation of breath seems to orchestrate or enliven a coincidence of bodily technique, tool movement, and percussive chop. In this moment, breath and tool are inextricably linked, as if the sound of air is produced by the tool itself. Take, for instance, the singing of "Katy Left Memphis" by the Parchman Farm inmate nicknamed "Crosseye":

Arkansas city did not—*hah*
A'have but ten *hah*
A'have but ten boys *hah* [*The percussive "hah" of this line also
    coincides with the sound of a wood chip flying from the tree trunk
    and striking Lomax's microphone*]
I have but ten (whoo) *hah*

Arkansas city did not—*hah*
Have but ten *hah*

A'little Joy said forty—*hah*
Well tha Katy was made *hah*
A'little Joy said forty—*hah*
Well tha Katy was made *hah*

Arkansas city gonna—*hah*
A'be her train *hah*
Arkansas city gonna—*hah*
A'be her train *hah*.

Oh Rosie—*hah*
Oh Gal (whoo) *hah*
Oh Rosie—*hah*
An' a ho-Lord Gal *hah*

The boats in the bayou turnin'—*hah*
Well-a'round'n'round
The boats in tha bayou turnin'—*hah*
Well-a'round'n'round *hah*

The drive wheel knockin' Ala—*hah*
Well'a-bama bound (whoo) *hah*
The drive wheel knockin'Ala—*hah*
Well'a-bama bound *hah*

You go-ta Memphis don't you—*hah*
Well ya act no whore *hah*
A'you go-ta Memphis don't you—*hah*
Well ya act no whore *hah*

A'buy you a-ticket n'catch tha—*hah*
Well tha yellow dog (whoo) *hah*
I buy you a-ticket n'catch tha *hah*
Well'a yella dog *hah*

Oh Rosie *hah*
An'a oh girl (whoo) *hah*
Oh Rosie *hah*
An'a oh-Lord girl *hah*[23]

The organizing force of song under labor conditions of extreme duress recalls Marcel Mauss's 1934 lecture to the French Psychology Society,

"Techniques of the Body." At a crucial point in his talk, Mauss describes the "remarkable feats of hunting endurance" displayed through an Aboriginal hunter's ability to outrun kangaroos, emus, and wild dogs.

Continuing his description, Mauss says:

> One of these running rituals, observed a hundred years ago, is that of the hunt for the dingo or wild dog among the tribes near Adelaide. The hunter constantly shouts the following formula:
> Strike (him, i.e. the dingo) with the tuft of the eagle feathers (used in initiation, etc.)
> Strike (him) with the girdle
> Strike (him) with the string round the head
> Strike (him) with the blood of circumcision
> Strike (him) with the blood of the arm
> Strike (him) with menstrual blood
> Strike him to sleep, etc.[24]

Through this example, Mauss proposes that ritual breathing techniques open a particular space of "confidence" and "psychological momentum." Ritual techniques of respiration emerging from the performance of song propels the human body into extraordinary feats of endurance, granting access to prodigious reserves of power.[25] Moreover, Mauss concludes his lecture with yet another gesture to the relationship between ritual efficacy and techniques of breath. Citing Marcel Granet's work on China and the respiratory rhythms associated with Taoism, he elaborates on the interrelationships between "breath technique" and "mystical states." Proceeding with his call for continued psycho-technical exploration of these ritual forms of breath, he evocatively states: "I think there are necessarily biological means for entering into 'communication with God.' Although in the end breath technique, etc., is only the basic aspect in India and China, I believe this technique is much more widespread."[26]

The phenomenon of Gandy dancing provides fruitful terrain to give further consideration to Mauss's interest in the "confusion" among techniques of the body, ritual forms of breath, and exterior objects. Because Gandy dancing seems to perpetually tack between sacred calls invoking religious motifs and other calls heavy with sexual innuendo, as if to constantly hop between both sides of the track, it seems always on the boundary of ritual efficacy, not only because of its close association with automaticity, but because of its sustenance and relation to older forms of work calls and spirituals.[27] In fact, not only do the calls of the Gandy dancers invoke biblical motifs and phrases from spirituals, but the practice of calling itself has been generally described as a form of preaching. For example, in a description of the mental and physical fatigue associated with track lining, one retired railroad crewman states:

> Yea, they done give out already! When you sing, that make them uplifted. So the fella' asked me, "how do you feel when you're singing?" I say, "I feel alright and they feels alright. And that make the job go easy." That's the way that was. *You got to have somebody to preach to 'em. That old man told me to talk my Latin.*[28]

Other firsthand accounts from the Gandy dancers themselves attest to the relation between the form of the railway chant and religious performance. Speaking of the singing prowess of a longtime railway straw boss he knows, Cal Taylor, a retired railway man from Mississippi, says: "And he got a voice too. And he's the man that trained mighty near all the men that's on these bridge gangs and trained em how to keep from getting caught with a piece of timber. *He can preach to a piece of timber*. Just like the sermons you hear, he can preach to 'em."[29]

In addition to the structural similarities between the rhythmic breath techniques of the Gandy dancer and the anointed respirations of the preacher, the labor history of the southern railroad and its associated industries of timber production and bituminous coal extraction suggest significant points of communication between poor whites in southern Appalachia and black laborers from the flatlands and coastal regions of North Carolina, Virginia, Georgia, Tennessee, South Carolina, and Alabama. Toward the end of the nineteenth century, large numbers of black workers were recruited by the railway and mining industries—employing recruiting tactics that were not only dishonest but often violent.[30] Poor whites in Appalachia would have had close interaction with southern black laborers in the mines, timber operations, and railway infrastructures, which were heavily exploiting the region of southern Appalachia for its natural resources. Although more historical work is needed at this point, it is plausible that the technology of the railroad is intimately linked to the spread of certain sermonic styles among predominantly white religious communities within the mountains of southern Appalachia.[31]

Brother Pearl's Preaching

Although Brother Raymond Pearl's preaching style stands out as particularly gifted, even among the numerous ministers who preach to the microphone in the live studios of radio station WGTH in Richlands, Virginia, the introductory remarks of his sermons seem somehow impeded. More specifically, this imposition is characterized by shallow, clipped breaths and a quivering tone of voice that falters somewhat, as if he were suffering from the subtle tremors of weakness or disease. Once again, the sensitivities of the artificial ear (microphone) reveal these acoustic intimacies unregistered by our natural capacities of hearing. A slight tremble in his voice and the sound of superficial respirations suggests that this is the voice of an elderly brother. This shallowness and fragility in the character of Brother Pearl's voice, however, quickly gives way to robust and forceful articulations sustained by the deep inhalations characteristic of the anointed breath.

Several stylistic elements come together in the poetic form of Brother Pearl's anointed performance. Once his sermon has gained momentum, for example, his voice finds a "tonal center" and remains in this intense monotone while he rhythmically chants out the words given to him by the spirit. As the poetic inspiration falls upon him, the colorful intonations of each word cede their place to the demands of meter and rapid pronunciation. The droning effect created by this chanted monotone is reinforced by the repetitive use of words such as "Amen" to introduce the next chanted line. This type of chanted monotone, which is a recurrent prosodic element in sermonic styles throughout southern Appalachia and beyond, bears a striking sonic resemblance to the chanted performances heard in tobacco and livestock auction houses throughout the American South. Indeed, several scholars have proposed that the specific prosodic styles of southern auctioneers—a unique combination of monotone chant and occasional intoned words—emerged out of a southern tobacco tradition of auction that placed the spirituals of southern slaves in close proximity to the English tradition of chanted bids.[32]

As is characteristic of many of the preaching styles in southern Appalachia, the end of the sermonic line is punctuated by the percussive grunt. Brother Pearl's technique of breath at the end of the chanted line is particularly interesting, however, because the second phase of this technique, the rapid inhalation of air, is not only clearly audible, but it often creates a rasping or wheezing noise. At certain times during the delivery, this secondary sound of inhalation is equally as percussive and pronounced as the initial exhaled grunt described at the beginning of this chapter. In this case, each movement of the anointed breath-dance—the forward thrusting exhalation and the backward pushing inhalation—corresponds to clearly audible and percussive breaths. This raspy secondary inhalation only becomes audible and particularly pronounced once Brother Pearl's sermon has reached its zenith of emotional intensity; in these moments his breath technique achieves its deepest and most regulated respirations.

When into the breath-groove, the radio listener becomes intimately attuned and aware of his respiratory cycles. There is a loose rhythmic form to his percussive breaths, but there is also something always eerily mechanical, jerky, or somehow off-kilter about the sound of his breath *through* the loudspeaker. Once again, the technical capacities of the radio apparatus seem to amplify the presence of the spirit, enabling the listener to literally hear the force of the Holy Ghost as it works the lungs of the orator like a bellows. To the ears of the listener, the microphone reveals an auditory close-up of the sacred pneumatic gesture, as if the ear of the listening faithful has entered inside the anointed mouth of the preacher.

Through this repetitive structure of multiple "Amens," the ear of the listener is lulled by the monotonous warmth of the chanted sermonic line. Yet this rhythmic warmth of the chanted line is periodically interrupted by another distinctive mark of Pearl's poetic style, the sudden explosive intonation of "*Whoop-Hal-le-lu-yer—ahh*":

> Amen because the Bible said to let ever-man—ahh
> Amen work out his own soul's salvation—ahh
> Amen with fear and with trem-ble—ahh
> Amen they's commin' a day friend—ahh
> Amen you're gonna stand up before'em—ahh
> Amen praise the Lord and the books are gonna be opened—ahh
> *Whoop-Hal-le-lu-yer—ahh*!

Requiring one breath unit, or a total expenditure of air from the lungs to voice the line, this phrase reveals how a single word is stretched, cut, and re-formed in the process of anointed poetics to both accommodate the demands of rhythmic cadence and announce the presence of the Holy Ghost. A recurrent poetic motif in the chanted sermons of this region, this coupling of warmly chanted sections with the sudden appearance of intoned sounds or words adds particular poetic intensity and affect to the sermonic performance. Like the marked pronunciation of the word power (*par*) when referring to the force of the Holy Ghost, Brother Pearl pronounces the prayer formula "Hallelujah" with a particular emphasis upon the end of the word (*yer*). This particular pronunciation of the "jah" seems to prepare the way for the corresponding end-of-the-line percussive exhalation of air (*yer—ahh*). To put this another way, the usual pronunciation of the "jah" would create a slight impediment to the explosive force of the percussive "ahh." At the end of Brother Pearl's sermon, when the poetic inspiration has flown and he has once again taken up his everyday conversational style, he gives a standard pronunciation to this word of praise: "May God bless you 'till the next time, honey. Stay in church friend. Pray. Seek the face of God. Hallelujah."[33]

At other points in the sermon, the chanted line is interspersed with a kind of routinized tongue, or glossolalia, that announces a deeper level of poetic inspiration. I employ the term "routinized" because this appearance of tongues does not derail the sermonic progression or throw it off-kilter. Moreover, this phrase of tongue speech often has a set pronunciation that is occasionally repeated during the sermon.

> Amen but when the books are open—ahh
> I've had people to tell me well—ahh
> I'm gonna stand there and I'm gonna argee—ahh
> Amen with God, this is just how silly—ahh
> Amen some people is—ahh
> Amen praise the Lord whoop-hal-le-lu-yer—ahh
> Amen but I believe today friend—ahh
> Amen when the book of life is opened—ahh
> Amen when ya stand before the Lord of Lords—ahh
> *Hak-cod-da-ee-oh-sai—ahh*[34] [*Speaking in tongues*]

After many months of listening to the voice of Brother Pearl over the radio and through tape recordings of his radio sermons, I was repeatedly impressed by his forceful anointed poetics and deep techniques of breath. Yet it was not until I visited his home church outside of Raven, Virginia, that I understood the implications of those faltering, shallow breaths that were clearly audible during the early moments of his sermon. Can you imagine my amazement and newfound appreciation for the force of the inspired poetics of breath when I realized that the elderly man, at least in his early eighties, hunched over on the front pew of the church visibly struggling for air, was Brother Pearl. His mouth, whose space had been filled many times with remarkable force and poetic capacity, was now covered by the translucent plastic cup of an oxygen mask attached to a large metal cylinder mounted on a small hand truck. In that moment, I was unable to connect the compelling force of Brother Pearl's anointed voice with the fragile old man laboring for breath in the front pew.

Like the prodigious force generated through the chanted songs of the manual laborers, Brother Pearl's preaching testifies to the tremendous psycho-physiological momentum released through the percussive technique of breath. Through this *pneumatic gesture*, the intertwining of bodily movement, song, and breath grants access to mnemonic surfaces and linguistic-formulaic capacities inaccessible to the everyday faculties of awareness and embodiment. Deep down in the pit of the stomach, an elementary form of religious life announces itself with a guttural, percussive clap whose noise signals that the gap between the sacred and the everyday has been unbroken. In this dance of pneumatic gesture, the force of the sacred presses close upon the domain of psycho-technics. And, thus, we are left once again with Marcel Mauss's concluding remarks during his lecture on techniques of the body ringing like an auditory after-image: "I think that there are necessarily biological means of entering into 'communication with God.'"[35]

A particular force of attraction resonates between the history of Pentecostal worship practices and the radio apparatus. The emergence of Pentecostalism in the early twentieth century was saturated in metaphors and practices organized around enraptured tongues and possessed mouths quickened by the divine power of the Holy Ghost. In fact, the manifestation of tongues is, according to the majority of commentators on the history of this movement, the preeminent practice and theological doctrine.[36] Just as the rap-tap-tappings of the American Spiritualist movement embodied a particular affinity to the communicative technology of the mid-nineteenth century, the anointed mouths of Pentecostalism seemed to find a particularly compelling voice through the mouth of the radio loudspeaker.[37] Through a kind of mechanical translation, the mouth of the radio loudspeaker mimicked the anointed organs of vocalization so characteristic of Pentecostalism.[38]

At the same time, the radio loudspeaker, animated by forces from elsewhere, not only provided a means to think about possessions of the Holy Ghost, but the mechanical apparatus itself enlivened the anointed Pentecostal mouth producing amplifications and other special effects specific to its radiophony. The apparatus of radio, translating experience through the loudspeaker (receiver) in what Rudolf Arnheim describes as experiential "blindness," provided the listener an intimate aural close-up of the anointed mouth.[39] Through the sensitivities of the radio microphone, the listener heard the anointed articulations of the preacher in striking new ways. The radio apparatus translated the experience of a congregation member sitting in the front pew during an enthusiastic sermon, feeling the fine droplets of saliva shoot from the mouth of the anointed orator. Through the sensitivities of the microphone-loudspeaker complex, it was as if the distanced radio auditor were inside the aural cavity of the preacher, inundated by the minute sounds of vocalization: the clicks, smacks, and pops of the lips, the moist flapping of the tongue, the visceral wheeze of inhalation, and the spray of saliva.[40] The apparatus of radio focuses in upon the "acoustic grain" of the anointed voice, translating its inspired force in particularly moving ways.[41]

Returning to Brother Aldie's sermon on the story of the dry bones in the desert, which were enlivened through the force of divine wind and prophetic words, it seems as if his preaching has ended prematurely. The brother claims that the power of poetic inspiration has been quenched and that the performative force of divine breath has been withheld:

> ALDIE: An' I told ya if anointin' come I'd preach, an' if it didn't I won't. Well guess what, the anointin' ain't come, an' I ain't gonna preach. [*In a very low, soft voice, almost a whisper, disconsolate*] I'm not gonna bust myself open. God knows all thangs.[42] [*Aldie begins closing Bible*]

Once again, through the radio loudspeaker the listener hears the slow methodical sound of the metallic teeth of Aldie's leather-bound Bible gnashing together as the sacred word is closed. And although Brother Aldie claims that the power of the Holy Ghost did not fall upon his faculties of vocalization this particular Sunday afternoon, one does wonder if the sensitive capacities of the radio apparatus were able to register and amplify a presence that was running through the mouth of the preacher, yet was unable to be heard in the space of the studio.

INTERLUDE

Sermon 3

The Breath of Brother Pearl—"Are You Ready?"

You pray for us today. In Revelations 20 and chapter 12, and it said: I saw the dead small and great standing before God and the book was opened and another book was opened which was the book of life. And the dead were judged out of those thangs which were written in the book according to their works. And the sea gave up the dead which were in it and the dead in hell delivered up the dead which was in them and they were judged every man according to his works. And the dead in hell were casted into the lake of fire, this is the second death. And whosoever was not fount written in the book of life is casted into the lake of fire.

 Amen, praise the Lord.
 I'd like to preach just a little bit today, amen.
 Are you ready, praise the Lord.
 I thought about it this mornin', praise the Lord, and last night amen.
 I was prayin' and seekin' the Lord
 Seemed like he lead me to this scripture—ahh
 Amen and I've prayed and I've cried
 Amen praise the Lord
 But are we ready to face it, amen.
 When that book is opened friend it's gonna mean somethin'—ahh
 Amen when ya stand before God, amen—ahh
 I've had people tell me, well—ahh
 If so-and-so can make it to heaven—ahh
 I haven't got anything to worry about amen—ahh
 Honey but I'll tell ya somethin' today, we better be worryin'—ahh
 Whoop-Hal-le-lu-yer—ahh
 Amen about our own soul—ahh
 Amen because the Bible said to let ever-man—ahh
 Amen work out his own soul's salvation—ahh

Amen with fear and with trem-ble—ahh
Amen they's commin' a day friend—ahh
Amen your gonna stand up before'em—ahh
Amen praise the Lord, and the books are gonna be opened—ahh
Whoop-Hal-le-lu-yer—ahh
Amen were it's for you—ahh
Are where it's against you—ahh
Amen you'r gonna stand there speechless—ahh
Amen praise the Lord—ahh
I've had people say well, God—ahh
Won't send me to hell, no—ahh
Amen ya send yourself—ahh
Amen ya don't obey—ahh
Amen what says the word of God—ahh
Hal-le-lu-yer—ahh
Amen but when the books are open—ahh
I've had people to tell me well—ahh
I'm gonna stand there and I'm gonna argee—ahh
Amen with God, this is just how silly—ahh
Amen some people is—ahh
Amen praise the Lord Whoop-Hal-le-lu-yer—ahh
Amen but I believe today friend—ahh
Amen when the book of life is opened—ahh
Amen when ya stand before the Lord of Lords—ahh
Hak-cod-da-ee-oh-sai—ahh [*A moment of speaking in tongues*]
And the King of Kings—ahh
Amen your gonna stand there speechless—ahh
Whoo-Hal-le-lu-yer—ahh
I feel somethin' in here this mornin'—ahh
Whoa glory to God—ahh
I want my record to be clear—ahh
Amen praise the Lord—ahh
I wanna do everything friend—ahh
That I can do—ahh
Amen to uphold the standards—ahh
Amen of God because—ahh
Amen one day after-awhile—ahh
Amen we're gonna stand—ahh
Amen before him—ahh

Whoop-Hal-le-lu-yer—ahh
And we're gonna give an account of it.
Amen
We can live like the devil if ya want to
Whoop-Hal-le-lu-yer
Amen you can live any kind of life
Amen you wanna live—ahh
Amen die and go to hell lost without God—ahh
Whoop-Hal-le-lu-yer—ahh
Amen but I'm here to tell you today friend—ahh
Amen if you wanna go to heaven—ahh
Amen you better come separated—ahh
Amen from the things—ahh
Whoop-Hal-le-lu-yer—ahh
Amen and get your mind—ahh
Amen set on heavenly thangs—ahh
Whoo-Hal-le-lu-yer—ahh
And forget about—ahh
Amen the things of this world—ahh
Amen my God—ahh
I ain't got the world's riches—ahh
And I don't need'em friend—ahh
Hal-le-lu-yer—ahh
Oh glory to God—ahh
It's enough down here—ahh
Amen to get by with—ahh
Whoop-Hal-le-lu-yer—ahh
Amen because—ahh
I b'lieve I got a mansion—ahh
A'waitin' on me.
Hal-le-lu-oh-se-de-oh-saii [*Hallelujah gives way to speaking in tongues*]
Hal-le-lu-yer
Friend it's gonna be somethin'—huh
Whoop-Hal-le-lu-yer—ahh
Amen ta stand before'em—ahh
Amen'n give an account—ahh
Amen of ever idle word—ahh
Amen man'll be judged by the deeds—ahh

Amen that he done by the life—ahh
Amen that we've lived—ahh
Amen we're gonna give an account of it—ahh
Oh yea you'll get a righteous judge—ahh
Amen you'll get everything—honey—ahh
'At's commin' to you—ah
Amen you will not be left out—ahh
Amen praise the Lord—ahh
Where it's good—ahh
Are where it's bad—ahh
Amen praise the Lord—ahh
Amen God will give the righteous judge—ahh
Whoop-Hal-le-lu-yer
Amen because—ahh
He is the Lord of Lords—ahh
And he is the King of Kings—ahh
Amen my God—ahh
He's gonna have the last say—ahh
Amen in mine'n'your life friend—ahh
Amen were we make it—ahh
Amen or were we don't
Oh glory to God—ahh
He done too much for me friends—ahh
He brought me too far—ahh
Whoop-Hal-le-lu-yer—ahh
Amen he's been too good ta me—ahh
Amen ta turn away from 'em—ahh
Amen all I want—ahh
And everything I can get a'holt of—ahh
Amen from the word of God—ahh
I don't need the world's goods—ahh
Amen praise the Lord—ahh
Amen because one day after awhile—ahh
I'm gonna leave here—ahh
I'm gonna leave it all behind—ahh
And it's not-ta-gonna do me no good.
Hal-le-lu-yer
Whoo-Glory!
Hal-le-lu-yer

I b'lieve the Bible tell us—ahh
Amen ta lay up our treasures in heaven—ahh
Amen were the moths'n'the rust—ahh
And the thieves cain't get it—ahh
Amen ya lay it up down here—ahh
And you worry about it—ahh
Whoop-Hal-le-lu-yer—ahh
I wanna lay it up there—ahh
Oh thank God—ahh
Amen when I part this life—ahh
Hal-de-oh-saii—ahh [*Speaking in tongues*]
I can go home friends—ahh
Amen and enjoy—ahh
Amen the blessings of God—ahh
Hal-le-lu-yer—ahh
I'd live in a shack—ahh
Amen just ta make it to heaven—ahh
Amen praise the Lord—ahh
But I don't b'lieve they's gonna be any there—ahh
Whoop-Hal-le-lu-yer—ahh
Amen but Jesus said in my father's house—ahh
Are many mansions—ahh
If it were not so—ahh
I would have told you—ahh
Whoop-Hal-le-lu-yer—ahh
Amen praise the Lord—ahh
We can have a mansion—ahh
A'waitin' on us—ahh
Amen praise the Lord—ahh
If we'll straighten up—ahh
Amen and live 'cordin'—ahh
Amen to the word of God—ahh
Hal-le-lu-yer—ahh
I ain't got no high school—ahh
Amen edge-jur-cation—ahh
But I'll tell ya somethin' today friend—ahh
I'm servin' the world's greatest teacher—ahh
Whoop-Hal-le-lu-yer—ahh
Amen he said ask—ahh

And I shall receive it—ahh
He said to seek and that shall find—ahh
Oh my God today—ahh
All we gotta do's ask for it—ahh
Whoo-n'ask in faith believen'—ahh
Amen praise the Lord—ahh
Amen without faith—ahh
It's impossible—ahh
Amen to please the Lord—ahh
Amen but friend—ahh
It's time to get ready—ahh
Amen we're leavin' here—ahh
I believe time is right up on us—ahh
Amen praise the Lord—ahh
I don't b'lieve we got the time left—ahh
That we think we have—ahh

Praise the Lord. This is Brother Pearl—huh. Sayin' we love you. May God bless you 'till next time honey. Stay in church friend. Pray, seek the face of God. Hallelujah. Brother Brown . . .

[*As Brother Brown arrives at the microphone and begins to announce prayer requests, Brother Pearl is heard once again in the background breathing out one final vivacious "Whoo!" as if the breath of the Holy Ghost had not fully left his lungs.*]

CHAPTER 4

Standin' in the Gap
The Materialities of Prayer

Both branches of magic, the homeopathic and the contagious, may conveniently be comprehended under the general name of Sympathetic Magic, since both assume that things act on each other at a distance through a secret sympathy, the impulse being transmitted from one to the other by means of what we may conceive as a kind of invisible ether, not unlike that which is postulated by modern science for a precisely similar purpose, namely, to explain how things can physically affect each other through a space which appears to be empty.
—SIR JAMES FRAZER, *The Golden Bough*, 1890

Man has, as it were, become a kind of *prosthetic* God. When he puts on all his auxiliary organs he is truly magnificent, but those organs have not grown on to him and they still give him much trouble at times.
—SIGMUND FREUD, *Civilization and Its Discontents*, 1930

IN THE LAST CHAPTER, we saw how the open mouth of the preacher, that hollow cavity of linguistic potentiality, is filled with the inspired words of the Holy Ghost. "Open wide your mouth and I will fill it," reads the popular passage from the book of Psalms (81:10). At the same time, however, there is always the precarious potential that this gaping mouth will remain empty, the tongue held fast in the clutches of silence. As we heard in the closing words of Brother Aldie, there are times when the anointing power of the spirit will not make itself manifest in the organs of vocalization. Prayer, yet another instance of efficacious words, is also beholden to the precarious contingencies of the *gap* between the sacred and the everyday.[1] According to many practitioners of intercessory healing prayer in southern Appalachia, the force of divine communication is often encumbered by demonic blockages, the inertia of unbelief, and the fickle hearing capacities of the divine ear.

During the rite of healing prayer, a preeminent performance among many Holiness-Pentecostal, charismatic, and Independent-Baptist churches in southern Appalachia, one theurgical technique is repeatedly invoked to help mitigate the precarious contingencies inherent in this gap. Literally a physical substitution of one body for another, the practice of "standin'-in" during the performance of healing prayer connotes the use of the body of a congregation member who is present, to act as a proxy representative for the sick patient who is not physically present in the worship space. When the actual imposition of hands upon the sick patient is not physically possible within the space of worship, the stand-in supplements this absence, and the healing rite of laying on of hands proceeds with another physical conduit. The term "stand-in" is a shortened version of the phrase "to stand in the gap." Within the space of the radio station live studio, for example, this process of embodied substitution is often invoked:

> DOROTHY: [*Speaking the prayer requests into the studio microphone*]
> We wanna remember Brother Henry today, he's not feelin' well.
> And he's been a real trooper, you know, he's been a real soldier for the Lord.
> An' the Devil's tryin' ta knock'em down'n keep'em down.
> I've had so many people tell us, that when Brother Henry *laid his hands up- on'em,*
> You know, he *got a prayer through on their behalf.*
> He had the faith, you know.
> He *stood there in the gap*, you know.
> An' we miss'em this mornin'.

The stand-in, therefore, has a doubled function: he or she provides a physical substitute for an absent body, while simultaneously providing a material conduit for the communication of divine healing power to the sick patient. The stand-in prefigures a doubled distance between the sick patient and the healing efficacy of the Holy Ghost. In this way, the stand-in acts as a kind of miraculous transmitter, translating healing virtue from the sacred elsewhere to ameliorate bodily suffering in spaces of the everyday.[2]

A recent recording from a live in-studio worship service at radio station WGTH in Richlands, Virginia, offers an example of the practice of "standin'-in." This particular instance of physical substitution occurred early in the broadcast during preparations for the ritual of healing prayer.

BROTHER ALDIE: I'm gonna ask Landis if he'd stand in for my cousin, Ursul Blankenchip.

He had five bypasses less than a year ago.

He had a hip replacement, and they put the ball in—they put it in one end too small.

And now they gotta do the complete hip.

And they cain't do that 'till March because they said it had to be a year after the bypass before they would 'tempt it.

But I'm goin' tell ya somethin' 'bout this man real fast; not tryin' to give him no honor'n'glory—it all goes to the Lord.

He was actually on TV a few years back.

He had a blood clot in a'arteries, and the arteries was too small.

Said they never seen arteries that small on a man.

They didn't have a stint small enough to go in it.

And on TV some preachers come in, prayed for him, and God moved.

They said, "You'll have to be back in two years an' we'll have to do open heart surgery."

He said, "Well they was wrong, it's thirteen years later. I did have to go back, but its thirteen years later."

And they did five bypasses but they had to take his heart outta his body and lay it up on his chest ta get to the one they had to fix.

So now he's in bad shape with his hip.

He's still movin' around goin', goin' to church.

Went to church last night and I thank he's gonna be listenin' this mornin' on the way to church if he's able to go.

But anyhow, I told'em we'd pray for'em.

He said, "Aldie I'd 'preciate that."

He said, "If them people just call my name before the Lord I'd appreciate it."

He's got the faith, and that's what the Bible said.

He said, "If you got the faith, by your faith you shall be made whole."

By your faith, not by mine, not by yours.

But he also said if two or three would touch and agree askin' the father anything in my name it shall be done.

That's what the Lord said.

Eh I'll tell ya, if he b'lieves it, if we b'lieve it, God said it, then why cain't it happen!

It can if we will believe.

So we're gonna lay hands on Brother Landis, *'cause Brother Landis has had hip surgery* here two weeks ago, I guess it was.
Two weeks tomorrow.
And he's with us today, and disappointed 'cause he couldn't be here last Sunday, but he was in church with us Thursday night.
But he's gonna stand in for my cousin.
I wanna ask you's people out in radioland to help us out.
If ya don't b'lieve, don't pray.
You're wastin' your time and ours too.
But if ya do b'lieve then lift your hands and pray with us and be parta this program.[3]

With the ritual stand-in in place, the congregation commences with the practice of enthusiastic communal prayer, which I have elsewhere termed "skein prayer" because of the entangled nature of the sound. The vivacious practice of all the congregants praying individual prayers out loud is also accompanied by rapid disjointed clapping, cries, singing, and other vocalizations. A cacophony of noise results that is believed by the congregants to be one of the most efficacious theurgical techniques to span the gap and "get a prayer through" to the divine ear. Just before the skein prayer gathers enough sonic momentum to render all meaningful articulations indiscernible to human ears, Brother Aldie is overheard giving final instructions to Ursul, who is about to hear the sacred force of communal prayer though the loudspeakers of his automobile radio:

ALDIE: Ursul, if you're listenin' lay ya hands on the radio, b'lievin' for your miracle.

At this point, skein prayer commences in earnest: its sacred noise resonating through the radio loudspeaker for several minutes until it gradually loses momentum and abruptly ends. The stand-in, however, whose sensitivities to the efficacy of the prayer seem to be amplified in this intermediary position between the patient and the divine, senses a communicative breakdown in the healing prayer. As the communal prayer begins to decrease in intensity, the stand-in suddenly claims that the prayer has not "gone through":

LANDIS: Let's do that again.
Let's do that again.
Dorothy, Dorothy, let's do that again.

Let's do that again, they was a big block somewhere.
We gotta get that block outta here.
[*Beginning the healing prayer once more*] Oh Jesus, Lord.
Jesus in your name, Lord, Jesus we come to ya Lord.
Lord in your holy sweet name . . . [*Din of skein prayer overwhelms the words of Brother Landis*]

Not to be deterred by the perceived failure of the first cycle of prayer, the congregation commences a second attempt at healing prayer, this time with even greater sonic force, intensity, and boisterous noise.

As suggested by this instance of healing prayer, the practice of standin'-in substitutes another body to literally stand in the space of an absent and distanced recipient of healing power. This theurgical practice of substitution, however, does not proceed at random, with just any person within this space of the gap. The specific decision to use Brother Landis as the stand-in suggests the potential to enliven through prayer certain sympathetic resonances between distant bodies. Through a mimetic or imitative association, Brother Landis is the most propitious stand-in because he has recently undergone a total hip replacement surgery. In an ironic way, therefore, the visceral process of hip replacement seems to thematize the substitutionary practice of standin'-in as an efficacious technique of healing prayer.

The theme of the prosthetic, moreover, announces several overarching experiences of displacement at work in this technique of divine communication. On the level of human sensory capacities, for example, this cycle of healing prayer anticipates the simultaneous extension and voicing of the prayer somewhere else, so that the distanced patient could possibly experience the prayer on his or her behalf in and through the technological extensions of the radio apparatus. To further mitigate the precariousness of prayer, not only is Brother Landis used as a stand-in, but the absent Ursul is instructed to make tactile contact with the automobile radio to facilitate the miraculous transmission of healing force. The technical capacities of the radio apparatus, just like a prosthetic organ, enable a particular sensory experience of divine communication. Ursul can literally feel the distant prayer through his hands. Though the studio congregation is unable to lay hands upon Ursul's disjointed artificial hip socket, the technical prosthetic of the loudspeaker allows Ursul to make tactile contact with the distant voices of the prayer warriors. In yet another bodily and sensory substitution, the artificial organ of the voice (the radio apparatus) translates and extends a manual experience of tactility across a distance. Recalling the fact that the mouth itself is a massive organ of touch, the crucial charismatic practice of laying on of hands is extended through the mouth of the radio loudspeaker.[4] Like an internal organ taken outside the natural boundaries of the body, the naked capacities of the ear are "armed" and extended with the sensitivities of the microphone and the amplifications of the loudspeaker.

Just as surgical replacement of bodily organs opens to the possibility of a disjointed fit or slippage—in this case a maladjusted ball socket necessitates a total hip replacement—the manifold substitutionary layers during the performance of healing prayer at times fail to successfully span the gap between Holy Ghost power and the exigencies of the everyday. Brother Landis, whose sympathetic resonance with Ursul seems to grant the charismatic capacity to detect or discern the communicative success of the prayer, senses a "big block somewhere," which has prevented the prayer from reaching both its divine destination and the ailing body of the patient. Sometimes during the end of a prayer cycle, when the noise of skein prayer decrescendos to a brief though forceful silence, one of the participants within the skein prayer will exclaim, "That prayer didn't go through!" and the congregation will perform the communal prayer once again with more intensity.

This potential for breakdown in the performance of healing prayer demands material conduits and embodied techniques to help buttress the unsteady contingencies of divine communication. Yet it is precisely in this performative moment, when faith, like a clogged artery, seems to be *bypassed* by practices of material substitution and supplementation, that an overt insistence upon the necessity and primary force of faith is invoked. Despite the many techniques and physical conduits that "stand in," the narration of healing prayer quickly reasserts the primacy of faith in the performance of divine communication. At certain moments, therefore, it seems as if the practice of faith alone grants access to healing efficacy:

> He's got the faith, and that's what the Bible said.
> He said if you got the faith, by your faith you shall be made whole.
> By your faith, not by mine, not by yours. . . .
> Eh I'll tell ya, if he b'lieves it, if we b'lieve it, God said it, then why cain't it happen!
> It can if we will believe. . . .
> I wanna ask you's people out in radioland to help us out.

> If ya don't b'lieve, don't pray.
> You're wastin' your time and ours too.
> But if ya do b'lieve then lift your hands and pray with us and be parta this program.

This performance of healing prayer marks the constant oscillation between corporeal detail and material substitutes, on the one hand, and explicit calls for the performance of an internalized, spiritual, and intellectualized belief on the other. At the crucial moment during the healing prayer, however, when Ursul is instructed to perform the rite of manual imposition upon the radio, the two seemingly discrete and mutually exclusive moments almost collapse into one another:

> ALDIE: Ursul if you're listenin' lay ya hands on the radio, b'lievin' for your miracle.

At the point where the efficacious healing power of the Holy Ghost is unleashed, manual gestures of tactility and the intellectualized performance of belief become almost indistinguishable.

The song "A Meeting in the Air" is often sung during the communal practice of healing prayer:

> Well there is going to be a meeting in the air
> In the sweet, sweet by and by
> Oh I am going to meet you, meet you over there
> In that home beyond the sky
> Such singing you will hear, never heard by mortal ear
> Twill be glorious I do declare
> And God's own Son will be the leading one
> At that meeting in the air
>
> You have heard of little Moses in that bulrush
> You have heard of fearless David and his sling
> You have heard the story told of dreaming Joseph
> And of Jonah and the whale you often sing
> There are many, many others in the Bible
> I should like to meet them all I do declare
> By an' by the Lord will surely let us meet them
> At that meeting in the air
>
> [Repeat first verse]

Many things will be there missing in that meeting
For the mourners' bench will have no place at all
There will never be a sermon preached to sinners
For the sinner has refused to heed the call
There will be no mourning over wayward loved ones
There will be no lonely nights of pleading prayer
All our burdens and our anguish will be lifted
At that meeting in the air. [*At this point in the performance, a wave of ecstatic emotion almost completely derails the song*]

[Repeat first verse]

ALDIE: Gonna be a meeting in the air, you gonna be there? [*Loud congregational exhortations fill the background*]
Jesus makes it possible we could all be there.
He said it wasn't his will, that any should perish.
But that we all come to repentance.
An' I'll tell ya today it's alot better felt than told,
It's alot better felt than told today.
He's a good God, he's here today. [*At this point, Aldie's voice is almost drowned out by the enthusiastic sounds in the background: Glory! Whoo! Yes Lord!*]
We thank God for all of yens.
All of yens got us tuned in.
An' I hope you're feelin' what we're feelin'.
Sister Donna said lift your hands, praise the Lord.
[*Vehement and guttural voice*] Let'em have his way with ya!

DOROTHY: Ya'll come on up and lay hands on Landis for that man who just fell.
Hallelujah, Glory.
This is fer Donna's husband. [*As Dorothy leaves the mic, she is overheard organizing the upcoming prayer. Donna preaches in the live studio during the airtime slot just before the* Jackson Memorial Broadcast *of Brother Aldie and Sister Dorothy*]

ALDIE: Ever-body in radioland lay ya hands on tha radio real fast.
We're gonna lay hands on Landis in behalf of Donna's husband,
He fell here a minute ago in tha studio,

Ah, that he'll be alright.
Lay hands on'em [*In a voice of clear and emphatic command; skein prayer begins*]

These examples of the practice of standin'-in suggest a basic characteristic of the healing prayer performance. The "spirit" of the prayer is its improvisatory form, a kind of off-the-cuff spontaneity and resourcefulness in regard to the exigencies of the situation at hand. In this way, whatever elements or resources are at hand are used to help instantiate the healing power of the Holy Ghost. Like a remnant of cloth taken from one context and used to patch the hole worn in a miner's coveralls, the practice of standin'-in recalls Stewart's description of "foolin' with thangs": a creative process whereby disparate or unanticipated elements are combined to form an ensemble that fulfills everyday necessity.[5]

Thus, a healing prayer is precipitated by an accidental occurrence within the space of the radio station. Shortly after the accident, the prayer warriors are organized around the sympathetic substitute (Brother Landis), whose associative chain of homologous elements (hip surgery, use of walker, older male, unsteady on feet, prone to falls, and so on) identifies him as the most efficacious stand-in within the immediately assembled congregation. In this way, the prayer is orchestrated to meet the sudden exigencies of the situation at hand. The hasty, improvised organization of the prayer, its orchestration "on the fly," so to speak, is embodied in the casual yet forthright tone of Sister Dorothy's voice as the microphone registers her informal instructions for specific congregation members to come up and lay hands upon the stand-in.

Further evincing the improvised spontaneity at the root of this practice of prayer, Brother Aldie voices a call for the participation of the distanced members of the listening audience: "Ever-body in radioland lay ya hands on the radio *real fast.*" The end of this instruction, "real fast," is the kind of expression that would be employed in a phrase such as "come and help me fix this gutter real fast," or "let me use your hammer real fast." This expression is used in everyday situations of mending, improvised patching, brief borrowing, and quick fixes that are called for in order to keep everyday actions and objects moving. Combining the sacred power of the Holy Ghost with the creative resourcefulness of the *bricoleur*, the stand-in bridges, if only temporarily, the gap between healing virtue and the painful actualities of everyday life.

These practices of radio prayer in Appalachia bear important resemblances to the techniques of faith healing espoused by Oral Roberts and others during the Charismatic Revival of the late 1940s.[6] The practices of standin'-in and manual imposition upon the radio apparatus are often explicitly referred to by radio preachers in southern Appalachia as "points of contact." This phrase was disseminated on a mass scale through Roberts's popular radio broadcast, *Healing Waters*, which by 1954 was reaching an estimated listening audience of over 100 million.[7] In order to shed light on the particular substitutionary practices of prayer during many live charismatic broadcasts in southern Appalachia, it will be useful to examine the place of similar practices within the broader context of mass faith-healing movements of the mid-twentieth century.

In what is perhaps the most influential treatise on the techniques of charismatic faith healing, *If You Need Healing Do These Things*, Oral Roberts explains "the point of contact," emphasizing that it is "the master key to healing." The point of contact is a crucial element within the broader history of technologically mediated prayer and practices of faith healing, and Roberts's description is worth quoting at length:

> *3. Use a Point of Contact for the Release of Your Faith*
>
> God is the only healer. Doctors perform a good work but they only assist nature while God can actually bring deliverance. The authority of Satan's oppression over human life is in God and in His children. But God is a spirit and sometimes we are confused because he is not directly before us in human body. He does not come into your room as your family physician with medical potions and instruments, you cannot see Him with the human eye, nor can you take a trip to heaven and present your case as you would go to your doctor's office. How then can we reach Him? *By establishing a point of contact.* Faith is the meeting ground between your limited self and your limitless God. A point of contact is given as a means of steadying and helping you to release your faith.[8]

Note how the question of faith is immediately described in terms of the sensory capacities of the "limited self" to register the presence of the divine spirit. This inability to perceive the presence of the spirit with our natural sensory faculties creates a "confusion" within the subject. This disorientation, moreover, seems especially related to the perceptual capacity of vision and its inability to sense the spirit: "You cannot seem Him with the human eye." In this confusing situation of perceptual blindness to the spirit, the "self" must establish a point of contact as a means of "steadying" a subject literally thrown off balance by a lack of visual grounding. The point of contact, therefore, seems to suggest a new way for the limited sensory capacities of the self to register the unseen omnipresence of the spirit. Indeed, Roberts's description of the limited capacities of the "human eye" announces the theme of augmented and extended sensory capacities that will be accessed through the point of contact. Whatever the case may be, this key passage frames the question of faith and divine healing in terms of limited sensory capacities and the possibility of transcending these perceptual inadequacies.

After this initial description of the point of contact, the reader of *If You Need Healing Do These Things* turns the page to see a cartoon illustration of this master key to healing. In this representation of a miraculous cure, the point of contact is the radio apparatus (see fig. 3). The bottom half of the drawing features a sick bedfast patient who reaches out a hand to make contact with the radio receiver. At the top of the panel is Oral Roberts himself, whose discerning right hand of healing power seems drawn toward the artificial sensitivities of the "radio station" microphone. Mediating between these two distanced actions is the divine hand of Christ, outstretched to communicate "healing virtue" into the sick patient. In both parts of the illustration, the artist has attempted to convey the simultaneous voicing of the crucial phrase "only believe" in the space of the *Healing Waters* live studio and the private sphere of the afflicted patient.

In this technological infrastructure of transmission and reception, the cartoon's depiction of the healing hand of Christ embodies the unseen presence of the electromagnetic waves circulating between the microphone and the loudspeaker. After a description of this image of radio healing, the previous passage describing the point of contact now resonates with new interpretive possibilities. This crucial passage is not simply a rumination upon the challenges of perceiving God's spiritual presence but is in fact a veiled commentary on the "confusing" sensory experience of registering the presence of the disembodied voice that has "come into your room." These themes of disembodiment, sensory blindness, or lack of visual grounding and the question of the communicative relation between the limited self and the limitless or unplaceable divinity seem strikingly similar to the basic elements of radio experience described by early theorists of the apparatus such as Arnheim and Adorno. Small wonder, therefore, that Roberts would directly relate the question of faith and the point of contact to the radio apparatus, as the two seemingly discrete instances seem, upon further inspection, to be mutually constitutive. Even under the auspices of a theological description of the challenges of faith, the point of contact can be seen as a particular appearance of the demand of faith in an age of the technological emancipation of the voice from its "body."[9]

Continuing this exploration into the point of contact and its relation to the sensorial capacities to experience faith and the presence of the sacred, the figure of the hand, or manual experience, ironically emerges within the heart of a phenomenon saturated by the disembodied voice. Recall the place of the divine hand in the mediation between patient and healer, as well as the specific forces of attraction between tactile experiences of power (note in the cartoon the representation of force radiating from the right hand of Roberts and at the interface between the patient's left hand and the radio set) and the technological infrastructure of the radio broadcast (microphone/receiver).[10] Other technological infrastructures as well informed Roberts's theologico-technical elaboration of the point of contact. Take, for example, his description of this tactile healing technique from the Evangelical film *Miracles Yesterday, Today, and Forever* (1994):

> The point of contact was given to me in a rather extraordinary experience. When I went to the little church I was pastoring and in the small office fell down and was seeking God as he was leading me into the healing ministry, because I didn't know what to do. I felt the call; but feeling the call and knowing what to do with it are different things. And ah, as I lay there I sought God, and ah, I forgot about time. I have no idea how long I lay there, but pretty soon everything faded away and was just God and me. And finally I heard the Lord's voice say, "From this hour, you'll feel my presence in your right hand. And my presence will enable you to detect if there's a demon present. The presence of God through your hand, will be a point of contact"—and there I was wonderin' what a point of contact was. What was he saying?
>
> So when I got home, I was led to notice that when I wanted the light on I flipped the switch. The power was not in the switch, the switch led to the power plant. But the switch was the connection to the power plant. It was the point of contact. It was where you made contact with the power of electricity in the power plant, that turned on the bulbs, the electric lights. Or if I took the key in my automobile and turned it the motor would turn over; it was the point of contact with the power of the motor. So He said my presence com-

ing into your hand will be a point of contact for you, so you'll feel a connection with me, strong enough for whatever comes against you: for whatever you come against in sin and sickness and disease and demons and fear and the torments of the people. Secondly, he told me it would be a point of contact for the people. When I touched them, I would say, let all the faith you have come out of your heart and go to God, because He's the power. I am a point of contact to you, and usually it works through my right hand into their bodies. They would just loose their faith because they become aware they were connected now to a greater power than Oral Roberts. They were connected to God himself and their faith, then, did the job. It brought the healing power, the supernatural miracle, into their lives.[11]

Through the *charismata* of a divine sensory capacity, the tactile sensitivities of Oral Roberts's right hand were miraculously attuned to become the first "point of contact." Even at its origin, therefore, the point of contact revolves around the theme of divinely augmented sensory capacities that grant tactile access to spiritual presence, both divine and demonic. Through this divine prosthesis, Roberts's right hand is able to "detect" the presence of the illness-causing demons within the sick patient.[12] As if he had yet to fully emerge from the trance state in which he heard the oneiric voice instructing him in his new sacred sensibilities, when Roberts returned home he was "led to notice" that when he wanted the light on he flipped the switch.[13] Through an automatic gesture directed by the spirit, Roberts is given a divine revelation, or desublimation, of an everyday gesture that enlivens a massive hidden and unremarked infrastructure. Through a kind of somnambulistic movement, the hand that operates the apparatus (switching the machine on, regulating the dials or knobs, as examples) is drawn to the light switch under the pull of some ineluctable force of attraction. In what could be seen as a critical parody or inversion, the instrumental gesture of "flipping the switch" not only reveals the repressed infrastructures underneath, but also suggests the way in which technological infrastructures are always organizing the perceptual and interactive capacities of the so-called user. This everyday instrumental gesture, now divinely guided like the jerky movements of a healing puppet, desublimates the vast machine ensemble of a hidden electrical infrastructure:

The power was not in the switch, the switch led to the power plant. But the switch was the connection to the power plant. It was the point of contact. It was where you made contact with the power of electricity in the power plant, that turned on the bulbs, the electric lights.

This divine revelation through the everyday manual gesture of flipping the switch also invokes a history of the organization of the modern bourgeois interior with forces and machine ensembles exterior to it. The sudden illumination of the electric bulb recalls the anxieties of the emergence of industrial gas light and its accompanying infrastructures of pipelines and gas preparation plants in the nineteenth century.[14]

This experience of doubling or manifold processes collapsed into one small gesture of the hand, the flick of the switch, the strike of the match, the push of the button, the pull of the trigger, also suggests an anxiety with regard to not only the traumatic shock of immediacy but also the force of automaticity at work behind everyday life.[15] Once again, Roberts's account of the formation of the point of contact clearly suggests that modern technological infrastructures have had an important role in informing and organizing this crucial theologico-technical practice within the global history of Charismatic faith healing.

This metaphor of the electric current is also evoked by Roberts to emphasize the way in which the tactile point of contact is an actual *physical conduit* for the transmission of efficacious healing power. As a specific technique of divine communication, the point of contact signals not only the kinesthetic "turning loose," "unleashing," and "releasing" of faith, but a concomitant surge of healing virtue or power into the body of the sick patient.[16] This surge of divine force is often compared to electrical phenomena, as in the popular description of the woman with the "issue of blood" from the book of Mark (5:25–34) invoked by many prominent twentieth-century Charismatic faith healers:

> The crowd moved back for her and she plunged on through and then . . . there He was. She had made it through to Him. She bent low, reached out a trembling hand and touched the hem of His garment. *It was like touching a live wire*, the mighty healing virtue of Christ surged out of Him into her. It went all though her, into every fibre of her being and spent its force against her affliction.

Continuing with the electrical metaphor several pages later, Roberts elaborates:

6. She Made Contact with Healing Power

"*She felt in her body that she was healed of that plague.*" Contact was made between her faith and the healing virtue resident in Jesus Christ. *Like plugging in an electrical connection*, making contact with the distant *powerhouse*, faith that is released—put into action—makes contact with God's power and releases the healing power. This power healed the woman of a literal disease.

This experience of an actual flow of energy through the body is an important aspect of the point of contact: "You tap the source of healing power causing it to *flow* into your body where it will destroy disease and affliction."[17] With its emphasis on the physical, palpable transmission of force through actual tactile contact, the point of contact provides a classic instance of the efficacious transmission of force, communication at a distance, and contagiousness of the sacred that occupied an important place in the early ethnological literature. And here, E. B. Tylor's interest in the spiritualist telegraph and Oral Robert's use of the ecstatic potential of the radio press close.[18] Although this force of attraction between ethnographic description and theorization of the contagiousness of the sacred and modern technology would perhaps take us too far afield from the immediate study, it is important to note the undercurrent circulating between the two seemingly discrete phenomena.

At a basic level, therefore, the point of contact is a tactile experience that emerges between, or at the interface of, the sensory capacities of the subject and an exterior object. And although "embodied" on an elementary level, this sensation gains a particular force of experiential intensity precisely because it cannot be located squarely within the perceptual boundaries of the subject, but it seems to emerge at this strange interface *between* the subject and object, the sacred and the everyday.

This efficacious unleashing of faith through the point of contact also invokes a crucial temporal dimension in the practice of divine healing. In his elaborations of this tactile practice of faith, Roberts often refers to the way that "the point of contact *sets the time*" for healing. Another passage from this curative instruction manual, *If You Need Healing Do These Things*, will help elaborate the key temporal dimension of the practice.

4. Turn Your Faith Loose—Now!

So many times I have seen the need of saying, "Believe now and you may have deliverance." On the other hand, many captives, when asked when they expect to get healed, will reply, "Oh, when God gets ready, I am." God has been ready all the time; it's your move next. Others reply, "I'm expecting God to heal me anytime." On the face of that statement is a certain amount of reasonable value, but I remind you that it is not scriptural. *There is a definite time when faith works and unless you set a time*, it is doubtful if you will ever be delivered. . . . God will respond and work in our behalf when we believe and *set the time*.

In and through a particular experience of tactile sensation, the point of contact performs a temporal actualization of faith, ritually instantiating faith in the embodied "here and now." A ritualized gesture of tactility and a particular attention to time or temporal awareness are thus intimately related.

This actualization of faith through a self-conscious action or human volition has a long history within American practices of "faith curing." In her work on the history of faith healing, historian Heather Curtis demonstrates that the curative rhetoric of "acting faith," or the performative realization of human agency within practices of divine healing, emerged in the 1870s and coincided with changing conceptions of human suffering and the force of the miraculous.[19]

Although the point of contact certainly draws from earlier historical precedents and practices of "acting faith," the specific temporal and tactile registers thematized by this healing technique, as we have seen, suggest specific relations with modern technology. Another specific instance of the point of contact will help flesh out this threefold relationship between tactility, temporality, and technology. Recall once again the preeminent point of contact through which millions of Americans experienced the tactile sensation of faith:

> Many lay their hands on their radio as a point of contact during our Healing Waters broadcast. Through this means they release their faith and through faith they are healed during the "prayer-time"' of the broadcast.[20]

How are we to understand this particular temporal awareness that is actualized through tactile contact with the radio apparatus during the most important "prayer-time" of the *Healing Waters* radio program? Likewise, how does this sacred experience of temporality relate to the actual physical gesture of tactile "steadying" that Roberts first uses as a term to describe the point of contact? This need for the gesture of tactility within both the experience of radio audition specifically, and the challenge of faith more generally, emerged from a spectral presence that could not be discerned by the natural perceptual capacities. The technique of the point of contact "steadied" a bodily awareness disoriented and thrown off-kilter by a disembodied voice. Seen in terms of the specificities of this disembodied radio voice, the point of contact steadied the listener who was perceptually separated from the physical immediacy and visual presence of the body of the speaker. And yet it is precisely in this moment when the "confused" or disoriented self attempts to buttress or supplement this sensory disjuncture by steadying the body, which has technically realized the ideal sacred bodily attitude of prayer—with eyes closed—that the subject experiences the crucial tactile-temporal awareness of the "setting" of the faith-time. Ironically, however, this experience of "steadying" produces the most compelling sensations of immediacy and temporal actuality *precisely in the moment when tactile sensation registers a rupture or doubling between the resonating immediacy of the radio loudspeaker and an awareness of forces that remain hidden behind the immediate sound of the radio voice.* Thus, the crucial moment of ritual temporality performs this rupture between perceptual immediacy and a vague awareness that there are forces at work outside the experiential frames of audile-tactile sensation through the radio apparatus.

By focusing in upon the performance of divine communication during the crucial prayer time of the radio broadcast and allowing the patient to experience the prayer in a different sensory register—a hand for an ear— the legerdemain of radio tactility marks the curious ritual coincidence of a distanced patient and absent healer. In this way, the point of contact is a wonderful example of what Marcel Mauss and Henri Hubert called "the moment of prestidigitation."[21] In a moment of technological artifice and a manual gesture, the distance between the patient and healer is collapsed in a release of healing efficacy.

The prayer time of the *Healing Waters* broadcast and the particular techniques of radio tactility involved can be seen as yet another instance of the performative manipulation of the disembodied voice for the purposes of healing. Like the shamanic throwing of the voice or the curative efficacy unleashed through the ventriloquism of the healing puppet, the mouth of the radio loudspeaker allows the sick patient to experience the prayer in an unanticipated way. Just as ritual performance often conjures grotesquely enlarged images and narrative techniques of "slow motion," opening a space of anti-temporality that seems to characterize many ritual forms, the radio loudspeaker amplifies the visceral sound of the mouth at prayer to monstrous and disconcerting proportions.[22] Likewise, the sensitive capacities of the studio microphone grant access to new forms of perceptual awareness and experience by sounding the unheard resonances of the acoustic unconscious. Even more than this, the ritual technique of radio tactility allows the patient to experience the sonic resonance of prayer through the hand, and thus miraculously substitutes a hand for an ear.[23] The point of contact, therefore, is the moment of divine communication when, through a manual gesture and a technological artifice, the experiential gap between the "limited self" and the "limitless God" is filled with a resonance outside the frames of everyday temporal awareness.

Although the divine gift of the point of contact was given to Oral Roberts to help dispel the "confusion" surrounding the practice of healing and the exercise of faith, a close reading of *If You Need Healing Do These Things* suggests an unanticipated or unacknowledged locus of faith itself. To be sure, everyday understandings and kinesthetic terms such as "turn loose" and "unleash" and "release" locate the standing reserve or potentially active faith within the interior of the subject. This religious subject, in turn, is able to exteriorize this standing reserve of faith through embodied techniques of prayer and performances of belief.

Yet the very heading that introduces this key theologico-technical performance suggests an unplaceability at the heart of this practice: "USE A POINT OF CONTACT FOR THE RELEASE OF YOUR FAITH."[24] This unanticipated locus of faith is also suggested further in that key section: "How then can we reach him? By establishing a point of contact. Faith is the meeting ground *between* your limited self and your limitless God." This passage, along with the examples invoked to explain and elaborate the point of contact, ironically point to the radical exteriority of faith itself. The potential standing reserve is not located within the interior of the religious subject but circulates outside the "believer," who through proper bodily attitude and techniques of manual gesture must orient him or herself to this exterior potentiality. Faith therefore makes its appearance in this precarious space of alterity *between* the "limited self" and the "limitless God." Faith emerges and circulates at this indeterminate "point" or interface between the subject and the divine. In this way, Roberts's highly influential phrase "point of contact" not only resonates with classic ethnological descriptions of the emergence of the compelling force of belief in and through the exchange of physical objects, but seems to press close to the phenomenological considerations of touch described by Maurice Merleau-Ponty and Jean Luc Nancy.[25]

Although crucial moments in the articulation of the point of contact suggest the exteriorities of faith, the practice of belief is quickly recuperated to the interior of the religious subject through the rhetoric of self-conscious action and individual agency to "declare your healing," "write your ticket with God," "set the time," and so on. Thus, the point of contact, that space between the sacred and the everyday, marks the oscillation at the heart of charismatic practices of faith healing between the agency of an autonomous subject and the precarious forces of automaticity and exteriority.

Though the point of contact demonstrates a particular force of attraction to the radio apparatus, Roberts claimed, as we have seen, that the originary point of contact was located in his right hand. The efficacious transmission of healing power through the practice of laying on of hands, of course, has been a crucial technique throughout the history of Christian healing practices. On the surface of things, therefore, it would seem that Roberts was merely continuing a long-standing tradition of curing through manual contact. Roberts's manual technique of the point of contact, however, thematized and described the older practice of manual imposition with new, *specifically modern, resonances*. More than fifty years before several academic disciplines would identify the theme of "religious sensations" as a particularly fruitful ground for studying religious experience and subjectivity, Oral Roberts was describing in vivid detail the particular tactile senses of "discernment" that enabled him to "detect" sickness and other spectral presences:

> God has not left Himself without human instrumentalities to deliver this generation. I have heard His voice: first that I was to be healed, next, that I was to bring healing to the sick and demon-possessed, and that His healing power would be felt in my right hand for all who would believe. It is happening just as the Lord said. I seldom feel anything in my left hand, but through my right hand I feel the healing virtue of the Son of God. Thousands have witnessed this power as it surged through every fiber of their being. God uses this human agency as a point of contact. The time is set when I lay my right hand upon the captive and adjure the afflictions to come out of him in the name of the Master, Jesus Christ of Nazareth. I feel the pressure of the disease rising to meet my right hand, but then as God's healing

virtue surges into the person, this pressure is relieved and deliverance is wrought.[26]

Not only the site for the efficacious transmission of healing virtue, Roberts's healing hand thematizes the place of sensory capacities and perceptual experience in the performance of healing. Through a preternatural sensory capacity, the great healer is able to "detect the presence" of that which is normally unregistered by the naked or unarmed perceptual faculties. The preeminent point of contact is a sacred sensory augmentation or extension, a kind of divine prosthesis appended to the body of the healer, that allows him to register through the tactile surface the presence of that which resides outside the enframement of the natural sensory capacities: "With a keen sense of discernment the Spirit enables him to detect the presence of demons, to ascertain their number and names. It is amazing to see people set free from demon spirits."

The point of contact marks a new technologically organized and imprinted interpretation of the influential passage from 1 Corinthians:

It was Paul who describes the nine gifts of the spirit in 1 Corinthians 12, including the gift of healing, the gift of miracles and the gift of discerning of spirits. These three gifts are given to certain believers, principally ministers, for the direct purpose of healing the sick and casing out demons. These gifts are additional stimulants to faith and will bring deliverance when other means fail.[27]

The *charism*, or divine gift of "discerning of spirits," is articulated by Roberts on the level of sensory perceptions, inflecting the older curative practice of the laying on of hands with notions of preternatural sensory extensions and amplified tactile capacities. Once again, however, the discerning right hand of the healer seems drawn, as if by some unseen force, to the radio apparatus. Thus, both the hand of demonic discernment and the radio receiver "detect" spectral presences, which remain imperceptible to the everyday sensory faculties. The radio extends the "natural" capacities of the ear, while the Holy Ghost augments the tactile sensitivities of the hand.

The Prosthesis of Prayer; or, The Apparatus of Belief

As the preeminent point of contact in the explosive early years of the Charismatic Revival, the radio became a central *apparatus of belief*. Just as Oral Roberts required a divine tactile enhancement to sense the presence of the spirit, the particular sensory experience generated through the radio apparatus helped to produce an appearance of belief, which was registered by the listener. The special effect of belief generated through the radio apparatus gave the listener a particular sensory experience of doubled immediacy, in terms of both a praying voice that was immediate yet distant, and the sensory disjuncture between the sound of the radio voice and warm vibrations registered through the hand. By enframing the experience of the disembodied voice and tactile sensation in particular ways, the special effect of radio produced a compelling sensation of immediacy, precisely in the moment that it suggested a force just behind or beyond perceptual access, which the listener was not quite able to fully perceive yet which was somehow registered or communicated by the radio apparatus itself. As an apparatus of belief, the radio produces on the level of sensory disjuncture between the capacities of touch and hearing what older modes of belief enlivened though the physical exchange and circulation of objects. Belief in an age of the faith apparatus is no longer temporally articulated through a system of deferral, but instead through the thematization of sensory disjuncture and the concomitant special effect. Belief moves and has its being beyond the religious subject, and thus the very possibility of sensory access and recognition of "faith" is given in and through the extended sensory prosthesis of the radio apparatus.[28]

This theme of sensory extension and the disconcerting awareness of a presence that persists just outside the perceptual frame recalls Freud's account of the emergence of faith, in the essay "Animism, Magic, and the Omnipotence of Thought."[29] In this description of the shift from magic to religion, Freud articulates how the automatic self-enclosed system of magical thinking became plagued or threatened by a disjuncture between our immediate perceptual experience and a recognition of latent memory surfaces capable of recalling the dead after immediate perception of them had ceased. The radio apparatus, as well, produces this rupture between perceptual immediacy and external storage and transmission capacities, and it is for this reason that early radio theorists such as Adorno are constantly invoking themes of spectrality, "spooks," atavistic residues, and divinatory arts to think about the phenomenological experience of the radio voice.[30]

Oral Roberts, therefore, should be taken quite literally when he claims that making tactile contact with the radio apparatus during healing prayer "unleashes" faith. Faith emerges not from within an interiority of a religious subject, but at the interface between the body's perceptual limit and its sensory prostheses. Once again, Freud makes the prescient association when writing in 1929 that there is an intimate force of attraction between an experience of the divine and mankind's prosthetic extensions. It is not so much that we have become prosthetic gods, but that the performative embodiment of belief has been exteriorized into the operations of machines. In this way, the increasing technological reproduction of the voice and the ever-expanding surface of exteriorized memory processors will only continue to set up the subject for new calls of faith and the threatening presence of that which persists just beyond the frame of perception, mechanical or otherwise.

The "Laying On of Hands" in the Age of Mechanical Reproduction

This section traces the crucial shift in charismatic prayer and associated healing-line techniques through Walter Benjamin's classic essay "The Work of Art in the Age of Mechanical Reproduction." Through a description of this transformation in curative performance, I explore the relation between the manual charismatic healing technique of the "laying on of hands" and what Benjamin terms "tactile appropriation" in an age of mechanical reproduction.

Tracing the history of pictorial reproduction techniques early in the essay, Benjamin announces that the hand, through a gradual process of technical abstraction, had finally become "freed" from the most important artistic functions in the process of pictorial reproduction by the lens of the camera. In this way, the sheer representational speed of the machine seemed to sever the hand from the body, taking its once-autonomous technique into its own sphere of repetitive machinations. Yet, in a way that resonates deeply with Freud's description of the logic of the uncanny, the hand, this severed, abstracted, and surmounted body part, seems to reemerge at the conclusion of Benjamin's essay with an unanticipated new force.[31] Like the famous accounts of the hand that obstinately and automatically maintains its grip on the throttle of the machine even in death, the abstracted hand of the machine reasserts its force once again, albeit in a strange and unanticipated new form.

In order to flesh out this history of manual abstraction, a history of technique whose intimate other is the collapse of traditional spaces of consecration that once isolated the auratic power of the sacred, Benjamin evokes the difference in therapeutic technique between the magician and the surgeon. In a descriptive move that signals a fascinating moment of coincidence between the preeminent charismatic healing technique and the curative hand of the magician, Benjamin twice invokes "the laying on of hands."[32] Here again, the tension between a literal and symbolic distancing and a compulsion to draw close constitute the difference in therapeutic technique. The touch of the magician maintains and reasserts symbolic hierarchies and power precisely in the moment of tactile contact, while the hand of the surgeon transgresses this traditional distance, penetrating beyond the dermal surface of the body. What is crucial here, however, is not so much a literal penetration of the hand from the surface into the interior of the body, but the way the very notion of the "operations" of the surgeon no longer approach the patient face to face, "man to man." In this penetrating moment of operation, the hand of the surgeon literally touches the body *through an optical apparatus* such as the laryngoscope.[33] In and through the optical device, the hand of the surgeon takes on a new magical resonance, performing "technical sleights of hand" and other adroit "acrobatic tricks."[34]

Through this new kind of "operational" therapy, the traditional attentive structure of eyes focused on hands, synchronized and working in unison, is broken, abstracted by the mechanical eye of the throat scope. The hand, therefore, in a kind of somnambulism, seems to be moving on its own, habitually, while the attention of the surgeon is oriented toward the optical image on the screen. In a very literal way, he thus makes contact with his hands through the aid of a prosthetic eye that is looking into the body for him.[35] Through the use of a very literal and concrete detail—the image of the surgeon looking upon a screen as his hands perform a seemingly disjointed operation—Benjamin begins to articulate a new mode of haptic attention that signals the specifically modern rupture between the immediate coordination of hand and eye.

Just as new orientations and possibilities of sensory awareness were opened through the mechanical eye of the optical device, mechanical devices of transmission and reception also wrought transformations in the ritual of healing prayer. In several significant ways, these pervasive shifts in the performance of prayer were portended within the technical environments of the charismatic healing revival tent. Part of the gospel infrastructure of Oral Roberts's Tent Cathedral, which seated over 9,000 and at the time (1949) was the largest gospel tent in the world, included a public address system with loudspeakers mounted on support beams throughout the tent. This system of voice amplification allowed the charismatic sermons and healing prayer of the revivalist to resound throughout the tent and beyond. Many eyewitnesses to the healing revivals, moreover, commented on Roberts's prowess and intimacy with the microphone, which he "clutched as if it were a broom sweeping sin from the tent."[36]

The key performative moment underneath these amplified revival tents was the miraculous healing of the sick through techniques of prayer and ritual gesture. One by one, each patient approached the elevated dais to receive the "laying on" of Roberts's hands and the accompanying prayer. As Roberts prayed out loud into the large steel microphone that stood between him and the patient, he often gripped the microphone stand with his left hand while pressing the palm of his right hand of spiritual discernment forcefully upon the forehead of the patient. In this moment of tactile contact between patient and healer, the sensitive capacities of the microphone clearly registered the performative modulations of the healer's voice: "Oh God! Oh, it's coming out now. Father, I ask for this miracle, I ask that . . . the Lord . . . HEAL!"[37] The phrase "Oh, it's coming out now" was spoken in a soft, almost matter-of-fact conversational tone. The following line was broken up and spoken as if to reflect the laborious effort expended by the healer in the moment of casting out the demon of infirmity. Finally, the efficacious word "HEAL!" was forcefully enunciated into the microphone. In this way, Roberts actively utilized the capacities of the public announcement system to help "effect" the force of the miraculous.

In what could be considered an intermediate theurgical form within the amplified space of the revival tent, the healing prayer had already undergone a kind of doubling or displacement, not only in terms of a message that was believed to resonate in the space of a divine elsewhere, but the displaced voice of the healer simultaneously resonated from individual loudspeakers located throughout the massive cloth architecture of the revival tent. In this way, the moment of enunciation of the healer signaled a doubled displacement, both within the immediate space of the tent and in the sacred beyond of a divine elsewhere. Through the system of voice amplification, moreover, the mouth of the evangelist was miraculously supplemented, resonating powerfully from above as if it were the voice of God.[38]

In this way, *both* the prayer and the crucial moment of laying on of hands were significantly augmented by the technology of voice amplification. The insinuation of the microphone/loudspeaker system into the traditional patient/healer relationship seemed to announce or foreshadow the curious reversal of this performative healing technique in an age of radio.[39] Yet, even in this intermediary or transitional form in the mediated environment of the tent, traditional forces of symbolic distance are maintained and reproduced through the healing technique of the prayer line. Recall how the patient is *standing below* Roberts, who is *seated above* upon the stage. On a basic level, therefore, the physical orientation of the patient-healer dyad reinforces symbolic hierarchies of high/low, sitting/standing, speaking/silent, and so on. Additionally, it is Roberts who touches the patient; he controls the healing agency and therapeutic force in this curative encounter. The further abstraction of the voice and hand from this ritual form would initiate a reversal that could be considered a profanation upon the more orthodox curative gestures.

Recalling Benjamin's well-known phrase "mechanical reproduction emancipated the work of art from its parasitical dependence on ritual," we could slightly reformulate this quote to describe the ritual technique of healing prayer mediated through the radio apparatus. This translation would read: "Ritual presence maintains a parasitical dependence upon mechanical reproduction." In so doing, the charismatic healing technique of "laying on of hands" in an age of mechanical reproduction presses close to the hand of the surgeon as described by Benjamin. Just as the technique of the surgeon's hand is mediated through the optical device, the prosthetic hand of the healer is only able to discern the body of the patient through the operations of the radio apparatus. In both cases, the "normal" sensory coordination and *habilité* of the hand has been supplemented by a sensory prosthesis or extension. The collapse of symbolic distance from what Benjamin calls the "face-to-face" relationship between surgeon and patient also characterizes the healing technique of tactile contact with the radio receiver during the performance of healing prayer. More specifically, it is no longer the healer who reaches out to touch the patient and thus reassert his symbolic force, but the sick patient who reaches out to make tactile contact with the resonating mechanical mouth supplementing the voice of the healer. More than this, however, the new orientations structured by the radio apparatus between patient and healer could be considered a transgressive reversal or inversion of earlier modes of efficacious healing gestures.

Thus, in an age in which the skin of the healer and its concomitant haptic gifts of spiritual discernment are extended by the prosthesis of radio, it is not the healer who touches the patient, but the patient who touches the healer. The tactile experience of the patient changes the traditional symbolic boundaries that once characterized the ritual milieu and associated curative techniques. Collapsing distance through a new grasp, the patient is also able to sense the healing resonances of divine communication in an unanticipated way. Through this profanation of *mediated immediacy* organized by the radio apparatus, a new sensation of devotional awareness is unleashed by the sensitivities of the microphone and the amplifications of the loudspeaker: the *acoustic unconscious*.

The force of attraction between the laying on of hands, tactile sensations, and the radio apparatus suggests the revelatory power of an "acoustic unconscious" operating at the heart of the phenomenon of radio healing. Though Benjamin's famous essay makes no explicit formulation of the notion of "acoustic unconscious," sonic themes resound throughout his text: multiple ruminations on sound film, descriptions of religious sounds resounding in the parlor, disembodied ears, prayer, and so on. Moreover, at that crucial moment in the text when Benjamin introduces the theme of tactility and distraction, he directly invokes the percussive shocks of Dadaist sound poems:

> From an alluring appearance or persuasive structure of sound
> the work of art of the Dadaists became an instrument of ballistics.
> It hit the spectator like a bullet, it happened to him, thus acquiring a tactile quality.

It is fascinating that he does not explicitly formulate a concept of the acoustic unconscious, especially given that at pivotal moments in his analysis it seems to be on the tip of his tongue.[40]

Just as the lens of the camera is able to isolate and access elements of visual phenomena inaccessible or imperceptible to the naked eye, the microphone and loudspeaker, technologies for the reproduction and amplification of sound, reveal aspects of sonic worlds that resound and echo underneath the "natural" sensory capacities of the unaided ear. Thus, early commentators on the microphone were fascinated by the account of the fly that landed upon the microphone's surface: through the system of electrical amplification, a sound which had never before been registered by human ears suddenly resounded as if it were the feet of an elephant.[41] Just as the photographic lens opened a world of vision upon new structural formations otherwise hidden in the "optical unconscious," the microphone made it literally possible to hear the "slip of the tongue" described by Freud in *The Psychopathology of Everyday Life* (1901). While technologies of voice recording enabled analysis on the symbolic level, the microphone extended the ear to perceptions of the visceral, corporeal, and elemental materialities of vocalization and language. Just as the camera lens isolated bodily movements so that even the most subtle muscular contraction could be isolated and analyzed, the microphone gave perceptual access to the saliva-soaked clacks, smacks, and watery undulations of the tongue itself as it slid and "slipped" among the teeth and moist oral cavity.

If the microphone reveals new structural formations resonating underneath the soundscapes of everyday life, what are the implications of this new prosthetic mode of hearing for the theurgical technique of prayer? Or, to pose this question another way, do the "faithful" experience the ritual of divine communication differently in an age of mechanical reproduction? Prayer and techniques of the body such as pious postures and sacred manual gestures seem always to be indissociably related. In this way, a material history of Christian devotional practices suggests a panoply of techniques for the material instantiation of the fleeting voice of prayer. In turn, these materializations of prayer always recall the disembodied voice through haptic sensations registered through the hand. Prayer beads, cloths, and leather phylacteries, for example, can be seen as translations of the aural performance of prayer into haptic devotional sensations.[42] Materialized prayers thus render the fleeting voice palpable and "record" its efficacy upon the surface of the body through the haptic sensations of rubbing, wrapping, pressure, fingering.

In terms of the relation between haptic sensation and the devotional object, mechanical reproduction initiates a new era in the material history of prayer. Through the amplified artificial mouth of the radio loudspeaker, the prayer is translated or decomposed into warm vibrations that can be haptically experienced through the hand as it touches the apparatus in a moment of divine communication. In this moment of healing prayer, as the radio trembles with power, the sick patient, through the operation of the radio apparatus, touches the healer-in-prayer like a deaf person feeling sound while touching the throat of the speaker. In this curious reversal, the patient makes transgressive contact with the prosthetically extended vocal organs through the operation of the radio apparatus. Just as the surgeon touches the patient through the mediation of an optical device, healing prayer in an age of mechanical reproduction is characterized by a new tactile relation between patient and healer. Accessing new haptic modes of devotional attention, radio prayer initiated a profound shift in the meaning and performance of faith and divine communication within the Christian tradition. The practice of healing radio tactility resonates with my reformulation of Benjamin's famous phrase: ritual presence maintains a parasitical dependence upon mechanical reproduction.

Let us return to the specificities of the practice of standin'-in within the context of charismatic communities in southern Appalachia. The sympathetic resonances between distant bodies that facilitate the communication of healing efficacy during the performance of intercessory prayer in Appalachia are organized and informed in intimate ways by the structure of the radio apparatus itself. More specifically, the practice of standin'-in cannot be abstracted from the specific experiences of technological communication at a distance and the longing to materialize the disembodied voice. This ritual technique of substitution mimics the materiality of transmission by inserting a physical body to help "receive" and "transmit" healing power. Just as the artificial sensitivities of the microphone are a crucial technical component in the material infrastructure of the radio broadcast, the sympathetic resonances embodied in the stand-in facilitate the communication of healing virtue from that sacred elsewhere to the abstracted body of the sick patient. The stand-in thus embodies a forgotten potentiality of the radio set: to both receive and transmit.[43]

The practice of standin'-in outside the space of the live studio marks the moment when the technological organization of prayer and techniques of divine communication insinuate themselves into other circumstances and environments of charismatic worship. Just like a voice transmitted over the airways, the practice of standin'-in leaves the confines of the live studio of the radio station and begins to resonate elsewhere, informing worship practices seemingly outside the specific media environments of radio transmission and reception.

During the practice of baptism in a river near the radio station in Richlands, Virginia, for example, I have seen participants being immersed in the chilly waters as stand-ins for other members of the congregation who were either physically absent or too sick or immobile to actually enter into the river. Within the space of actual churches and during prayer meetings in private homes as well, stand-ins are often employed to help "get a prayer through" on behalf of an absent family member, friend, or congregation member. Even within these worship spaces seemingly unorganized by forces of technological mediation, therefore, the experience and understanding of the practice of standin'-in can never be fully abstracted from the structure of the radio apparatus. As the radio broadcast comes to a close and the "altar call" is importunately voiced into the live studio microphone, the phrase "The Lord is a'comin' soon, just as sure as I'm a'standin' here" is often invoked to reinforce the urgent immediacy of the need for repentance and salvation. Yet, as this phrase is translated through the mouth of the radio loudspeaker, the theme of bodily presence and immediacy takes on new displaced and doubled resonances. Just like the prosthetic replacement of a bodily organ, the theurgical practice of standin'-in marks that moment when bodily capacities of sensation and awareness are extended beyond the "natural" boundaries. It is in and through this extended embodiment that the efficacious power of the Holy Ghost makes its appearance.

Altar Call
If You Ain't Blas-ah-phemed the Holy Ghost

EACH SUNDAY before the close of the *Jackson Memorial Hour* broadcast, a member of the congregation approaches the microphone to deliver the "altar call" to the listeners out in radioland. Both in the studio and out in that diffuse space of audition, "time is a'windin' up," and thus commences a call for the "sinners, backsliders, and the lost and undone" to repent and ask the Lord for forgiveness. This urgent plea to "get your sins under the blood," "get it fixed up," "get prayed-up," and "get ready ta go Home," is voiced into the studio microphone. Just as the clarion blast of Gabriel's trumpet is invoked to describe the commencement of the Second Coming that is "nigh at the door," the congregant giving the altar call casts an occasional furtive glance at the naked light bulb protruding from the wall that signals that the call for salvation is being communicated on-air. Time, after all, in both the everyday and the eschatological sense, is a'windin' up.

During the altar call, the all-encompassing potential for Christ's forgiveness, "no matter how far down in tha pit of sin you've gone," is broadcast to all the "lost" out in radioland. Yet this urgent plea for repentance and salvation "before it's ever-lastin' too late" is always tempered or qualified by an ominous exclusionary clause: "The Lord will forgive you no matter what ya done; as long as you ain't *blas-ah-phemed* the Holy Ghost." Although always invoked in passing during the altar call, this qualifying phrase is never elaborated or expounded upon and remains a vaguely ominous potential for breakdown even within Christ's seemingly all-encompassing power of redemption. Although I have never heard an exegesis of Holy Ghost blasphemy articulated during the altar call, during which this exclusionary clause is inevitably invoked, this passage from the book of Matthew seems to connote the act of attributing the miraculous workings of the Apostles to forces other than the Holy Ghost. In other words, to blaspheme the Holy Ghost, like the Pharisees who attributed the power to cast out demons and heal the sick to Beelzebub, would be to attribute the efficacious force of the miraculous to something outside or exterior to the operation of the Holy Ghost.

Upon hearing this clause of exclusion during the altar call, I am always struck by the way this exceptional transgression poses specific challenges to the practice of ethnographic interpretation. Indeed, it is precisely an ethnographic interpretation which relegates the presence of the Holy Ghost merely to the warm vibrations of a radio loudspeaker or the stark materiality of a devotional object that could be considered vulgar or blasphemous. Like the percussive sound of the bone as it suddenly collides with another object, the resonances of the Holy Ghost can never be located within a stable relation between the subject and the object, but instead in that sudden unleashing of an excessive presence when the subject is intertwined or interfaced with the object. The question of the presence and efficacious healing power of the Holy Ghost, therefore, is a question of subjectivity and the prosthetic extensions that allow this subject to sense a world. Like a mended bone that has the capacity to prefigure climactic events and accidental phenomena, or sense the presence of the unseen, the Holy Ghost appears in that strange space where human perceptual faculties are organized and extended by artificial organs of sensation, mnemonic devices, and materialized devotions. Until that day when the stones themselves cry out, the unremarked extensions and augmentations of the subject will continue to voice the calling of an excessive presence. The Holy Ghost resounds in that point of indistinction between subject and object, and it is through a performative evocation of this point that the healing *par* is unleashed into the spaces of the everyday.

Notes

Introduction

1. Stewart, *A Space on the Side of the Road*.
2. In what was to be his "great work," Marcel Mauss defines prayer as "a religious rite which is oral and bears directly on the sacred." Much of my theoretical insight into the history and nature of prayer is taken from Mauss's unfinished dissertation, originally published in limited print in 1909 but subsequently printed in an English translation in 2003. However, my work departs from Mauss's in considering the way that the oral performance of divine communication can never be fully abstracted from the materialities of the worship space. Mauss, *On Prayer*, 57.
3. The phrase "materialities of divine communication" derives from the work of several "post-Marxist" scholars in the field of literary studies, especially that of Hans Gumbrecht. See, for example, Gumbrecht and Pfeiffer, *Materialities of Communication*; and Gumbrecht, *Production of Presence*.
4. For an elaboration of the "sensational form," see Meyer, "Religious Sensations"; and Meyer, *Aesthetic Formations*. On the question of sensory regimes and religious experience, see also the influential work of Charles Hirschkind. Hirschkind, *The Ethical Soundscape*. Of course, Meyer has also been at the forefront of a resurgence of anthropological interest in devotional objects that continues to gain momentum. For an introduction to the "material turn" in anthropology and the social sciences, see, among many others, the opening sections of Houtman and Meyer, *Things*; and Morgan, *Religion and Material Culture*.
5. On the question of the "interfacing" of religion and media, also described as a structural intimacy between the "miracle and the special effect," see the work of Hent de Vries. See de Vries, *Religion and Media*.
6. "Obviously there are two subjective states of experience involved in these facts. And between the dreams of one and the desires of the other there is a discordant factor. Apart from the sleight of hand [*tour de passe-passe*] at the end, the magician makes no effort to make his ideas coincide with the ideas and needs of his client. These two very intense individual states coincide only at the moment of the conjuring trick [*a la moment de la prestidigitation*]. At this unique moment a genuine psychological experience takes place." Mauss, *A General Theory of Magic*, 152. Given that the crucial moment of curative efficacy was forged through the legerdemains of a specific type of technique, it comes as no surprise that Mauss and Hubert conclude their general theory with a rumination on modern industrial techniques. By struggling with the relation between the experience of magical techniques and the automatic efficacy of

specifically industrial techniques, these authors prefigure the contemporary debates on the "interfacing" of transcendence and tele-technology in crucial ways. For another analysis on this key moment, see Crapanzano, "The Moment of Prestidigitation," 102.

7. Boas, "I Desired to Learn the Ways of the Shaman," in *The Religion of the Kwakiutl*; Lévi-Strauss, "The Sorcerer and His Magic," in *Structural Anthropology*; Taussig, "Viscerality, Faith, and Skepticism."

8. I am thinking here especially of James Randi, whose work *The Faith Healers* (1987) gained wide public recognition and rekindled the debate on the place of faith healing in American popular culture. Following a long line of Enlightenment performances that demystified or disenchanted earlier forms of magic and "credulity" with new technologies and methods of science, Randi used a radio scanner to reveal that the famous faith healer Peter Popoff was receiving his divine "words of knowledge" through a hidden earpiece that received secret radio messages from his wife hidden backstage. Randi's account belies a deeper question as to the experiential efficacy of the performance of faith precisely in the face of the tricks of technological artifice. Given the forces of attraction between faith healing and the technologically mediated voice that I trace in this work, it is no surprise that Popoff chose a wireless earpiece to help facilitate his own healing performance. Signaling a departure from accounts such as these, my research sees the forces of doubt, suspicion, and technological artifice as crucial components to a phenomenology of faith in an age of mechanical reproduction. Incidentally, even after James Randi's technical revelations, Popoff continues to bring in millions of dollars a year for his healing ministry. See Randi, *The Faith Healers*.

9. Thomas Csordas's work on embodiment, somatic modes of awareness, and religious sensations has also been useful throughout my research. However, for all the phenomenological resonances of Csordas's work, the major trajectory of his argument seems beholden to an interiority that resists an engagement with the way objects and technologies exterior to the subject allow for the emergence of particular "somatic modes of attention." I find Csordas's emphasis on the way charismatic techniques enframe a particular experience of the "inertia" or "heft" of the bodily unconscious in terms of a religious presence very useful. While expanding on some of the insights of Csordas, my work explores the experience of sacred presence at that interface between body and object. Moreover, a basic premise of my work is that the very capacity of the body to sense an ecstatic presence appears in that strange umbilical linkage between the subject and its exteriorized perceptual capacities. See, for instance, Csordas, "Elements of Charismatic Persuasion and Healing," 121–42; Csordas, "Embodiment as a Paradigm for Anthropology," 5–47; Csordas, "Somatic Modes of Attention," 135–56; Csordas, *The Sacred Self*; and Csordas, "Asymptote of the Ineffable," 163–85.

10. Other influential works in the academic study of materialized devotions include Belting, *Likeness and Presence*; Chidester, *Authentic Fakes*; and McDannell, *Material Christianity*; as well as publications in the journal *Material Religion*. This interest in material devotional practice is part of a larger recent resurgence on the topic of materiality in general; see Miller, *Materiality*.

11. The thorough historical work of David Harrell has helped to inform my understanding of the explosion of charismatic practices of faith healing in the years following World War II. See Harrell, *All Things Are Possible*; and Harrell, *Oral Roberts*.

12. This attempt to hear the sound of the sacred builds upon an ever-growing body of scholarship on the historical specificities of listening and the sonic environment, or soundscape. In terms specifically related to the religious resonances of sound, see, for example, Chidester, *Word and Light*; Connor, *Dumbstruck*; Corbin, *Village Bells*; Peters, *Speaking into the Air*; and Schmidt, *Hearing Things*. Because my project is immersed in questions of orality, prayer, and other religious performances, an older body of scholarship on the question of sacred voicings also sustains my research in significant ways. Among this large body of scholarship on the transition from orality to literacy, we must include Goody, *The Domestication of the Savage Mind*; Havelock, *Preface to Plato*; Havelock, *The Muse Learns to Write*; Innis, *Empire and Communications*; Ong, *The Presence of the Word*; and Ong, *Orality and Literacy*.

13. "He that hath ears to hear, let him hear" (Matthew 11:15, King James Version).

Chapter 1

1. The Greek term *charismata* is usually rendered in English as "spiritual gifts." Elaborated in the New Testament, these divine gifts included, among other things, the miraculous ability to heal the sick and prophesy, and the ecstatic practice of speaking in unknown tongues (glossolalia). For more on the practice of glossolalia, see Hastings, *Encyclopaedia of Religion and Ethics*. I would like to thank Brian Larkin for his insightful commentary and helpful suggestions on an early version of this chapter presented at the Sheldon Scheps Memorial Library, Department of Anthropology, Columbia University, March 8, 2010. On the topic of Quranic recitation and the radio, see Larkin, *Signal and Noise*.

2. Hill, *The Cat's Whisker*; Schiffer, *The Portable Radio in American Life*.

3. Stewart, *A Space on the Side of the Road*, 44.

4. Once again, the abundance of metaphors of divine hearing capacities within the worship context is worth noting. (From Isaiah 59:1: "His ears are not too heavy to hear the cries of his people.") These auditory motifs within the orally saturated culture of early Christianity leads to the question of how the contemporary faithful experience and conceive divine capacities to hear prayer in an age immersed in technological extensions of sound and hearing.

5. Marcel Mauss explores the relationship between prayer and the nonrepresentational force of sounds produced by the vocal organs. See Mauss, *On Prayer*. Likewise, Mauss's famous articulation of "techniques of the body" concludes with a rumination upon the "psychological momentum" gained through the breathing techniques of prayer.

6. Blanton, "Augustine's Postal Demons"; Peters, *Speaking into the Air*; Schmidt, *Hearing Things*.

7. Meyer, *Aesthetic Formations*.

8. De Vries, *Religion and Media*.

9. Arnheim, *Radio*.

10. Tacchi, "Radio Texture."

11. Freud, *The Uncanny*.

12. From Luke 19:14: "I tell you, if these were silent, the very stones would cry out!"

13. Tape recording of live *Jackson Memorial Hour* broadcast, October 12, 2008,

WGTH 105.5 FM. Because this excerpt from the testimony of Sister Violet is part of an anointed rhetorical style characterized by specific pronunciations of words such as power ("par") and a rhythmic cadence that is heard by the listening faithful as a "sign" of Holy Ghost anointing, I have attempted to translate the sound of her voice issuing from the loudspeaker as faithfully as possible.

14. Sterne, *The Audible Past*.

15. Adorno, *Current of Music*.

16. Recall, for example, the history of furniture in the bourgeois household: phonograph, radio, and seating within railway cars all became upholstered and cushioned so that the apparatus could become a piece of household furniture. Once proudly displayed, the wires, tubes, and diaphragms now moved behind the black veil. Schivelbusch, *Disenchanted Night*.

17. Utilizing archival material such as letters, historian Tona Hangen has demonstrated that the mediated voice of twentieth-century evangelical preaching made it seem as if the preacher were actually present inside the privacy of the home. Hangen, *Redeeming the Dial*.

18. Roberts, *If You Need Healing*, 35.

19. Ibid. Another material of mass-mediated healing, the prayer cloth is the other most prominent object within the charismatic reliquary of faith prosthetics. Though more archival research is needed at this point, it seems that the supplying of prayer cloths by mail was increased through radio broadcasting and charismatic and Pentecostal publications. Of course, Roberts still had to rely on letters to generate funds for his healing empire, and prayer cloths were a crucial component for both the organization and the perpetuation of Pentecostal religious communities and the raising of money.

20. Hangen, *Redeeming the Dial*, 74.

21. Roberts, *If You Need Healing*, 33.

22. While conducting fieldwork with charismatic listening communities in Appalachia, I had the opportunity several times to participate in radio tactility while listening to live broadcasts within listeners' homes. My description of the sensations of vibration were registered through my ethnographic hand, a *gauche* one at best. For the "holy hand" of the charismatic, imprinted and cauterized through manual theurgical techniques, tactile metaphors of divine touch, and haptic "senses of detection," the experience produced through radio tactility is no mere vibration, but the trembling power of the Holy Ghost.

23. In this ritual of divine communication, the microphone stand recalls the stake that holds the sacrificial animal, as described by Hubert and Mauss. The stake thus marks the point or interface between the sacred and the everyday and is the object wherein the consecrated force is focused. See Hubert and Mauss, *Sacrifice*.

24. To this contemporary inventory of anxieties in relation to technologies of divine surveillance, we could add early Christian accounts of the inscriptive capacity of writing angels, angelic postal messengers, and the "listening birds" that convey every idle word into the divine ear.

25. Speaking of the psychological impact of the radio voice upon the isolated listener, Adorno says, "The deeper this voice is involved within his own privacy, the

more it appears to pour out of the cells of his most intimate life; the more he gets the impression that his own cupboard, his own phonograph, his own bedroom speaks to him in a personal way, devoid of the intermediary stages of the printed word; the more perfectly he is ready to accept wholesale whatever he hears. It is just this privacy which fosters the authority of the radio voice and helps to hide it by making it *no longer appear to come from outside*" (my italics). Adorno, *Current of Music*, 114.

Chapter 2

1. I am thinking here especially of Dorgon's account of a ritual foot washing within the space of an Old Regular Baptist church in Appalachia. See Dorgan, *The Old Regular Baptists*, 102. The specific passage that is interpreted as a call for the ritual ablution of the feet is John 13: "If I then, your Lord and Master, have washed your feet; ye also ought to wash one another's feet. For I have given you an example, that ye should do as I have done to you. Verily, verily, I say unto you, the servant is not greater than his lord; neither he that is sent greater than he that sent him. If ye know these things, happy are ye if ye do them."

2. As elaborated in my chapter on radio tactility, the ubiquitous phrase "prayer warrior" within the charismatic community was popularized by Charles Fuller on his radio program. This is one of many examples within the worship context that suggests the way mass-mediated practices such as radio prayer were actively incorporated into the space of the church.

3. Once again, this small detail seems to suggest the mutual interpenetration between so-called traditional Pentecostal practices and mass-mediated healing revivals of the mid-twentieth century. "Old Time Religion" is thus anachronistically infused and enabled through the modern apparatus of radio broadcasting and the automatic sorting machines of the postal system.

4. For more detailed analysis of the history of the massaging of fats and oils into the skin for the purposes of consecration and healing, see "unction" and "anointing," in Hastings, *Encyclopaedia of Religion and Ethics*.

5. This particular force of charismatic language to unconsciously organize practices of articulation recalls the work of Susan Harding. See, for example, Harding, *The Book of Jerry Falwell*.

6. Several of the most influential histories of prayer, for example, Friedrich Heiler's *Prayer: A Study in the History and Psychology of Religion* (1920), take up decisive apologetic and polemical positions in their articulations of prayer. Heiler, for instance, is constantly describing the ossified performances of Catholic prayer in comparison to the spontaneous and authentic outpourings of Protestant prayer techniques. In *On Prayer*, Marcel Mauss laments the fact that so much polemic energy was invested in these histories of prayer that their scholarship became weak and unreliable. My intention here is to explore the theme of tactile experience in religious devotion, using the density and technical instrumentalities of the bead as a foil or springboard to begin thinking about the material qualities and sensations offered through the texture of the prayer cloth. It is not my interest or intention here to make statements upon the legitimacy of the devotional object but instead to attempt to grasp the phenomeno-

logical texture or hand of the sacred thing. In the end, moreover, it should be kept in mind that the earliest manifestations of what we recognize today as Rosary beads were fashioned out of knotted rope and other long strips of cloth, and thus the two seemingly different objects are much more closely related than they initially appear.

7. Carroll, "Interview: Praying the Rosary," 436. "The appeal of a particular religious devotion is best understood by focusing upon those aspects of the devotion that are most immediate and most concrete from the point of view of those who engage in the devotion. In the case of the Rosary, for instance, this means a focus upon the excessive repetition of Hail Marys, the orderliness of the prayers, and *the tactile experience of fingering the beads*" (my italics). See also Carroll, "Praying the Rosary."

8. Carroll's argument draws heavily from Freud's essay on the relation between obsessive acts and religious rites. For a summary of Carroll's argument, see the section titled "Of Beads and Feces," in "Praying the Rosary," 491.

9. That the old English word for prayer was "bead" sheds crucial light on the constant oscillation in the history of divine communicative techniques between the oral vocalization of prayer and the drive to instantiate the voice into the material object. See Thurston, "Genuflexions and Aves," 441–52.

10. The monastic penitential technique of the body known as the genuflection (literally bending or hitting of the knees) relates to the phrase in Appalachia used to refer to the performance of prayer: "hittin' the prayer bones" connotes the falling upon one's knees in order to assume a traditional comportment of prayer.

11. See, for example, Lewis Mumford's analysis, "The Monastery and the Clock," in Mumford, *Technics and Civilization*, 12–18.

12. There is a rich early ethnological tradition interested in issues of string and its relation to efficacious vocalizations such as prayer, song, and rhyme. These investigations into the relationship between efficacious prayer and techniques of weaving, basketry, and string games have also provided useful insights into the intertwined relations among voice, manual gesture, and spiritual power.

13. For a description of the "remnant bag" and other aspects of quilting techniques in southern Appalachia, see Macneal, *Quilts from Appalachia*.

14. The creative recombinative possibilities evoked by the remnant bag resonate with Lévi-Strauss's notion of bricolage, as well as Stewart's elaboration of "foolin' with thangs." As in the act of prayer, the manual technique of sewing, stitching, weaving, and so on, cannot be separated from the poetics of "just talkin' on thangs." A communal bond and sociality is solidified/sutured in and through the process of stitching together fragments—words literally inscribed in the stitch through a simultaneous movement of the hand, needle, and tongue. For the intimacies between communal prayer and the manufacture of patchwork quilts in the African American tradition, see *Gee's Bend*. The single red fragment of cloth that can be found upon some of these patchwork quilts can be seen as a visual representation of the percussive hand clap that bridges the gap between the everyday and the sacred in many African American spaces of worship.

15. Harrell, *Oral Roberts*, 119.

16. Ibid.

17. I have yet to find the answers as to how Roberts's organization dealt with the growing logistical difficulty of how to anoint and "pray over" hundreds of thousands of prayer requests. The sheer size of this process necessitated that the early techniques of hand "manufacture" be changed. Did the mass circulation of prayer cloths through the postal system necessitate a kind of mass anointing where the pastor prayed over huge piles of cloth fragments at once? Or perhaps he prayed over the cutting and sorting machines themselves? More archival work is needed to explore these questions.

18. Harrell, *Oral Roberts*, 119.

19. Siegert, *Relays*.

20. Over the last thirty years, massive Pentecostal and Evangelical organizations have circulated many different textile variations on the prayer cloth, such as fragments of wool, fleece, burlap crosses, prayer rugs (both paper and cloth), prayer shawls, and fabric "prayer clouds."

21. Other mass healing campaigns, such as the ones organized by evangelists Jack Coe, William Brahnam, "Sweet" Daddy Grace, and A. A. Allen, also featured anointed cloths of similar size and ridged borders.

22. On the similarities between conceptions of that mystic potentiality known as *mana* and the heterogeneous force of the Holy Ghost, see Robert M. Anderson, *Vision of the Disinherited*. The transformation of a rag into a materialized prayer in the American Pentecostal tradition also bears striking similarities to the "spiritual medicines" described by Matthew Engelke in his influential work, *A Problem of Presence*. For the apostolic healers of the Masowe weChishanu Church in Zimbabwe who strive for a spiritual relationship with God unbeholden to scripture and material objects, one of the most effective forms of prayer is materialized in the substance of a mere pebble. According to Engelke, these prayer pebbles, readily available in the dirt surrounding the open-air spaces of worship, become the material conduits of healing prayer precisely for their "non-specialness" or lack of prior associative links with other therapeutic and religious systems. See Engelke, *A Problem of Presence*, 234. For another insightful account of the apostolic prayer pebble, see also Engelke, "Sticky Subjects and Sticky Objects," 118–39. Both the Pentecostal prayer cloth and the Masowe apostolic prayer pebble are revealing examples of the paradox of prayer and its relation to materiality described by Marcel Mauss in *On Prayer*: "Prayer in religions whose dogmas have become detached from all fetishism, becomes itself a fetish." Mauss, *On Prayer*, 26.

23. Harrell, *Oral Roberts*, 91.

24. Several participants in the early Oral Roberts healing campaigns commented upon the specific soundscape of the revival tent: "The tent provided a remarkably fine acoustic setting"; ibid., 95. The insertion of "high speed" film cameras within the revival tent allowed the space of the tent to enter into the domesticity of the living room, and without the oppressive heat of special technical lighting needed for the older types of film cameras. Not only did the presence of TV cameras in the healing tent sound the death knell for the Golden Days of radio, it also altered the form and speed of the healing line itself. Ironically, the high-speed film slowed the healing line because Roberts wanted to give the TV viewing audience a sense of the intimacy of the

healing experience. Likewise, it is important to note that Roberts could reproduce the presence for the TV viewing audience in the "live" tent revival, but he failed to convey this presence when he tried to reproduce the radio format in the television studio.

25. Ibid.

26. Baker, "Miracle Magazine in the Sixties," 204–18.

27. This specific employment of the prayer cloth took place in 1963. By then, not only had the charismatic tactics for raising funds become more sophisticated and aggressive, but the prayer cloth had become more and more closely associated with the augmentation of "financial blessings," upon both the sender and the receiver. I discuss this shift in greater detail at the conclusion of this chapter.

28. Perhaps the most influential early ethnological reference (1889) would be the numerous references to blood and ritual purity in William Robertson Smith's *Lectures on the Religion of the Semites, First series, The Fundamental Institutions*.

29. Helpful sources for the history of practices of tactile contact, or "handlaying," within early Christianity include Robinson, *The Laying On of Hands*; and Whitehouse, "Manus Impositio."

30. For useful histories of the handkerchief, see Braun-Ronsdorf, "The Handkerchief"; Braun-Ronsdorf, *History of the Handkerchief*; and Peri, *The Handkerchief*.

31. Indeed, the handkerchief's absorbent properties and use to soak up bodily fluids make it an especially apt object for profane and secret magical purposes. Of course, this aspect of the handkerchief opens the field of analysis to a much more pervasive and dangerous form of "magic" than that connoted by a domesticated form of modern magical "entertainment."

32. The etymological accounts of the phrase "hanky-panky," like the history of prayer and divine communication that it supposedly mimics, end up replicating many of the apologetic and polemical debates between Protestants and Catholics that get subtly played out in the discourses on magic and the history of prayer. What I want to emphasize in this section is the way these seemingly innocuous etymologies reveal the underlying *tension that also resides* at the heart of the Pentecostal prayer handkerchief.

33. Bellew, *The Art of Amusing*, 134.

34. Of course, the telegraph was not the only modern apparatus that seemed particularly attracted to the spiritual communiqués and appearances of the spiritualist movement. The new optical technologies of photographic lenses and gelatin plates also had an uncanny ability to register spectral presences otherwise imperceptible to the naked eye. See, for instance, Gunning, "Phantom Images"; and Chéroux, *The Perfect Medium*.

35. Chéroux, *The Perfect Medium*, 179.

36. Schrenck-Notzing, *Phenomena of Materialisation*.

37. Ibid.

38. Reactions such as this also characterized the reception of these images at the exhibition of spiritualist photographs entitled *The Perfect Medium*; see exhibition catalog: Chéroux, *The Perfect Medium*.

39. Indeed, the importance of speaking in foreign and unknown tongues within the American Spiritualist tradition prefigured the irruption of Pentecostal tongues

in 1906 in significant ways. Leigh Schmidt makes this point in his work; see *Hearing Things*, 236.

40. My use of the phrase "spiritual storyin'" resonates with Stewart's notion of "talkin' on thangs." As this phrase suggests, the figure of materiality always seems to persist in the heart of these otherwise strictly oral performances. In this way, "talkin' on spiritual thangs" always suggests the particular objectile dimensions and their moments of surfacing or desublimation within the narrative poetics of the testimony. For another devilish encounter and its spiritual implications, see Stewart, *A Space on the Side of the Road*, 162–63.

41. Mauss, *A General Theory of Magic*.

42. De Certeau, "What We Do When We Believe."

43. Anointing the sheet from the Dollar Store invokes the intimate relations between the prayer cloth and magical notions of accumulation and circulation associated with the prayer cloth. As a commodity, the sheet *already* has a specific spectral quality and metaphysical subtlety operating within it. In this way, perhaps we could think of the necessary process of cutting or rending the fabric in the process of sacred manufacture as a release of spiritual force *already* accumulated in the fabric commodity. This releasing of preexisting spiritual presence then opens a space for the creative reconfiguration of the fabric remnant into new contexts and categories. In many ways, the dollar bill itself resembles the prayer cloth. The devotional gesture of rubbing the prayer cloth between the thumb and fingers, for instance, is also a manual gesture for money—thus both objects convey a particular haptic sensation that is associated with magical accumulation and the force of objects that seem to move on their own. In the history of evangelical and charismatic organizations, the prayer cloth became increasingly associated precisely with the accumulation of dollar bills. Now "green prosperity handkerchiefs" are circulated by the thousands to facilitate the miraculous accumulation of wealth made possible by the power of the Holy Ghost. Thus, if Marx were to write his essay on the commodity within our contemporary setting, he would update his equation: 1 revival tent = 5,000 coats = 1,000,000 prayer cloths. I would like to thank Allen Shelton for suggesting this relation between Marx's famous equation and the prayer cloth. For an exploration of the circulation and agency of other material objects used to communicate with that spectral elsewhere, see the remarkable chapter, "Planchette, My Love," in Shelton, *Dreamworlds of Alabama*.

44. Indeed, several sources on the history of prayer suggest that the word "prayer" originally referred to a cutting of the flesh in the act of divine communication. The phylactery, for example, can be seen as a symbolic representation of an earlier form of cutting and scarification associated with techniques for contacting the divine. See "prayer" and "phylactery," in Hastings, *Encyclopaedia of Religion and Ethics*.

45. The insight of Walter Benjamin resonates deeply with this story of miraculous automaticity: "The invention of the match around the middle of the nineteenth century brought forth a number of innovations which have one thing in common: one abrupt movement of the hand triggers a process of many steps. This development is taking place in many areas. One case in point is the telephone, where the lifting of a receiver has taken the place of the steady movement that used to be required to crank the older models. Of the countless movements of switching, inserting, pressing, and

the like, the "snapping" of the photographer has had the greatest consequences. A touch of the finger now sufficed to fix an event for an unlimited period of time. The camera gave the moment a posthumous shock, as it were." See Benjamin, *Illuminations*, 174–75.

46. Griffith, "Material Devotion—Pentecostal Prayer Cloths," 4. This idea of the immediacy of the prayer cloth is a recurrent theme in the few published descriptions in the field of religious studies. These accounts rely on the printed testimonials of Pentecostal publications such as magazines and pamphlets, which all tend to repeat this theme of immediate efficacy for the purpose of publication space and to quickly convince the audience of their curative force. Scholars in the fields of American history and religious studies should take this into consideration when making pronouncements about practices of devotion based on the published accounts in the official Pentecostal literature. My ethnography demonstrates that the force of "immediacy" that is claimed by scholars such as Griffith appears with most compelling force in and through particular structures of deferral, habituation, and temporal articulation through systems of exchange and narrativity.

47. My notion of the temporal articulation of belief has been informed through the work of Michel de Certeau. See de Certeau, "What We Do When We Believe."

48. The information on coal and its associated industries of extraction, transportation, and processing has been taken largely from Summers, *Anthracite*; and Bogen, *The Anthracite Railroads*.

49. The themes of coincidence, automaticity, and the efficacy of the prayer cloth that I outline in this chapter are inspired by Pemberton's essay on the forces of attraction between ritual performance and the geared machine ensemble of an Indonesian sugar refinery. See John Pemberton, "The Spectre of Coincidence," 75–90.

50. In the early 1900s, extraction technologies such as the electric locomotive and the automatic drill greatly increased the productive capacities of the mining industry. These advancements in mechanization, however, also produced new potential for explosive accidents within the mine in the form of fine coal dust and the rapid release of methane gas—both of which were highly volatile when released or stirred up within the dark subterranean atmosphere of the mine. For an account of the catastrophic explosion in the Red Ash mine, as well as a history of government-regulated safety practices in the bituminous coal extraction industries of West Virginia, see Rakes, *Acceptable Casualties*. My return from the field coincided with yet another explosion within the mines of West Virginia: twenty-nine miners were instantly killed when a faulty ventilation system allowed sufficient methane gas to accumulate and explode. The company that owned the mine, Massey Energy, has a long history of federal safety violations. The politicians of West Virginia continue to turn a blind eye to egregious safety conditions and severe environmental degradation in favor of financial gain for both themselves and the coffers of the state.

51. The work of Lewis Mumford elaborates on the intimate relations between the artificial environments of the coal mine and everyday modern life "above ground." See Mumford, *Technics and Civilization*. For another useful account of the psychological impacts created in situations of everyday life oriented and organized around the coal extraction industry, see, for instance, Gaventa, *Power and Powerlessness*.

52. The center of this sacred hub of manual gesture as that place where the diffuse potentiality of the Holy Ghost is focused seems reminiscent of the post or stake to which the sacrificial animal is tethered. For an analysis of the demarcation of sacred space and its relation to rites of entry and exit, see Hubert and Mauss, *Sacrifice*.

53. Here I am working from the concepts of belief and faith elaborated by de Certeau, "What We Do When We Believe."

54. A portion of this analysis of the anxieties surrounding the intrusion of infrastructures of illumination into the bourgeois interior is informed by the work of Wolfgang Schivelbusch. See Schivelbusch, *Disenchanted Night*.

55. In his famous work, *The Idea of the Holy*, Rudolf Otto describes the uncanny "numinous" experience of the "creeping flesh." In the strict sense of the term, Freud's notion of the uncanny describes an experience of un-placeability that persists in situations of modernity that have "surmounted" older symbolic forms in which the irruption of the sacred could be schematized within discernible classificatory systems and categories of awareness. In the end, therefore, Holy Ghost bumps are *not uncanny*. Note the ecstatic pleasure in the descriptive accounts given by Pentecostal congregants—this is not the unplaceable anxiety of the uncanny.

56. This "somatic awareness" seems very different from the ones that provide the recurrent themes in the work of Thomas Csordas.

57. In this way, the bumps of the Holy Ghost could be seen as sacred magnifications of the sweat glands themselves. Indeed, on several occasions, Sister Violent has described one of the most forceful anointings as a literal secretion of oil from the palms of the hands. This motif of secretion of holy unction from the body also has a long tradition in Catholic veneration of both icons and living saints.

58. The flapping of the tongue inside the viscous cavity of the mouth is an incredibly tactile experience and cannot be abstracted from the tactile sensations of articulation, especially in contexts of the anointed mouth and tongues that flap under the power of divine winds. For more on orality and sensations of tactility, see Connor, "Edison's Teeth."

Chapter 3

1. Of course, I am drawing heavily from Mauss's famous essay, "Techniques of the Body." The theme of dance and breath seems crucial to his argument, especially in relation to issues of the sacred. "I had to go back to ancient notions, to the Platonic position on technique, for Plato spoke of a technique of music and in particular a technique of dance, and extend these notions." Mauss, *Techniques, Technology, and Civilization*, 82.

2. One aim of this chapter is to compel the reader's ears to hear the particularly sacred resonances of this guttural grunt.

3. Jousse, *The Oral Style*, 31; Jousse, *The Anthropology of Geste and Rhythm*.

4. For useful descriptive accounts of this poetic dance within the context of Old Regular Baptists in southern Appalachia, see Dorgan, *Giving Glory to God in Appalachia*, 59–60; and Dorgan, *The Old Regular Baptists*, 55–56.

5. The intertwined relation of sound, breath, and possessed tongue is firmly es-

tablished in the preeminent passage from the second chapter of the book of Acts: "And when the day of Pentecost was fully come, they were all with one accord in one place. And suddenly there came a sound from heaven as of a rushing mighty wind, and it filled all the house where they were sitting. And there appeared unto them cloven tongues like as of fire, and it sat upon each of them. And they were all filled with the Holy Ghost, and began to speak with other tongues, as the Spirit gave them utterance" (King James Version).

6. My ethnographic exploration of the specific textures of the possessed voice has also been inspired and challenged by another account of the voice of possession that remains within the modulations of everyday speech: "Recalling the Dead on Mount Osore," in Ivy, *Discourses of the Vanishing*.

7. Barthes, *The Responsibility of Forms*.

8. See, for example, the sermon of Brother Pearl further in the chapter and included in its entirety in the third interlude.

9. Needham, "Percussion and Transition," 231–44; Rouget, *Music and Trance*.

10. After reviewing the tape of this broadcast several times, I was struck with the eloquence and conversational fluency of Sister Z's testimony, especially since she claimed to be such a young convert in the Lord. Part of her poetic fluency in this testimonial performance must have been gained from listening to other testimonials over the radio during her years in prison. Besides the force of oral transmission over the radio apparatus, however, Sister Z's testimonial prowess seems to point to an overarching form of narrative poetics that is practiced in southern Appalachia and elsewhere. The poetic force of the testimonial in southern Appalachia, therefore, could be thought of as sacred "talkin' on [spiritual] thangs." Stewart, *A Space on the Side of the Road*.

11. Because many of the elders of the radio congregation associated with the *Jackson Memorial Hour* suffer from severe back and hip problems, I was deputized to help with the baptizing. This capacity to participate, however, was only made possible after Aldie and the elder brothers first immersed me in the brisk waters of the river. I vividly recall the shock of the cold water and the green luminescence of afternoon sunbeams as they passed through the leaves of the giant walnut tree that grew from the riverbank. The shock of immersion into chilly water itself is enough to initiate a radical change in breathing technique. After helping the brothers dunk several initiates, I was struck by the force required to fully immerse the initiates' bodies into the flowing water. Within this worship context, it is absolutely necessary that the body be fully immersed in this ritual of symbolic death. Two attempts at immersion, for instance, had to be done over when the initial attempt at dunking did not immerse the body totally under the water. Several of those baptized were also put under multiple times in order to act as physical "stand-ins" for other congregation members who were absent or too weak/disabled to enter into the river. After the immersion of one middle-aged sister, I heard Brother Aldie exclaim, "Look at the Holy Ghost on her face!" in reference to the raised chill bumps upon the surface of her wet skin. The "Holy Ghost chillbumps" or "bumps" are often referred to when testifying of the visceral and somatic experience of the spirit.

12. Transcription of live WGTH broadcast, October 12, 2008.

13. Brother Aldie's play on words here recalls another colloquial expression in southern Appalachia in reference to the phenomenon of speaking in tongues. No other phrase seems to render the phenomenon of glossolalia more "faithfully" than the phrase "cuttin' loose the tongue" or the power of the Holy Ghost "cuttin' the tongue loose."

14. Freud, *Jokes and Their Relation to the Unconscious*, 188.

15. For more on the performative spaces opened through the theme of bodies "got down" and spaces of critical dialogue opened though "back talk," see Stewart, *A Space on the Side of the Road*, 3.

16. See the first interlude for this particular sermon transcript in its entirety.

17. The excerpts from Sister June's sermons are all taken from various recordings of her live, in-studio preaching at radio station WGTH. Though I have actually been present in person within the radio station studio to hear Sister June's preaching, these particular recordings were taped on a cassette player from the radio.

18. This sermon was recorded off the radio, March 21, 2009, from the 2:00 pm broadcast originating from radio station 105.5 FM, WGTH, in Richlands, Virginia.

19. Useful descriptions of Gandy dancing include Brown, "Negro Folk Expressions: Spirituals, Seculars, Ballads, and Work Songs," 45–61; Ferris, "Railroad Chants: Form and Function," 1–14; Jackson, *Afro-American Work Songs in a Texas Prison*; Jackson, "Prison Worksongs: The Composer in Negatives," 245–68; Jackson, "Wake Up Dead Man: Afro-American Worksongs from Texas Prisons"; Manning, "Railroad Work Songs," 41–47; and Sloss Furnace Association, *Spirit of Steel: Music of the Mines, Railroads, and Mills*.

20. Holtzberg-Call, *Gandy Dancers*, 4-5 (my italics).

21. For the history of African American labor practices in southern Appalachia, see, for instance, Eller, *Miners, Millhands, and Mountaineers*; Lichtenstein, *Twice the Work of Free Labor*; Nelson, *Steel Drivin' Man*; and Wormser, *The Rise and Fall of Jim Crow*.

22. Holtzberg-Call, *Gandy Dancers*, 4.

23. Lomax, *Prison Songs*. The last portion of the liner notes to this particular selection read: "The train reference may indicate a late-nineteenth century origin for this song, as countless black convicts were leased by the state to perform dangerous railroad work at that time." To listen to this track, go to http://amso.alexanderstreet.com/View/377666, track #14.

24. Mauss, *Techniques, Technology, and Civilization*, 82. Here Mauss is quoting from the work of Teichelmann and Schurmann (1840), *Outlines of a Grammar, Vocabulary, and Phraseology, of the Aboriginal Language of South Australia*, spoken by the Natives in and for some distance around Adelaide, published by the authors at the Native Location, Adelaide.

25. Interesting both in its invocation of the prodigious psycho-physical capacities instantiated through song and its political implications in the United States, Mauss also includes in this section a wonderful description of Native American endurance: "Running. Position of the feet, position of the arms, breathing, running magic, endurance. In Washington I saw the chief of the Fire Fraternity of the Hopi Indians who had arrived with four of his men to protest against the prohibition of the use

of certain alcoholic liquors in their ceremonies. He was certainly the best runner in the world. He had run 250 miles without stopping. Henri Hubert, who had seen them, compared them physically with Japanese athletes. The same Indian was an incomparable dancer." Mauss, *Techniques, Technology, and Civilization*, 84, 89, 93.

26. Mauss's interest in techniques of breath and its relation to ritual cannot be abstracted from his earlier project on the history of prayer. His insistence on the importance of breath as a special consideration for ethnographers and colonial officials is evinced in his lectures on the technique of ethnography: "Breath and breathing differ while running, dancing or performing magic: the rhythm of breathing should be noted, together with the associated stretching of arms and legs." Mauss, *Manual of Ethnography*, 25.

27. If another excursus were to be added to Schivelbusch's work *The Railway Journey: The Industrialization of Time and Space in the Nineteenth Century*, perhaps it would explore the phenomenon of Gandy dancing. The vast "machine ensemble" of the railroad is literally kept on track, aligned, by a song that coordinates movements of bodies and implements. The boiler-breath of steam as it blew from the whistle and percussively huffed from the pressure valves just as the drive wheels began to pull the machine out of the station was made possible through the rhythmic breath of the black section crews who aligned portions of track through the organizing force of the "hah" at the end of the sung line. Small wonder, therefore, that the history of American folk music seems not only saturated with metaphors of this mechanized transportation, but resonates on a deep level with the sound of the whistle and rhythm of locomotion as it is mimed through the harmonica, pounded on the guitar box, and channeled through the voice. In addition, does not the rhythmic technique of the Gandy dancer seem to run parallel to the concepts of traumatic shock, repression, and other forces of automaticity cauterized upon the modern perceptual faculties? The synchronized and coordinated rhythm generated through the work song is a powerful work technique, not only to muster the tremendous force necessary to move the entire track assemblage but also to accomplish this feat in a state of distraction or displacement from the immediacies of the harsh reality of forced labor. When an adaptation of spiritual song and preaching style is sung in order "to get the worker's mind off work," are we not already on our way to notions of ritual automaticity pressing upon the religious or the magical? And like the scalded hand of the engineer who holds fast to the throttle of the machine even in death, the deep distraction generated through the rhythmic form of breath that characterizes the work chant demonstrates yet another manifestation of the forces of attraction between repetition in the field of ritual and the mechanical movements of the train's drive wheel.

28. Holtzberg-Call, *Gandy Dancers*, 4 (my italics).

29. Ferris, "Railroad Chants: Form and Function," 10.

30. Eller, *Miners, Millhands, and Mountaineers*; Lewis, *Black Coal Miners*; Shifflett, *Coal Towns*; Trotter, *Coal, Class, and Color*.

31. Of course, the fervent and enthusiastic revivals of the early nineteenth century in this region of Appalachia must have also played a significant role in the oral transmission of the chanted sermonic form. My emphasis on the importance of the railway helps to account for the regional specificity and resilience of this performative

practice in southern Appalachia, as well as to suggest new ways to theorize the poetic and affective import of the percussive breath. At this point, more historical research is needed. The history of this sacred breathing technique is part of an ongoing project into the origins and spread of the anointed grunt.

32. Tillis, "The Chant of the Tobacco Auctioneer," 141–49.

33. See the third interlude for the complete transcript of Brother Pearl's sermon.

34. In his seminal work on the chanted folk sermon, Bruce Rosenberg terms phrases such as Brother Pearl's "Whoop-hal-le-lu-yer-ahh" as "stall formulas" that function as sonic space holders. These stall formulas supposedly occupy the audience while giving space to the preacher to compose the next sermonic line. Yet if we take the numerous personal accounts of the preachers themselves describing the experience of anointed preaching seriously, it seems that Rosenberg's (and the entire Perry-Lord tradition of formulaic composition to which his work responds) analysis of the stall formula is too cognitive and instrumental. Taking into account the particular temporal lag described by preachers such as Brother Aldie between the articulations of the anointed mouth and the conscious awareness of meaning "in the mind," could we not begin to propose a theory of formulaic composition that sees the techniques of pneumatic gesture inherent in recurrent phrases such as the "Whoop-hal-le-lu-yer-ahh" as mnemotechnics that themselves grant access to surfaces of memory and poetic force not located within the space of conscious linguistic modes of articulation? Rosenberg, *The Art of the American Folk Preacher*.

35. Upon editing this section on Brother Pearl's anointed poetics of breath, I realized that my account had replicated the narrative testimonial form often performed in southern Appalachia to recount appearances of the miraculous. Mauss, "Techniques of the Body," in *Techniques, Technology, and Civilization*.

36. Robert M. Anderson, *Vision of the Disinherited*; Hollenweger, *The Pentecostals*.

37. Of course, the early history of Pentecostalism does not display a direct technological coincidence, as with Spiritualism and the telegraph; however, the general Pentecostal spirit emerging in 1906 seemed to speak prophetic words about the radio and all its explosive religious potential in the near future to come. For a description of some of the early charismatic figures of radio, see Hangen, *Redeeming the Dial*.

38. My description of the "mouth" of the "loudspeaker" and the peculiar resonances involved draws heavily from Adorno's work on radio. Adorno, *Current of Music*, 80–86.

39. In a section of his book on radio entitled "In Praise of Blindness: Emancipation from the Body," Arnheim describes useful aspects of radio "relay": "It is true that it [everyday radio relays of current events] hardly makes an entirely satisfactory impression, but at least it conveys distant happenings to the listener by the most direct method conceivable to-day, that is to say, it artificially cuts out slices of reality, by this isolation making them the object of special attention, sharpening acoustic powers of observation and drawing the listener's attention to the expression and content of much that he ordinarily passes by with deaf ears." Arnheim, *Radio*, 140–41.

40. Indeed, I experienced this insufflation of anointed spittle several times while sitting in the front pews of church revivals in southern Appalachia.

41. In a series of articles on the recitation of Islamic poetry by Muslims in Mauri-

tius, the linguistic anthropologist Patrick Eisenlohr has also brought attention to the way technologies of sound reproduction such as audio cassette and CD are able to reproduce crucial stylistic elements of the religious performance. In the Mauritian context, the proper recitation of these poems (*na't*) is intimately related to textures of the voice and the pious sensations that are elicited through these stylistic elements. Attending to the particular assumptions about media technology and performative authenticity held by Mauritian Muslims, Eisenlohr demonstrates how technologies of sound reproduction become "domesticated" in culturally specific ways. Indeed, attention to ways theological orientations and assumptions about technology shape media practice is a crucial analytical tool for the anthropology of media. I am equally as interested, however, in an attempt to describe the way devotional objects and media technologies organize experiences of the transcendent in bodily rhythms and somatic attunements that resonate well beneath or beyond the conscious structures of belief characterized by the so-called semiotic ideology. For Eisenlohr's insightful accounts of the relation between pious recitational style and technologies of sound reproduction, see, among others, Eisenlohr, "Technologies of the Spirit," 273–96; Eisenlohr, "Materialities of Entextualization," 314–33; and Eisenlohr, "Mediality and Materiality in Religious Performance," 330–48.

42. Recorded from live studio broadcast, WGTH, Richlands, Virginia, February 8, 2009. Pastors in southern Appalachia often employ visceral pulmonary metaphors to describe the act of preaching. Take, for instance, another phrase of Brother Aldie: "They're preachers out there today bustin' their lungs open—ahh/Preachin' tha true word a'God" (WGTH, January 2011).

Chapter 4

1. Once again, Max Muller's etymological analysis of the word "prayer" and its intimate link with the term "precarious" suggests the gap, or potential for communicative breakdown, at the heart of this technique of divine communication. Muller, "On Ancient Prayers," in *Last Essays*. For a further description of the efficacious ritual act of prayer and the force of the spoken word, see Mauss, *On Prayer*, 50–54.

2. A crucial practice within the live studio of the radio station, the act of standin'-in recalls the technological capacities of early radio sets to both receive and transmit. On this forgotten capacity, see, for example, Brecht's essay "The Radio as an Apparatus of Communication" (1932), in Strauss, *Radiotext(e)*.

3. Tape recording of the *Jackson Memorial Hour* radio broadcast, 105.5 WGTH, Richlands, Virginia, Sunday, December 12, 2010.

4. On the mouth as an organ of tactility, see, for instance, Connor, "Edison's Teeth: Touching Hearing," 153–72.

5. Stewart, *A Space on the Side of the Road*, 44. One might indeed invoke Lévi-Strauss's notion of *bricolage* here as well. Lévi-Strauss, *The Savage Mind*.

6. For thorough descriptions of the history of the early days of the Charismatic Revival, see Harrell, *All Things Are Possible*; and Harrell, *Oral Roberts*.

7. Harrell, *Oral Roberts*, 120.

8. Roberts, *If You Need Healing*, 32. I am quoting here from the revised second

edition of 1950. The first edition of the healing treatise placed even more emphasis on the place of demons in the etiology of illness.

9. Here I am working from Arnheim's chapter "In Praise of Blindness: Emancipation from the Body," in Arnheim, *Radio*. See ibid., 30.

10. On this longing for a return of the corporal presence of the body in the experience of radio listening, see Peters, *Speaking into the Air*, 214–18. For further consideration of tactile experience in and through the radio apparatus, see my description in Chapter 1, as well as the section on "the laying on of hands" in this chapter.

11. *Miracles Yesterday, Today, and Forever*.

12. This recurrent concept of spectral "detection," moreover, cannot be abstracted from the popular technical terminology of radio reception, crystal detectors, valve-detectors, and so on.

13. *Miracles Yesterday, Today, and Forever*.

14. Schivelbusch, *Disenchanted Night*.

15. Says Benjamin, "Comfort isolates; on the other hand, it brings those enjoying it closer to mechanization. The invention of the match around the middle of the nineteenth century brought forth a number of innovations which have one thing in common: the abrupt movement of the hand triggers a process of many steps. This development is taking place in many areas. One case in point is the telephone, where the lifting of a receiver has taken the place of the steady movement that used to be required to crank the older models. Of the countless movements of switching, inserting, pressing, and the like, the 'snapping' of the photographer has had the greatest consequences. A touch of the finger now sufficed to fix an event for an unlimited period of time. The camera gave the moment a posthumous shock, as it were." Benjamin, *Illuminations*, 174–75.

16. In this way, the preeminent ritual gesture of charismatic faith healing thematizes on the level of sacred efficacy what Canetti describes as the most basic of human manual techniques: grasping and letting go. Canetti, *Crowds and Power*.

17. Roberts, *If You Need Healing*, 110, 106, 79 (my italics).

18. See, for example, the essay "Animism in Theory and Practice: E. B. Tylor's Unpublished 'Notes on Spiritualism,'" in Stocking, *Delimiting Anthropology*, 116.

19. Roberts, *If You Need Healing*, 32 (his italics), 38–39 (my italics). Curtis, "Acting Faith." See also Curtis, *Faith in the Great Physician*; and Porterfield, *Healing in the History of Christianity*.

20. Roberts, *If You Need Healing*, 35.

21. Mauss, *A General Theory of Magic*, 152.

22. Turner, "Images of Anti-temporality," 243–65; Hubert, *Essay on Time*.

23. My analysis of certain experiences of disjointed radio time departs from many of the accounts of so-called radio temporality by scholars such as Paddy Scannell and Jo Tacchi. Perhaps this significant difference in the temporal potentialities of the radio apparatus, and concomitant scholarly descriptions, can be attributed to the fact that Scannell and Tacchi listen to the sounds issuing from the loudspeaker in Great Britain and therefore have not heard the sound of ecstatic communal prayer erupting from the radio apparatus. See, for instance, Scannell, *Radio, Television, and Modern Life*; and Tacchi, "Radio Texture."

24. Roberts, *If You Need Healing*, 30.

25. Ibid., 30 (my italics); Merleau-Ponty, *The Visible and the Invisible*; Nancy, *Corpus*; Derrida, *On Touching*.

26. Roberts, *If You Need Healing*, 35–36.

27. Ibid., vi, 78. Here is the specific passage to which Roberts refers: 1 Corinthians 12:4–10: "Now there are diversities of gifts, but the same Spirit. And there are differences of administrations, but the same Lord. And there are diversities of operations, but it is the same God which worketh all in all. But the manifestation of the Spirit is given to every man to profit withal. For to one is given by the Spirit the word of wisdom; to another the word of knowledge by the same Spirit; to another faith by the same Spirit; to another the gifts of healing by the same Spirit; To another the working of miracles; to another prophecy; to another *discerning of spirits*; to another divers kinds of tongues; to another the interpretation of tongues" (King James Version, my italics).

28. For a thorough exploration of the religious resonances informing the history of the concept of "apparatus," see Agamben, *What Is an Apparatus?* In her essay "The Cinema Screen as Prosthesis of Perception: A Historical Account," author Susan Buck-Morss traces the origin of the word "prosthesis" to the table upon which the Eucharistic elements were prepared. Buck-Morss, "The Cinema Screen," 45–62.

29. Freud, "Animism, Magic, and the Omnipotence of Thought," in *Totem and Taboo*.

30. Adorno, *Current of Music*.

31. Benjamin, *Illuminations*; Freud, *The Uncanny*. Overarching thematic motifs within this section have also been informed by Pemberton, "The Spectre of Coincidence," 75–90.

32. "The magician heals a sick person by the laying on of hands; the surgeon cuts into the patient's body. The magician maintains the natural distance between the patient and himself: though he reduces it very slightly by the laying on of hands, he greatly increases it by virtue of his authority." Benjamin, *Illuminations*, 233. For other useful accounts of the history of the tactile communication of healing virtue in the practice of Christian healing, see Porterfield, *Healing in the History of Christianity*; Robinson, *The Laying On of Hands*; and Whitehouse, "Manus Impositio."

33. In the particularly revealing footnote 14, Benjamin quotes Luc Durtain: "I refer to the acrobatic tricks of larynx surgery which have to be performed following the reversed picture in the laryngoscope. I might also speak of ear surgery which suggests the precision work of watchmakers." Benjamin, *Illuminations*, 248–49.

34. Ibid.

35. We also see other parallels in the history of technology on the level of voice and hand. Think, for instance, of the stenographic sound hand that prefigured the technological speed-up of the stylus in the phonograph. Early in the essay, with his rumination on sound film and the surpassing of the human hand by the speed of the machine, all these notions are invoked by Benjamin. This freeing of the hand through technical speed-up creates an uncanny sensation in the viewer of these new abstracted operations. Perhaps there is an attraction to knitting on the subway train, but still there is something dissonant or disconcerting about hands moving through

this extremely delicate, complicated, and automatic weaving operation while gazing lazily at one's reflection in the opaque subway window. Children learn this talk of manual dissociation at an early age through the incessant harping of the typing teacher, "Don't look at the keys!" Even to this day, the image of someone typing at a computer terminal while looking away from the screen still strikes some as strange or somehow disquieting—but this residue of older attentive forms is quickly disappearing. A new mode of distraction has become the normal sensory orientation; this can be readily seen as the screen of the cellular phone radically alters techniques of walking and structures of awareness on the street. Direct eye contact is now more easily achieved by the metropolitan through a constant gaze upon the screen of the cellular phone or other handheld device. Thus, the narcissistic interiority of the folding compact makeup mirror has become a perpetual self-reflection through the screen of a cellular phone.

36. Harrell, *Oral Roberts*, 97. Indeed, almost all of the iconic photographs of Roberts seem to draw attention to his intimacies with the microphone, both the grip of his hand and its close proximity to his mouth. In the iconography of the Charismatic Revival, the two—Roberts and the microphone—are almost inseparable.

37. Transcribed from a live recording from Oral Roberts's revival tent: *Miracles Yesterday, Today, and Forever*.

38. Of course, the very moment of enunciation itself always performs a displacement from the source of utterance. The public announcement system in the healing tent is thus a technological realization of older forms and techniques of curing that utilized and thematized the force of the abstracted or displaced voice in the service of curative efficacy. Take, for instance, the shamanic techniques of "throwing the voice." As this history suggests, therapeutic efficacy cannot be abstracted from these technologies of voice and the moment of artifice or prestidigitation.

39. Here it is important to note that the *Healing Waters Broadcast* and the mass tent crusades were not separate but were both developing and gaining mass momentum on parallel tracks. Roberts's intimacy with the microphone in the revival tent and his awareness of the force and presence created by the public announcement system must have helped inform his almost preternatural ability to reproduce "presence" through the unforeseen or unacknowledged potentialities of the radio apparatus.

40. Benjamin, *Illuminations*, 238. See, for example, Benjamin's ruminations on sound and synchronization in early film at the beginning of the essay. Ironically, many of these sonic motifs in this pivotal text have fallen upon commentators and theorists with no ears to hear these acoustic resonances of modernity. Neglecting this sonic aspect of the text, in turn, has led many scholars of media and the senses to write about the perceptual/phenomenological impact of the cinematic in Benjamin's work as if it were still silent.

41. Numerous publications from the late 1870s recounted various instances of the sound of the fly: "But its extreme sensitiveness to minute sounds is perhaps best shown by enclosing a fly in an empty matchbox, when, upon listening at the attached telephone, every movement of the fly is heard as a loud noise." Barrett, "The Microphone," 711.

42. This notion of the intertwining of prayer and manual technique recalls a large

body of work within the ethnological tradition on the relation between manual techniques and efficacious words. The work on string games (cat's cradle) by Evans-Pritchard and many others demonstrates how these games are survivals of older manifestations of manual skills where the weaving of baskets for hunting was accompanied by prayer and song—to both facilitate construction and render effective the snare, the net, and the trap.

43. Brecht, "The Radio as an Apparatus of Communication." See also Hill, *The Cat's Whisker*; Aitken, *Syntony and Spark*; and Schiffer, *The Portable Radio in American Life*.

Bibliography

Adorno, Theodor W. *Current of Music: Elements of a Radio Theory.* Frankfurt am Main: Suhrkamp Verlag, 2006.
Agamben, Giorgio. *What Is an Apparatus? And Other Essays.* Stanford: Stanford University Press, 2009.
Aitken, Hugh. *Syntony and Spark: The Origins of Radio.* New York: Wiley, 1976.
Anderson, Benedict. *Imagined Communities: Reflections on the Origin and Spread of Nationalism.* London: Verso, 1983.
Anderson, Robert M. *Vision of the Disinherited: The Making of American Pentecostalism.* New York: Oxford University Press, 1979.
Arnett, Paul, Joanne Cubbs, and Eugene Metcalf, eds. *Gee's Bend: The Architecture of the Quilt.* Atlanta: Tinwood Books, 2006.
Arnheim, Rudolf. *Radio: An Art of Sound.* New York: Da Capo Press, 1972.
Askew, Kelly, and Richard Wilk, eds. *The Anthropology of Media: A Reader.* Malden: Blackwell Publishers, 2002.
Auslander, Philip. *Liveness: Performance in a Mediatized Culture.* London: Routledge, 1999.
Baker, Ronald. "Miracle Magazine in the Sixties: Mass Media Narratives of Healing and Blessings." *Journal of American Folklore* 118 (Spring 2005): 204–18.
Barrett, W. F. "The Microphone." *Good Words* 19 (January 1878): 711.
Barthes, Roland. *The Responsibility of Forms: Critical Essays on Music, Art, and Representation.* Berkeley: University of California Press, 1991.
Bellew, Frank. *The Art of Amusing: Being a Collection of Graceful Arts, Merry Games, Odd Tricks, Curious Puzzles, and New Charades; Together with Suggestions for Private Theatricals, Tableaux, and all Sorts of Parlor and Family Amusements.* New York: Carelton, 1866.
Belting, Hans. *Likeness and Presence: A History of the Image before the Era of Art.* Chicago: University of Chicago Press, 1994.
Benjamin, Walter. *Illuminations.* New York: Schocken Books, 1986.
Bird, Charles. "Heroic Songs of the Mande Hunters." In *African Folklore*, edited by R. M. Dorson. Bloomington: Indiana University Press, 1972.
Blackman, Winifred. S. "The Rosary in Magic and Religion." *Folklore* 29, no. 4 (1918): 255–80.
Blanton, Ward. "Augustine's Postal Demons: Reflections on a Theologico-Postal History of the West." Paper presented at the European Science Foundation Exploratory Workshop "Technology and Religion: Structural Affinities and Cultural Challenges." Glasgow, October 14–16, 2009.

Boas, Franz. *The Religion of the Kwakiutl*. New York: Columbia University Press, 1930.

Bogen, Jules I. *The Anthracite Railroads: A Study in American Railroad Enterprise*. New York: Ronald Press Company, 1927.

Borwick, John. *Microphones: Technology and Technique*. London: Focal Press, 1990.

Braun-Ronsdorf, Margarete. "The Handkerchief." *Ciba Review* 89 (December 1951): 3198–222.

———. *The History of the Handkerchief*. Leigh-on-Sea: F. Lewis, 1967.

Brown, Sterling. "Negro Folk Expressions: Spirituals, Seculars, Ballads and Work Songs." *Phylon* 14 (Winter): 1953.

Buck-Morss, Susan. "The Cinema Screen as Prosthesis of Perception: A Historical Account." In *The Senses Still: Perception and Memory as Material Culture in Modernity*, edited by C. Nadia Seremetakis. Chicago: University of Chicago Press, 1996.

Canetti, Elias. *Crowds and Power*. New York: Viking Press, 1972.

Carroll, Michael. "Interview: Praying the Rosary." *Journal for the Scientific Study of Religion* 27, no. 3 (September 1988): 429–41.

———. "Praying the Rosary: The Anal-Erotic Origins of a Popular Catholic Devotion." *Journal for the Scientific Study of Religion* 26, no. 4 (December 1987): 486–98.

Chéroux, Clement. *The Perfect Medium: Photography and the Occult*. New Haven: Yale University Press, 2005.

Chidester, David. *Authentic Fakes: Religion and American Popular Culture*. Berkeley: University of California Press, 2005.

———. *Word and Light: Seeing, Hearing, and Religious Discourse*. Urbana: University of Illinois Press, 1992.

Classen, Constance. *The Book of Touch*. Oxford, UK: Berg, 2005.

Clements, William. "The Rhetoric of the Radio Ministry." *Journal of American Folklore* 87, no. 346 (Fall 1974): 318–27.

Connor, Steven. *Dumbstruck: A Cultural History of Ventriloquism*. Oxford, UK: Oxford University Press, 2000.

———. "The Help of Your Good Hands: Reports on Clapping." In *The Auditory Culture Reader*, edited by Michael Bull. New York: Berg, 2003.

———. "Edison's Teeth: Touching Hearing." In *Hearing Cultures: Essays on Sound, Listening, and Modernity*, edited by Veit Erlmann. Oxford, UK: Berg, 2004.

———. "Incidents of Breath: Pneumatic and Electric Ventriloquisms." In *Articulate Objects: Voice, Sculpture, and Performance*, edited by Aura Satz. Bern: International Academic Publishers, 2009.

———. "The Machine in the Ghost: Spiritualism, Technology, and the 'Direct Voice.'" In *Ghosts: Deconstruction, Psychoanalysis, History*, edited by Peter Buse. New York: St. Martin's, 1999.

Corbin, Alain. *Village Bells: Sound and Meaning in the 19th-Century French Countryside*. New York: Columbia University Press, 1998.

Crapanzano, Vincent. "The Moment of Prestidigitation: Magic, Illusion, and Mana in the Thought of Emile Durkheim." In *Prehistories of the Future: The*

Primitivist Project and the Culture of Modernism, edited by E. Barkan and R. Bush. Stanford: Stanford University Press, 1995.

Csordas, Thomas. "Asymptote of the Ineffable: Embodiment, Alterity and the Theory of Religion." *Cultural Anthropology* 45, no. 2 (April 2004): 163–85.

———. "Elements of Charismatic Persuasion and Healing." *Medical Anthropology Quarterly* 2, no. 2 (June 1988): 121–42.

———. "Embodiment as a Paradigm for Anthropology." *Ethos* 18, no. 1 (March 1990): 5–47.

———. *The Sacred Self: A Cultural Phenomenology of Charismatic Healing.* Berkeley: University of California Press, 1994.

———. "Somatic Modes of Attention." *Cultural Anthropology* 8, no. 2 (May 1993): 135–56.

Curtis, Heather D. "Acting Faith: Practices of Religious Healing in Late Nineteenth-Century Protestantism." In *Practicing Protestants: Histories of Christian Life in America, 1630–1965*, edited by Laurie Maffly-Kipp, Leigh E. Schmidt, and Mark Valeri. Baltimore: Johns Hopkins University Press, 2006.

Faith in the Great Physician: Suffering and Divine Healing in American Culture, 1860–1900. Baltimore: Johns Hopkins University Press, 2007.

Davis, Gerald. *I Got the Word in Me and I Can Sing It, You Know: A Study of the Performed African-American Sermon.* Philadelphia: University of Pennsylvania Press, 1985.

De Abreau, Maria. "Goose Bumps All Over: Breath, Media, and Tremor." *Social Text* 26, no. 3 (Fall 2008): 59–78.

Dean, Rebecca. "'I'll Meet You In the Air: A Cultural Study of Appalachian Pentecostal Radio Preaching." Ph.D. diss., University of Pittsburgh, 1998.

Derrida, Jacques. *On Touching, Jean-Luc Nancy.* Stanford: Stanford University Press, 2005.

De Certeau, Michel. "What We Do When We Believe." In *On Signs*, edited by Marshall Blonsky. Baltimore: Johns Hopkins University Press, 1985.

De Vries, Hent, ed. *Religion and Media.* Stanford: Stanford University Press, 2001.

Dix, Keith. *What's a Coal Miner to Do? The Mechanization of Coal Mining.* Pittsburgh: University of Pittsburgh Press, 1988.

Dorgan, Howard. *The Airwaves of Zion: Radio and Religion in Appalachia.* Knoxville: University of Tennessee Press, 1993.

———. *Giving Glory to God in Appalachia: Worship Practices of Six Baptist Subdenominations.* Knoxville: University of Tennessee Press, 1990.

———. *In the Hands of a Happy God: The "No-Hellers" of Central Appalachia.* Knoxville: University of Tennessee Press, 1997.

———. *The Old Regular Baptists of Central Appalachia: Brothers and Sisters in Hope.* Knoxville: University of Tennessee Press, 1989.

Durkheim, Émile. *The Elementary Forms of the Religious Life.* New York: Free University Press, 1996.

Eisenlohr, Patrick. "Materialities of Entextualization: The Domestication of Sound Reproduction in Mauritian Muslim Devotional Practices." *Journal of Linguistic Anthropology* 20, no. 2 (December 2010): 314–33.

———. "Mediality and Materiality in Religious Performance: Religion as Heritage in Mauritius." *Material Religion* 9, no. 3 (September 2013): 330–48.

———. "Technologies of the Spirit: Devotional Islam, Sound Reproduction, and the Dialectics of Mediation and Immediacy in Mauritius." *Anthropological Theory* 9, no. 3 (November 2009): 273–96.

Eller, Ronald. *Miners, Millhands, and Mountaineers: Industrialization of the Appalachian South, 1880–1930.* Knoxville: University of Tennessee Press, 1982.

Engelke, Matthew. *A Problem of Presence: Beyond Scripture in an African Church.* Berkeley: University of California Press, 2007.

———. "Sticky Subjects and Sticky Objects: The Substance of African Christian Healing." In *Materiality*, edited by Daniel Miller. Durham: Duke University Press, 2005.

Ferris, William. "Railroad Chants: Form and Function." *Mississippi Folklore Register* 4 (1970).

Freud, Sigmund. *Jokes and Their Relation to the Unconscious.* New York: Penguin, 1976.

———. *The Psychopathology of Everyday Life.* New York: Penguin Books, 2002.

———. *Totem and Taboo: Some Points of Agreement between the Mental Lives of Savages and Neurotics.* New York: Norton, 1952.

———. *The Uncanny.* New York: Penguin Books, 2003.

Gaventa, John. *Power and Powerlessness: Quiescence and Rebellion in an Appalachian Valley.* Urbana: University of Illinois Press, 1980.

Goody, Jack. *The Domestication of the Savage Mind.* Cambridge: Cambridge University Press, 1977.

Griffith, R. Marie. "Material Devotion: Pentecostal Prayer Cloths." Interview. *Material History of American Religion Newsletter* (Spring 1997): 1–3.

Gumbrecht, Hans. *Production of Presence: What Meaning Cannot Convey.* Stanford: Stanford University Press, 2004.

Gumbrecht, Hans, and Ludwig Pfeiffer, eds. *Materialities of Communication.* Stanford: Stanford University Press, 1994.

Gunning, Tom. "Phantom Images and Modern Manifestations: Spirit Photography, Magic Theater, Trick Films, and Photography's Uncanny." In *Fugitive Images: From Photography to Video*, edited by Patrice Petro. Bloomington: Indiana University Press, 1995.

Hangen, Tona J. *Redeeming the Dial: Radio, Religion, and Popular Culture in America.* Chapel Hill: University of North Carolina Press, 2002.

Harding, Susan. *The Book of Jerry Falwell: Fundamentalist Language and Politics.* Princeton: Princeton University Press, 2000.

Harrell, David. *All Things Are Possible: The Healing and Charismatic Revivals in Modern America.* Bloomington: Indiana University Press, 1975.

———. *Oral Roberts: An American Life.* Bloomington: Indiana University Press, 1985.

Hastings, James, ed. *The Encyclopaedia of Religion and Ethics.* New York: Charles Scribner's, 1919.

Havelock, Eric. *The Muse Learns to Write: Reflections on Orality and Literacy from Antiquity to the Present.* New Haven: Yale University Press, 1986.
———. *Preface to Plato.* New York: Grosset & Dunlap, 1967.
Heiler, Friedrich. *Prayer: A Study in the History and Psychology of Religion.* London: Oxford University Press, 1932.
Hill, Jonathan. *The Cat's Whisker: 50 Years of Wireless Design.* London: Oresko Books, 1978.
Hirschkind, Charles. *The Ethical Soundscape: Cassette Sermons and Islamic Counterpublics.* New York: Columbia University Press, 2006.
Hollenweger, Walter J. *The Pentecostals: The Charismatic Movement and the Churches.* Minneapolis: Augsburg Pub. House, 1972.
Holtzberg-Call, Maggie. *Gandy Dancers.* Cinema Guild, color video, 1994.
Houtman, Dick, and Birgit Meyer, eds. *Things: Religion and the Question of Materiality.* New York: Fordham University Press, 2012.
Hubert, Henri. *Essay on Time: A Brief Study of the Representation of Time in Religion and Magic.* Oxford, UK: Durkheim Press, 1999.
Hubert, Henri, and Marcel Mauss. *Sacrifice: Its Nature and Function.* Chicago: University of Chicago Press, 1964.
Hurston, Zora Neale. *The Sanctified Church.* New York: Marlow, 1981.
Innis, Harold. *Empire and Communications.* Toronto: University of Toronto Press, 1972.
Ivy, Marilyn. *Discourses of the Vanishing: Modernity, Phantasm, Japan.* Chicago: University of Chicago Press, 1995.
Jackson, Bruce. *Afro-American Work Songs in a Texas Prison.* Black and white film. Produced by Peter and Toshi Seeger. Folklore Research Films, Inc., 1966.
———. "The Glory Songs of the Lord." In *Our Living Traditions: An Introduction to American Folklore,* edited by Tristram Coffin. New York: Basic Books, 1968.
———. "Prison Work Songs: The Composer in the Negatives." *Western Folklore* 26, no. 4 (October 1967): 245–68.
———. *Wake Up Dead Man: Afro-American Worksongs from Texas Prisons.* Cambridge: Harvard University Press, 1972.
Jackson, J. M. "The Black American Folk Sermon and the Chanted Sermon: Parallels with a West African Tradition." In *Discourse in Ethnomusicology II: A Tribute to Alan P. Merriam,* edited by Caroline Card. Bloomington: Ethnomusicology Publications Group, 1981.
Jakobson, Roman. "Closing Statements: Linguistics and Poetics." In *Style in Language,* edited by Thomas Sebeok. Cambridge: MIT Press, 1960.
Johnson, James Weldon. *God's Trombones: Seven Negro Sermons in Verse.* New York: Viking, 1927.
Jousse, Marcel. *The Anthropology of Geste and Rhythm: Studies in the Anthropological Laws of Human Expression and Their Application in the Galilean Oral Style Tradition.* Edited by E. Sienaert. Durban: University of Natal, Centre for Oral Studies, 1997.
———. *The Oral Style.* New York: Garland. 1990.

Larkin, Brian. *Signal and Noise: Media, Infrastructure, and Urban Culture in Nigeria.* Durham: Duke University Press, 2008.

Leiris, Michel. *La Langue Secrète des Dogons de Sanga* (Soudan Français). Paris: Institut d'Ethnologie, 1948.

Leroi-Gourhan, Andre. *Gesture and Speech.* Cambridge: MIT Press, 1993.

Lévi-Strauss, Claude. *The Savage Mind.* Chicago: University of Chicago Press, 1966.

———. *Structural Anthropology.* New York: Basic Books, 1963.

Lewis, Ronald. *Black Coal Miners in America: Race, Class, and Community Conflict, 1780–1980.* Lexington: University Press of Kentucky, 1987.

Lichtenstein, Alex. *Twice the Work of Free Labor: The Political Economy of Convict Labor in the New South.* London and New York: Verso, 1996.

Lomax, Alan. *Prison Songs, Vol. 1: Murderous Home.* Historic recordings from Parchman Farm, 1947–48. Cambridge: Rounder Records, 1997.

Macneal, Patricia. *Quilts from Appalachia: An Exhibition Sponsored by the Palmer Museum of Art.* University Park: Pennsylvania State University, 1988.

Maffly-Kipp, Laurie, and Eric Schmidt, eds. *Practicing Protestants: Histories of Christian Life in America, 1630–1965.* Baltimore: Johns Hopkins University Press, 2006.

Manning, Ambrose. "Railroad Work Songs." *Tennessee Folklore Society Bulletin* 32 (June 1966): 41–47.

Mauss, Marcel. *A General Theory of Magic.* New York, Norton, 1975.

———. *The Gift: The Form and Reason for Exchange in Archaic Societies.* New York: W. W. Norton, 1990.

———. *Manual of Ethnography.* Oxford, UK: Durkheim Press/Berghahn Books, 2007.

———. *On Prayer.* New York: Durkheim Press/Berghahn Books, 2003.

———. *Techniques, Technology, and Civilization.* New York: Durkheim Press/Berghahn Books, 2006.

McDannell, Colleen. *Material Christianity: Religion and Popular Culture in America.* New Haven: Yale University Press, 1995.

Merleau-Ponty, Maurice. *The Visible and the Invisible; Followed by Working Notes.* Evanston: Northwestern University Press, 1968.

Meyer, Birgit. *Aesthetic Formations: Media, Religion, and the Senses.* New York: Palgrave, 2009.

———. "Religious Sensations: Why Media, Aesthetics, and Power Matter in the Study of Contemporary Religion." *Religion: Beyond a Concept*, edited by Hent De Vries. New York: Fordham University Press, 2008.

Meyer, Birgit. and Annelies Moors, eds. *Religion, Media, and the Public Sphere.* Bloomington, Indiana University Press, 2006.

Meyer, Birgit, and Peter Pels, eds. *Magic and Modernity: Interfaces of Revelation and Concealment.* Stanford: Stanford University Press, 2003.

Miller, Daniel. *Material Cultures: Why Some Things Matter.* London: UCL Press, 1998.

———. *Materiality.* Durham: Duke University Press, 2005.

Miracles Yesterday, Today, and Forever. Santa Ana: Trinity Broadcasting Network, videocassette (part 2), 1994.

Mitchell, Henry. *Black Preaching: The Recovery of a Powerful Art*. Philadelphia: Lippincott, 1970.

Morgan, David, ed. *Religion and Material Culture: The Matter of Belief*. New York: Routledge, 2010.

Muller, Max. *Last Essays by the Right Hon. Professor F. Max Muller*. London: Longmans, Green, 1901.

Mumford, Lewis. *Technics and Civilization*. New York: Harcourt, 1934.

Nancy, Jean-Luc. *The Birth to Presence*. Stanford: Stanford University Press, 1993.

———. *Corpus*. Paris: A.M. Métailié: Diffusion, Seuil, 1992.

Needham, Rodney. "Percussion and Transition." *Man* (New Series) 2, no. 4 (December 1967): 231–44.

Nelson, Scott Reynolds. *Steel Drivin' Man: John Henry, the Untold Story of an American Legend*. Oxford and New York: Oxford University Press, 2006.

Ong, Walter. *Orality and Literacy: The Technologizing of the Word*. New York: Methuen, 1982.

———. *The Presence of the Word: Some Prolegomena for Cultural and Religious History*. New Haven: Yale University Press, 1967.

Otto, Rudolf. *The Idea of the Holy: An Inquiry into the Non-Rational Factor in the Divine and Its Relation to the Rational*. New York: Oxford University Press, 1958.

Pemberton, John. "The Spectre of Coincidence." In *Southeast Asia over Three Generations: Essays Presented to Benedict R. O'G. Anderson*, edited by James Siegel. Ithaca: Cornell University Press, 2003.

Peri, Paolo. *The Handkerchief*. Modena: Zanfi, 1992.

Peters, John Durham. *Speaking into the Air: A History of the Idea of Communication*. Chicago: University of Chicago Press, 1999.

Pipes, William. *Say Amen, Brother! Old-Time Negro Preaching: A Study in American Frustration*. New York: William-Frederick Press, 1951.

Pitts, Ann. "A Prosodic Analysis of a Chanted Formulaic Sermon." *Rackham Literary Studies* 9 (1978): 89–96.

Pitts, Walter. "Keep the Fire Burnin': Language and Ritual in the Afro-Baptist Church." *Journal of the American Academy of Religion* 56, no. 1 (Fall 1988): 77–97.

———. *Old Ship of Zion: The Afro-Baptist Ritual in the African Diaspora*. New York: Oxford University Press, 1993.

———. "West African Poetics in the Black Preaching Style." *American Speech* 64, no. 2 (Summer 1989): 137–49.

Porterfield, Amanda. *Healing in the History of Christianity*. New York: Oxford University Press, 2005.

Raboteau, Albert. *A Fire in the Bones: Reflections on African-American Religious History*. Boston: Beacon Press, 1995.

———. *Slave Religion: The "Invisible Institution" in the Antebellum South*. New York: Oxford University Press, 2004.

Rakes, Paul. "Acceptable Casualties: Power, Culture, and History in the West Virginia Coalfields, 1900–1945." Ph.D. diss., West Virginia University, 2002.

Randi, James. *The Faith Healers*. Buffalo: Prometheus Books, 1987.

Roberts, Oral. *If You Need Healing Do These Things*. Tulsa: Healing Waters, 1950.

Robinson, Clayton. "The Laying On of Hands, with Special Reference to the Reception of the Holy Spirit in the New Testament." Ph.D. diss., Fuller Theological Seminary, 2008.

Rosenberg, Bruce. *The Art of the American Folk Preacher*. New York: Oxford University Press, 1970.

———. "The Formulaic Quality of Spontaneous Sermons." *Journal of American Folklore* 83, no. 327 (Spring 1970): 3–20.

———. "The Message of the American Folk Sermon." *Oral Tradition* 1, no. 3 (Spring 1986): 695–727.

———. "The Psychology of the Spiritual Sermon." In *Religious Movements in Contemporary America*, edited by Irving Zaretsky. Princeton: Princeton University Press, 1974.

Rouget, Gilbert. "African Traditional Non-Prose Forms: Reciting, Declaiming, Singing, and Strophic Structure. In *Proceedings of a Conference on African Languages and Literatures Held at Northwestern University*, edited by J. Berry. Evanston: Northwestern University, 1966.

———. *Music and Trance: A Theory of the Relations between Music and Possession*. Chicago: University of Chicago Press, 1985.

Scannell, Paddy. *Radio, Television, and Modern Life: A Phenomenological Approach*. Cambridge: Blackwell, 1996.

Schiffer, Michael Brian. *The Portable Radio in American Life*. Tucson: University of Arizona Press, 1991.

Schivelbusch, Wolfgang. *Disenchanted Night: The Industrialization of Light in the Nineteenth Century*. Berkeley: University of California Press, 1988.

———. *The Railway Journey: The Industrialization of Time and Space in the Nineteenth Century*. Leamington Spa: Berg, 1986.

Schmidt, Leigh Eric. *Hearing Things: Religion, Illusion, and the American Enlightenment*. Cambridge: Harvard University Press, 2000.

Schrenck-Notzing, Albert. *Phenomena of Materialisation: A Contribution to the Investigation of Mediumistic Teleplastics*. London: Kegan Paul, Trench, Trubner, 1920.

Seremetakis, Nadia. *The Senses Still: Perception and Memory as Material Culture in Modernity*. Chicago: University of Chicago Press, 1996.

Shelton, Allen. *Dreamworlds of Alabama*. Minneapolis: University of Minnesota Press. 2007.

Shifflett, Crandall. *Coal Towns: Life, Work, and Culture in Company Towns of Southern Appalachia, 1880–1960*. Knoxville: University of Tennessee Press, 1991.

Sloss Furnace Association, producer. *Spirit of Steel: Music of the Mines, Railroads, and Mills of the Birmingham District—An Educational Resource*. Birmingham: Sloss Furnaces National Historic Landmark and Crane Hill Publishers, 1999.

Siegert, Bernhard. *Relays: Literature as an Epoch of the Postal System*. Stanford: Stanford University Press, 1999.

Sienaert, Edgard. "Marcel Jousse: The Oral Style and the Anthropology of Gesture." *Oral Tradition* 5, no. 1 (Summer 1990): 91–106.
Smith, William R. *Lectures on the Religion of the Semites. First series. The Fundamental Institutions.* New York: Appleton, 1889.
Sterne, Jonathan. *The Audible Past: Cultural Origins of Sound Reproduction.* Durham: Duke University Press, 2003.
Stewart, Kathleen. *A Space on the Side of the Road: Cultural Poetics in an "Other" America.* Princeton: Princeton University Press, 1996.
Stocking, George. *Delimiting Anthropology: Occasional Essays and Reflections.* Madison: University of Wisconsin Press, 2001.
Strauss, Neil, ed. *Radiotext(e).* New York: Semiotext(e), 1993.
Summers, Leonard. *Anthracite and the Anthracite Industry.* New York: Pitman & Sons, 1922.
Tacchi, Jo. "Radio Texture: Between Self and Others." In: *Material Cultures: Why Some Things Matter*, edited by Daniel Miller. Chicago: University of Chicago Press, 1998.
Taussig, Michael. "Tactility and Distraction." *Cultural Anthropology* 6, no. 2 (May 1991): 147–53.
———. "Viscerality, Faith, and Skepticism: Another Theory of Magic." In *Magic and Modernity: Interfaces of Revelation and Concealment*, edited by Birgit Meyer and Peter Pels. Stanford: Stanford University Press, 2003.
Teichelmann, C. G., and Schurmann, C. W. *Outlines of a Grammar, Vocabulary, and Phraseology, of the Aboriginal Language of South Australia.* Adelaide: self-published, 1840.
Thurston, Herbert. "Genuflexions and Aves: A Study in Rosary Origins (Part 1)." *Month* 127 (1916): 441–52, 546–59.
Tillis, Fredrick, and Koenraad Kuiper. "The Chant of the Tobacco Auctioneer." *American Speech* 60, no. 2 (Summer 1985): 141–49.
Titon, Jeff Todd. *Powerhouse for God: Speech, Chant, and Song in an Appalachian Baptist Church.* Austin: University of Texas Press, 1988.
Trotter, Joe. *Coal, Class, and Color: Blacks in Southern West Virginia, 1915–32.* Urbana: University of Illinois Press, 1990.
Turner, Victor. "Images of Anti-temporality: An Essay in the Anthropology of Experience." *Harvard Theological Review* 75, no. 2 (1982): 243–65.
Vaughn-Cooke, Anna Fay. "The Black Preaching Style: Historical Development and Characteristics." In *Language and Linguistics Working Papers* 5, edited by W. K. Riley. Georgetown: Georgetown University, 1972.
Warner, Michael. *Publics and Counterpublics.* Cambridge: Zone Books, 2002.
Whitehouse, Michael. "Manus Impositio: The Initiatory Rite of Handlaying in the Churches of Early Western Christianity." Ph.D. diss., University of Notre Dame, 2008.
Wormser, Richard. *The Rise and Fall of Jim Crow.* New York: St. Martin's Press, 2003.

Index

Accident: on highway, 54; coal mining, 91; safety, 93–94; "Be Careful!," 95–96
Acoustic unconscious, 115, 173, 181
Adorno, Theodor W., 21, 166; "spooks" of radio voice, 176
African American, 9; work songs and spirituals, 140–44; influence on preaching styles, 140–44; forced labor, 144; prayer and quilting, 192 (n. 14)
Allen, A. A., 66
Amplification, 17–18; efficacy of prayer, 22; in tent revival, 24, 179; spiritual intimacies of, 146, 181
Anointing, 12; of prayer cloth, 55; with oil, 56, 58, 92, 93; cloth remnant, 61; handkerchief, 67, 78; bodily fluid, 67–68; as manufacture, 93, and Holy Ghost chills, 99–100; as secretion, 100; as rhetorical gift, 116, 119; absence of, 149. *See also* Breath; Grunt
Anorexia, 78
Apostle Paul, 67–68, 92
Apotropaic: prayer cloth as, 82–83
Apparatus of belief, 26; and postal system, 80; radio as, 175; special effect and sensory disjuncture, 176
Arnheim, Rudolf, 188–89; on radio blindness, 166
Articulation, 17
Automaticity, 55, 88–89; sacred, 91, 95, 97; and laughter, 128; and everyday life, 169

Baptism: in river, 122; story of, 123; rite of, 124
Belief: "Only Believe," 23, 166; and ritual efficacy, 27; locus of, 83
Benjamin, Walter, 177; mechanical reproduction, 77–83
Biomedicine, 131
Blasphemy: of sacrament, 70; of Holy Ghost, 185–86
Blindness: and radio audition, 18, 25; Arnheim's description of, 148–49
Blood: song about, 66; bodily fluid, 67; woman with issue of, 67, 169; like flow of electricity, 169
Bones, 53; sound of, 1; Elisha's, 2; song "These Bones," 2; embodiment, 3; prayer, 3; Ezekiel's dry, 9; and audition, 10; resurrection of, 11; fire in, 12; and honeycomb, 109, 112; mended, 186
Breath, 11, 104; prayer for, 116; body technique of, 118, 143, 145; "breath-unit," 118, 146; total poetics of, 120; breath-dance, 146; shallow, 147; momentum generated through, 148, 155
Brown, Clarence, 53

Carroll, Michael, 60
Catastrophe, 91
Certeau, Michel de, 85
Chant: of tobacco auctioneer, 132, 134, 145; rhythm and work, 140–44; monotone, 145–46

217

Index

Charismata (charism): of rhetoric, 12; of discernment, 23, 175; poetic, 136; Oral Roberts's point of contact, 168
Charismatic broadcast, 12
Charismatic Revival/Renewal, 7, 8, 165, 175
Children, 135
Coal mining: dust, 16; Red Ash Coal Company, 91; accident, 91, 196 (n. 50); "Be Careful!," 95; disaster, 95; electrical infrastructure, 97; railway, 140–44. *See also* Accident
Colloquialism, 136
Consecration: of everyday object, 87. *See also* Anointing; Cutting; Skein Prayer
Crowd phenomena, 65
Curtis, Heather, 171
Cutting: pinking shears, 56, 63; of cloth, 61; and charismatic theology, 64; process of, 64; ritual significance of, 87

Dance: respiratory techniques of, 117–18; in the spirit, 118; runnin' in the spirit, 124–25; Gandy dancing, 140–44; technique of body, 143; breath-dance, 146; as political protest, 199 (n. 25)
Dead, the, 150
Demon, 179, 185; of illness, 23, 167–68; possession, 174–75
Devil, 20, 106–7, 137, 152, 157; Satan, 29; torments child, 82–84
Disavowal: faith and the object, 27, 81, 83
Discernment, 68, 179–80; charismatic gift, 23; in revival tent, 24; Oral Roberts's hand of, 166; spectral detection, 174–75
Divination: apparatus of, 32
Dog: bulldog, 53, 137; bite of, 28–29
Dollar Store, 85
Doubled awareness, 22. *See also* Sensory disjuncture

Ecstasy, 28
Ectoplasm, 75–77
Engelke, Matthew: on prayer pebble, 193 (n. 22)
Exchange: theories of, 5; of hands, 59, 82; relation to testimony, 79; circulation of prayer cloth, 84; circulation and belief, 85

Faith: exteriorities of, 4, 72; and hearing, 10; doubled nature of, 27; objectile dimension of, 27; texture of, 59; as beyond subject, 80; unplaceability of, 83; insistence upon, 161; electrical metaphors of, 170; "faith cure," 171; ritual instantiation of, 171; locus of, 173; Freud's account of, 176; as interface, 177; shift in, 182
Faith healing: ethnographic theories of, 4; practices of, 14; scholarly assumptions, 27
Ferenczi, Sandor, 60
Fetish, 3
Fieldwork, 5–6
Film: high-speed camera, 193 (n. 24)
Floppin' Fish, 123
Flow: tactile communication, 67; sacred fluidity, 68; electrical phenomena, 169; point of contact as, 170
Foot washing, 53
Freud, Sigmund: *not* uncanny, 124; description of faith, 176; logic of uncanny, 177; on the prosthetic, 177; slip of tongue, 181

Gap: between sacred and everyday, 156; relation to "standin'-in," 157; bridging techniques, 159; between Holy Ghost and everyday, 161; between healing and everyday, 164
Genuflection, 1; and monastic regulation, 60
Gesture: "Holy hand," 16; demarcating

sacred space, 93; instrumental, 168; of listener, 172; curative, 180; inversion of, 180
Glossolalia, 17, 101, 128; from loudspeaker, 34; in tent, 66; early Pentecostal, 76; definition of, 77; as routinized tongue, 147; Pentecostal history, 148; example, 151. *See also* Tongues
Granet, Marcel, 143
Graveside, 113
Griffith, R. Marie, 90
Grunt: description of, 117; as respiratory spring, 118; growl of voice, 119; as pneumatic gesture, 120; shallow, 120; and clapping, 121; engastrimythic, 121; percussive drum, 121; as sacred laughter, 133; percussive punctuation, 145; as breath-dance, 146
Guitar, 124–25
Gun, 86, 87, 88

Hand: textile definition of, 52
Handkerchief: anointing of, 63; ancient *sudarium*, 67; hanky-panky, 69, 73; etymology and history of, 69–71; maniple, 71; testimony, 78; green prosperity, 195 (n. 43)
Healing prayer: testimony, 20, 22
Healing Waters broadcast, 8, 171–72; "prayer time" of, 23
Heavyset Woman, 126
Hell: dead in, 150–52
Holiness church, 53
Holy, 113
Holy Ghost: manifestation of, 10; revelatory remnant, 87; laughter, 128; "far" (fire), 138; possession of, 148; resonances of, 186
Holy Ghost chills, 98–104, 128, 198 (n. 11)
Honeycomb, 109, 112, 138
Hubert, Henri, 4, 172

If You Need Healing Do These Things, 23, 170, 173; explains point of contact, 165–66
Improvisation, 12–13, 15, 121; as spirit of prayer, 164
Independent Bible Church of God at Red Ash, 91, 95, 97
Infrastructure: of radio broadcast, 21; of revival tent, 64; of transience, 65; postal system, 80; of circulation, 82; coal-powered, 97; cartoon illustration of, 166; as faith metaphor, 167; instrumental gesture of, 168; anxieties around, 169

Jackson Memorial Hour, 5, 14–15, 90, 122, 163
Jousse, Marcel, 118

King James Bible, 136

Language: excess of, 72; exteriority of, 76
Laughter: belly, 120–21; laughing spirit, 120–21; and clapping, 121; self-effacing, 121; ritual aspects of, 124; sacred aspect of, 124; force of, 127; Holy Ghost, 128; smile, 128; in charismatic worship, 130; anointed, 132; guttural, 133
Lightbulb, 13, 16, 167, 169, 185; flicker of, 97
Lomax, Alan and John, 141
Loudspeaker: heat and pressure of, 25; sounds glossolalia, 34, 146

Magic, 69
Manual imposition (laying on of hands); healing techniques of, 5; sound of, 15; practices of touch, 22; on sick patient, 157; loudspeaker, 161; on radio, 162, 165; history of, 174–75; mechanical reproduction, 177; Benjamin's

invocation of, 178; and voice amplification, 179; mechanical reproduction, 180
Manual technique: of prayer, 56–57; fingering beads, 60
Mass Media: religious movements, 7
Mauss, M., 118, 172; *On Prayer*, 3–4; on gift, 55, 79; on magic, 83; technique of the body, 142–43; psychotechnics, 148; on breath, 200 (n. 26)
McDannell, Colleen, 5
McPherson, Aimee, 23
Mechanicity: sound of, 85; moment of coincidence, 88; machines, 91
Merleau-Ponty, Maurice, 174
Microphone, 5, 145, 149, 182–83; as altar, 15–16; ritual organizations around, 17–18; in revival tent, 24; ritual progression around, 31; sacred space, 32; and zipper, 115; Oral Roberts's intimacy with, 179
Meyer, Birgit, 3, 4, 18
Mnemotechnics, 58; rosary bead, 61; and preaching 136, 148
Muller, Max, 14

Nancy, Jean Luc, 174
Narrative: structure, 54, 80, 89; effects of, 55; temporal dimension, 79; as performance of faith, 132
Noise, 9, 17, 19; numinous, 10; as distortion, 19; warm vibrations of, 26; nonrepresentational 58, 122; efficacy of, 159–60

Objectile, 4, 10, 23, 27; renunciation of, 83

Pantomime, 73
"Par" (power), 85, 147, 186; Holy Ghost, 1; shaking radio, 20; and Holy Ghost chills, 99; warsh off, 103; at baptism, 123; and runnin' in the spirit, 125; par-a-God, 128; as "far" (fire) 138
Parable, 37

Patching, 9, 164; creative reuse, 62; and Pentecostal theology, 64; Holy Ghost power, 88
Percussion, 1, 74; clapping, 17, 87, 121; respiration, 117; Holy Ghost drum, 121; percussive architecture 121; and work calls, 140–44. *See also* Grunt
Photography, 75
Pneumatic gesture, 120, 146, 148
Pneumatology: charismatic, 64. *See also* Pneumatic gesture
Point of Contact, 9, 15; and healing prayer, 22; cartoon illustrations of, 23, 25–27, 166; instructions and history, 62, 165; and electrical infrastructure, 167–69; and energy flow, 170; temporal dimension of, 170; radio as, 171; temporal awareness, 173
Postal system, 6, 65, 68, 77, 79–80; Oral Roberts and prayer cloth, 62–63; writing letters, 81–82
Potter's wheel, 108, 137
Prayer: history of, 8, 14–15, 18; techniques of, 8, 16; sound of, 10; healing, 15; failure of, 20; machine, 60; recitation, 61; tent, 66; handkerchief, 69, 72; for breath, 116; breakdown of, 159, 161; material histories of, 182; technical organization of, 183
Prayer board, 102
Prayer cloth, 6, 8, 52–54; anointing of, 55–56; and voice, 57–58; exchange of, 59; texture of, 60; cutting of, 61; printed message on, 62; manipulation of, 64; relation to revival tent, 65; history of, 68; "prayer handkerchief," 72; cloth as an everyday object, 76; tongue shape, 77; wearing of, 86, 88, 90; as textile tongue, 87; critique of historical description, 90; anointing with oil, 92; colored bandanas, 93; portability of, 96. *See also* Cutting; Handkerchief
Prayer line, 24, 82

Prayer machine, 61
Prayer warrior, 15, 20, 29, 55–57
Preaching, 9; "stall formula," 201 (n. 34). *See also* Anointing; Breath; Grunt
Precarious: etymology of, 14, 27, 95
Prestidigitation, 71–72, 94, 187 (n. 6); moment of, 4, 172
Prison: women's penitentiary in Virginia, 122; Tennessee work farms, 140–44
Profanation, 96
Prosthesis, 10, 68, 88, 160, 184, 186; and charismatic gift, 23, 25; of prayer, 26–27, 175; and ecstatic movements, 86–87; divine, 168, 175–76; vision, 178; mode of hearing, 182. *See also* Discernment
PTL Club (Praise the Lord), 126–27
Possession: twitch of, 122

Radio: voice, 11; "radioland," 13; early sets, 15; listening practices and habit, 19, 21; divine vision, 34–35; prosthesis of, 180
Radio tactility, 6, 163, 173, 190 (n. 22); national scale of, 7–8; and charismatic touch, 22; new sensory mode, 26; interfacing of, 28; automobile radio, 160; ritual of 162; during "prayer time," 171; as legerdemain, 172
Railroad: track maintenance, 140; song about, 142; forced African American labor, 144
Raven, Va., 147
Red Ash, Va., 91–92
Remnant, 164; cloth fragments, 52, 56; and tactility, 57; transformation of, 58, 61; bag, 62–63; theological significance of, 64, 87; filthy rags, 66–67. *See also* Cutting
Resurrection, 113; of bones, 2

Revelations, 150
Rhythm: structure, 118; coordinated movements, 140–44
Richlands, Va., 122
Ritual: organization of, 6; circumambulation, 28, 30; technological transformations of, 32; performance, 32, 172; substitution, 56; healing instructions, 62; Eucharistic, 71; cutting, 87; of anointing, 93; and humor, 124; breathing techniques, 143; running, 143; gesture, 171; temporality, 172; antitemporality, 173; techniques of radio tactility, 173; technological transformations of, 178; reversal of gesture, 180; parasitical dependence, 180, 183; of divine communication, 182; technique of substitution, 183
Roberts, Oral, 7–9, 173; theological terms, 22–23; use of prayer cloth, 62–63; tent cathedral, 65, 178; "prayer tent," 66; faith healing technique, 165; cartoon illustration, 166; on discernment, 174–76; healing line, 180
Rosary bead, 60
Rosenberg, Bruce, 201 (n. 34)
Rust, 154

Sacred: sound of, 10
Saussure, Ferdinand de, 76
Schrenck-Notzing, Albert, 75
Sensation/senses, 10, 19, 21, 25–27, 98, 160, 174–75, 180, 184; structures of awareness, 99; artificial amplification of, 161; sensory capacity, 165–67, 170; divinely augmented, 168; devotional attention, 182
Sensational form, 3, 18
Sensory disjuncture, 19; and Holy Ghost power, 25; and distraction, 72; and magic, 73–74; and point of contact, 172; apparatus of belief, 176
Shelton, Allen, 195 (n. 43)

Skein prayer, 58, 64, 87, 121; definition, 16; efficacy of, 17–20; and tactile sensation, 26; numinous noise of, 57, 94, 161; and sonic momentum, 159

Snake, 138; serpent, 39; rattlesnake and copperhead bite, 109

Song: transition from chant to, 119, 133; and tool movement, 141; "a meeting in the air," 162

Special effect, 18–19, 22, 148; magic trick, 73; as sensory disjuncture, 176

Spiritualism: history of, 75; and relation to technology, 148

"Standin'-in," 9, 16, 28, 64, 86; descriptions of, 157, 159–61; and Stewart's "foolin' with thangs," 164, 183. *See also* Improvisation; Patching

Stewart, Kathleen: "foolin' with thangs," 16, 164

Stones, 19

Substitution, 16, 86, 157, 161; ritual, 56; force of, 59; and prohibited desire, 60; magical, 72, 94; and sympathetic resonance, 160; ritual technique of, 183

Sweat: in revival tent, 65; ancient *sudarium*, 67; Apostle Paul, 92; of preacher, 118

Sweeny, June, 135

Tactility, 5, 22–23, 52, 171; ritual inversion of, 24; radio heat, 25; texture, 57, 59; textile patterns, 63; profane/transgressive, 67–68; layering of hands, 94; and Holy Ghost chills, 101; across distance, 161; gesture of, 172; haptic attention, 178; and distraction, 181

Technological breakdown, 19–20

Temporality, 185; deferral, 55, 80, 89; of narrative, 79; "temporal articulation," 82, 85, 90; production of belief, 84; of divine healing, 170; ritual anti-temporality, 172–73

Tent revival: Oral Roberts healing campaign, 23–24; canvas architecture, 64–65; prayer tent, 66; Oral Roberts, 178

Testimony, 20, 54–55, 77, 79, 81, 83, 85–86, 89, 96–97, 122, 132; of healing, 26; repetition of, 59; and narrative structure, 80–81; and communal bonds, 84; effects of, 130; visceral elements of, 131

Theologico-technical, 173; point of contact as, 22–23, 167; global charismatic healing, 160

Tongues, 33, 77, 101, 119, 137–38, 148; as sword, 64; of spiritualist medium, 76; textile, 80; in narrative wind, 87; rollin', 99; control of, 108; deadly lyin', 109; routinized, 147; example, 151–52, 154; Freud on, 181; cuttin' loose, 199 (n. 13)

Trailer, 53

Transcendence, 3

Transduction, 21

Truck: engine, 52; breakdown, 123

Tylor, E. B., 170

Ventriloquism, 75

Vibration: and hearing, 26

Vocal exercises, 17

Voice: healing and displacement of, 172

Vries, Hent de, 4, 18

WGTH (radio station, 105.5), 5, 13, 126, 135, 145, 157

Zipper: sound of, 115, 149